THE NEW eco-ARCHITECTURE

Alternatives from the Modern Movement

Colin Porteous

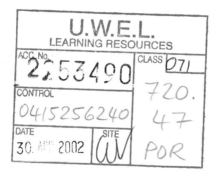

SPON PRESS
Taylor & Francis Group

London and New York

First published 2002
by Spon Press
11 New Fetter Lane, London EC4P 4EE

Simultaneously published in the USA and Canada
by Spon Press
29 West 35th Street, New York, NY 10001

Spon Press is an imprint of the Taylor & Francis Group

Typeset in Sabon by Wearset Ltd, Boldon, Tyne and Wear
Printed and bound in Great Britain by St Edmundsbury Press, Bury St Edmunds,
Suffolk

British Library Cataloguing in Publication Data
A catalogue record for this book is available from the British Library

Library of Congress Cataloging in Publication Data
Porteous, Colin.
The new eco-architecture : alternatives from the modern movement/Colin Porteous.
p. cm.
Includes bibliographical references and index.
ISBN 0-415-25624-0 – ISBN 0-415-25625-9 (pbk.)
1. Architecture, Modern–Environmental aspects. 2. Modern movement
(Architecture)
I. Title.
NA2542.35 .P67 2001
720'.47–dc21   2001049457

Contents

Foreword

No sensible person can doubt that in architecture, as in every other human activity, ecological values must be primary. There is now enough evidence to show all but the most bone-headed that radical changes are taking place in the climate of the planet, which will alter it from the one in which humanity evolved to a state that will almost certainly be inimical to our species. The process has started, and if change continues at its present rate, severe effects are to be expected soon. For the first time in the history of human beings, we can see the vital importance of planning and acting not just for next year or the next election, but for decades and even centuries. We must learn to live in harmony with the planet or perish, or at least face an environment that will become so progressively alien that the political conditions of survival will be horrendous. The professions, particularly architecture, have much to teach politicians.

Development in its widest sense, from destruction of natural habitats to the organisation of our individual dwellings, is by far the greatest force in driving ecological change, and construction of buildings is one of development's most important components. This book is a most important contribution to debates about ways in which we might build a more sustainable future.

Initially, its organisation seems strange, with the first part devoted to construction techniques of the heroic Modern Movement, and the second to the wider development of Modernism. The third part is a wide ranging (but often highly focused) *tour d'horizon* of many of the exciting possibilities thrown up by today's practice.

In fact, Porteous's structure allows many new insights. The historical analysis serves at least two main purposes. It shows that contemporary ecological concerns were often shared by our Modernist ancestors. The analysis gives environmentalism historical perspective, through which we can understand contemporary activity. And Porteous's history should give impetus to analysis of the performance of buildings over time: which, as he points out, is vital if we are to progress.

One of the most important aspects of the book is the way in which it emphasises the importance of architecture as a discipline. This is not professional one-upmanship, but an insistence that making the environment is something which is so important and complicated (in all human and environmental senses) that it cannot be handed over to people who specialise in particular disciplines. It must remain with those who continue to weave everything together: an essential way of thinking if we are to survive as a species.

Porteous's main virtue is his optimism. We are faced with potentially horrendous problems, but he has no doubt that we can design ourselves out of them with creative analysis of history and technology, and a generous input of ingenuity. This book stimulates essential imagination.

PETER DAVEY
Editor, The Architectural Review

Preface and Acknowledgements

The title implies a content concerned on the one hand with the ecological or 'green' issues of today, and how they might inform and influence new architecture. On the other hand, the use of the term 'The New Architecture', as used by Gropius *et al.* during the heroic period of the Modern Movement, suggests a green past that could have relevance for the present. Thus this is a quest concerning the origins and development of modern environmentally conscious architecture. It does not, as some might expect, look back to indigenous and other precedents from the more distant past. It has been the 20th century that has exponentially abused the biosphere to the endangerment of natural eco-systems. Moreover the consequences of such relentless interventions by humankind have engaged architects from the outset of modernism. Now, despite national reforms, standards and controls, the hostile eco-impacts of buildings continue to invisibly accelerate. Architects must therefore play a more vigorous part in global amelioration.

My career has been split between practice, teaching and research, the last mainly within the relatively narrow sphere of solar architecture, and with the emphasis on techniques applicable to mass housing. The scientific aspect to my persona belies a passion about the more subjective sensory aspects of architecture. These come into play between the hard-edged pragmatics of logic and the boundless aspirations of instinct. My father, who set much store on both tenets, inculcated a notion of climate-sensitivity within me from an early age. He was forever talking about the orientation of houses in their particular context. At any rate, when aged fourteen, I was inspired to order *Architectural Design*. The first issue to arrive was March 1956. Its theme was The Modern House. It introduced me to Le Corbusier in France, Argentina and India, Richard Neutra as well as Marcel Breuer in the USA, Powell and Moya, The Architects' Co-Partnership, Peter Womersley and Alison and Peter Smithson in the UK, and others from other countries. For example, I loved the transparent serenity of three houses in Oslo which led the issue (Eames-influenced, I was later to discover), two being designed for themselves by Arne Korsmo and Christian Norberg-Schulz. Later that same year, I was able to see 'in the flesh' the Smithson's plastic House of the Future at the Ideal Home Exhibition in Edinburgh.

What fascinated me in particular was the range of radicalism of solutions – the reinvention of the house as I knew it. Some were more difficult to assimilate than others. Maison Jaoul in Paris and Maison

Shodhan in Ahmadabad did appear brutal, especially in black and white photographs. Others, which seemed to embrace the natural world more wholeheartedly, were more sympathetic to young eyes. This included Le Corbusier's urban house for Dr Curutchet, as well as Neutra's lush rural or suburban setting for the Kronish residence, and the sylvan woodland site of the weekend house near Chichester by The Architects' Co-Partnership. The dissolution of expected inside–outside boundaries was incredibly seductive, as was the dissolution of rooms within. Interest with the opaque components lying between inside and outside at this early stage was understandably superficial – to do with surface and texture only. Having said that, there were clues as to the insulated construction of the houses in Oslo, which made sense of the woodwool slabs discovered while exploring a building site during the previous summer.

Taking this cue, the first part of the book investigates what is hidden, examining the attitudes and deeds of leading players of the Modern Movement with respect to the unglazed skin of their buildings, and recognising aspects that still hold relevance to critical green indicators of today such as energy efficiency and air quality. The next two parts open the discourse out to what is generally less hidden physically, and trace a green architectural lineage to the present. They are consistent in examining ideas and polemics during a period when artificial ecological impacts have steadily intensified, always with the aim of gaining new or renewed environmental insights in terms of today's needs.

In the course of writing the book, I am particularly indebted to the thoughtful comments of my partner, Mary Patrick, as well as to those of a close colleague and friend, Paul Simpson. The content has formed the core of a course for a few years now at the Mackintosh School of Architecture, Glasgow School of Art and the feedback from students has also been invaluable. Further, with respect to illustrations, I wish to thank The Graphics Company, Edinburgh, all those who agreed to reproduction and, within the School, Craig Laurie and other support systems such as the library.

Colin Porteous

Introduction

We rely on Yorke (1934) to tell us that the walls and roofs of Le Corbusier's and Jeanneret's housing at Weissenhofsiedlung in Stuttgart in 1927 were not simply constructed of solid concrete, rather than Le Corbusier himself (1960) or architectural historians such as Blake (1960) or Jencks (1973). The fact that the enclosing walls have been released from their loadbearing function by the concrete frame is known to all, but their insulating, multi-layer nature in the 1920s and 1930s, whether non-loadbearing or loadbearing, is not so well appreciated. Similarly it might be reasonable for a student of architecture to imagine that 'passive solar' design had its birth in the experimental houses of Trombe and Michel in 1967, rather than Mies van der Rohe's Tugendhat Haus in Brno in 1930. They might also forget just how important it was to the architects of the early Modern Movement that their revolution in design included as a matter of course innovative methods of servicing, particularly with respect to heating and ventilating.

The basic proposition in this book is to fill a gap with the benefit of hindsight. This is a gap that looks at the environmental concerns of today which impinge directly on architecture by examining origins in the Modern Movement. The contention is that although some of the semantics may only date back a decade or so, the issues were an intrinsic part of the birth pangs of modern architecture in the early part of the 20th century, and that some of the tensions and contradictions still confront us today. This process of sifting history to separate out the essential from the inessential for those who disseminate it is inevitable, but it means that there is a recurring need to re-evaluate in order to avoid relevant omissions, misrepresentation, myths and distortions. To validate this view it is perhaps as well at the outset to discuss two particular terms in use today – 'sustainable development' and 'sustainability'. Both are contentious. Their scope extends beyond the built environment and are now firmly embedded in the socio-political arena. Their ascendancy has been rapid, while various definitions fail to satisfy critics.

Pawley (2000) argues that the first is an oxymoron, the second is ill-defined and both are impossible to achieve. However, medically we know precisely what is required to sustain life, and architecturally we have a good grasp of what is needed to sustain comfort, well-being and health. For example, surveys from many different parts of the world consistently show a correlation between damp housing, ill health in general, and respiratory disorders such as asthma in particular. Therefore it can be said with confidence that damp dwellings are not sustainable, or we might say that they are below a tolerable standard.

If we view the terms as absolute, a building development either being sustainable or not sustainable, we run into difficulty. The Brundtland definition, 'development that meets the needs of the present without compromising the ability of future generations to meet their own needs', leaves much scope for interpretation. 'Need' invokes *some course of action*; 'meeting' can imply intersection of movement in opposite directions; 'compromise' may be defined as *exposing liability to harm by injudicious action*; and 'ability' as *adequate capacity to do something*. The solution to the conundrum of sustainable development must lie in accepting the reality of relativity and shifting boundaries. For all we may attempt to regenerate existing buildings, new ones are always going to be a fact of life, and a proportion of these are bound to be built on 'greenfield' as opposed to 'brownfield' sites. Availability of resources is also bound to vary with time as well as geography. This does not invalidate designing to optimise energy efficiency and minimise environmental impact at any given time in any given location. The legal profession has long used the words 'reasonable' and 'reasonably' to assist in litigation. There is no reason why architects should not take this up with respect to sustainability. For example, the materials used for a building could be described as *reasonably sustainable*, implying a relatively low embodied energy, relatively low use of non-renewable resources and relatively low impact in terms of pollution. The recurring consumption of fuel over the life of a building can be described in the same terms. Inevitably it will be necessary to refer to norms or benchmarks in order to support a case for *reasonably sustainable*, but it should not be necessary to get bogged down in a plethora of detailed standards. Indeed the concept can be given authority today in just the same way that Le Corbusier approached the making of concrete blocks from industrial waste, the sourcing of local gravel and lime for floor slabs, or the use of turf to protect expensive and vulnerable waterproof membranes.

Although the word 'sustainability' has the very specific implication of infinite capability in the same way as the cyclical loops of nature, in practical terms of what it means to the architect, there is a very fine difference compared with another topical term, 'green design'. The conceptual idea of relative greenness has also been given credence by Cooper at a conference entitled 'The Challenge of Sustainability' (1993). Cooper presented a diagram which moved from grey culture, which was pro-science and included rationalism and reductionism, through grey/green culture to green culture, which at the extreme end was anti-science and embraced mysticism as well as holism. One can argue that holism is wrongly grouped along with anti-science 'eco-warriors' and that indeed holism is an entirely rational scientific concept. Nevertheless, this does not undermine the concept of relative greenness in architecture or its very close conceptual association with relative sustainability. At any rate, this is the assumption made here. The use of the word 'alternatives' in the sub-title of the book is similarly open, alluding to much more than energy.

The first of three parts, entitled *the multi-layer phenomenon* discusses the nature of the solid or opaque envelope, excluding glazing. It considers the heroic period of modernism in the 1920s, and its impacts through the 1930s and beyond, in order to better understand the tenacity of these roots relative to the issues of today. The main question to be answered here is to what extent was the materiality driven by scientific logic, and to what extent by the visual dictates of surface and other aesthetic ideologies, these aspects subjugating what lay inbetween, inside and outside to a degree of random pragmatism. This then embraces the degree to which structure was exposed or concealed, and the degree to which energy efficiency and climatic appropriateness were considered. A subsidiary question is to what extent has the well-publicised deterioration of many icons of the Modern Movement been due to poor initial detailing, including the specification of materiality and ordering of constructional layers, and to what extent due to lack of adequate care and maintenance. The need to seek answers to these questions is driven primarily by recent failures and attitudes. Although the term 'life-cycle analysis' has gained currency, we are still faced with serious tectonic mishaps, sometimes due to initial financial constraints, sometimes to ignorance, and sometimes to both. There also seems to be an astonishing reluctance on the part of the architectural press to adequately disseminate building construction. This inevitably leads to a climate of disinterest, or an undermining of confidence in this area, among students of architecture. The first part then does indulge in some rudimentary comparative thermal appraisal and classification of a representative range of buildings, confining the geographical arena mainly to Europe and North America. The intention is to use this data, alongside recorded statements of intent by some of the architects of this period, and to an extent the propositions of historians and theoreticians, to assist in the process of engaging with the questions. Definitive answers do not necessarily result, but lessons are learned.

The second part, *the glass is greener...*, explores whole buildings in their climatic setting, starting with the impact of replacing the window, as a hole in a wall, with a window-wall. It embraces pioneering passive solar design, use of materials, components and techniques. Again it re-examines the heroic period of modernism in the 1920s, but within a less constrained time-frame. The methodology is similar to the first part and environmental science still lies at the core of the discourse. But it is not so reliant on quantitative indicators for comparisons. Critical differences and commonalities between leading figures such as Wright and Le Corbusier are again explored, but in a more holistic architectural context.

The last part, *adventitious propagation?*, suggests a dialectic between continuity and intermittence. Just as the seeds of some wild flowers remain interred and dormant for years, only appearing once the ground is disturbed, so also environmental architecture reacts at least partly to major economic or political crises. These chapters thus progress to tracing impacts of metaphorical flowerings from the 1960s to the 1990s.

References

Blake P. (1960), *Le Corbusier Architecture and Form*, Gollancz, UK, 1960 and Pelican Books, 1963.

Cooper I. (1993), Teaching Sustainability in UK Schools of Architecture: Home Thoughts from Abroad, proceedings The Challenge of Sustainability, 15th September, University of Edinburgh EH1 1JZ.

Jencks C. (1973), *Le Corbusier and the Tragic View of Architecture*, Allen Lane, (Penguin Books).

Le Corbusier (1960), *Le Corbusier My Work*, The Architectural Press, London.

Pawley M. (2000), *Sustainability: Today's Agenda for Tomorrow*, The Architects' Journal, No. 1, Vol. 2.

Yorke F. R. S. (1934), *The Modern House*, The Architectural Press, London.

The multi-layer phenomenon

PART ONE

CHAPTER 1

1927 – a chronological milestone

In order to begin a fresh historical investigation, it is sometimes useful to identify a chronological milestone, a particular year that is significant to the topic in hand. In this context 1927 was such a year. It was the year of the first English publication of *Towards a new Architecture* by Le Corbusier,[1] as well as building the Stein house at Garches.[2] It was also the year of the Weissenhofsiedlung in Stuttgart, with notable contributions by Le Corbusier, Walter Gropius[3] and other leading figures. Although the new Bauhaus building in Dessau was officially opened in December 1926, its department of architecture was not occupied until April 1927[4] with Hannes Meyer at the helm. It was the year Jan Duiker (with Bijvoet) completed plans for an open-air school in Amsterdam,[5] and a year when Eileen Gray's '*maison en bord de mer*' at Roquebrune[6] was under construction. It was the year marking the completion of Karl Marx Hof in Vienna by Karl Ehn,[7] and the Van Nelle factory in Rotterdam by Brinkman and van der Vlugt.[8] Moreover, with specific relevance to *the multi-layer phenomenon*, it was the year when van Doesburg,[9] in appraising Weissenhofsiedlung said: 'Every material has its own energy force, and the challenge is to enhance this energy force to its maximum by proper application.' Expanding on materiality and extolling the decisiveness of *ultimate surface*, he said: 'The ultimate surface is in itself the result of construction. The latter expresses itself in ultimate surface. Bad construction leads to bad surface. Good construction produces a sound surface with tension.' Finally, later in the same critique he said: 'the correct, logical use of the modern materials will cause the new form of architecture to emerge quite involuntarily'.

In the USA it was a year of continuing financial crisis for Frank Lloyd Wright,[10] the year he set up Camp Ocatillo in Arizona, and marks the beginning of the period when he wrote his autobiography. It was the year that Richard Neutra's Health House for Dr Lovell[11] started on site, and the year after completion of Rudolph Schindler's Beach House[12] for the same client (not to mention the year of formal separation of Rudolph and Pauline Schindler). The year of 1927 marked a nadir for Buckminster Fuller[13] with the collapse of the Stockade Building System company, whose application for patent had just been filed that year. But it was also the year of Fuller's initial sketches of the 4-D tower, heralding the Dymaxion House,[14] which was thereafter first exhibited in 1929, the year of the Wall Street Crash.

In the UK, 1927 was the year after the General Strike, and heroic modernist landmarks are difficult to find. However, it does coincide with the publication of three hefty and very orthodox volumes[15] describing the state of building technology. The significance of this set lies more in its omissions than its content. 'Insulation' is not indexed and lightweight materials are only included under 'fire-resisting construction'. The worthy tomes serve to emphasise the extent of bold constructional experimentation embarked on by leading modernists, and it is partly this boldness that will be metaphorically ploughed and rotovated.

The fundamental difference between what van Doesburg wanted in terms of 'sound surface with tension' and traditional methods of construction was the stripping away of external projections. The paradox is that many decorative features of then and now, such as cornices or dripstones above lintels, have a practical function – shedding water away from a façade. So also do more purely functional features such as copings and cills. Thus it tended to be the terminating or joining horizontal edges that made van Doesburg's 'sound surfaces' particularly vulnerable.

However, setting aside wall-heads, cills and so forth, the other area of vulnerability was associated with the layering of different materials between inside and outside. In spite of the acknowledgement that 'bad construction leads to bad surface', the preoccupation of van Doesburg and other modernists in 1927 actually lay with what was visible, endorsing a new aesthetic parity of external and internal surfaces. Patterned wallpaper gave way to painted plaster inside, and smooth stucco was used outside rather than stone, brick, timber, tiling, etc. However, as soon as more than one material lay between inner and outer finishes, differences between their respective thermal properties could become critical. For example, if in the plane immediately behind the stucco, we had a reinforced concrete frame with an infill of breeze-blocks, the differential thermal movement could rapidly cause the finishing layer to crack. The usual way to overcome this was to cover all joints with some form of lath, but if this in turn suffered any form of corrosion, it could then part company with its covering. Similarly, if a continuous layer of insulation is introduced next to a dense structural material, differences in respective thermal and vapour resistances could cause interstitial condensation. This could in turn lead to the deterioration of some part of the construction. The control of quality on site also then becomes critical. For example, if reinforcement is too close to the surface of concrete in a zone vulnerable to interstitial condensation. Alternatively, in a zone subject to intermittent saturation from rain, the external coating will again break down.

Moreover, the mix of materials was to a large extent driven by a desire for slimness on the part of the modernists. Slimness was associated with lightness and efficiency. Thin reinforced concrete walls, with steel bars inevitably not far below the surface, could also function as beams spanning large openings. A thin backing of a material such as cork could serve as shuttering during construction, and give the wall the same thermal efficiency as a much thicker traditional one of stone or brick. However, in practice there were significant variations in both thermal performance and constructional vulnerability, and this was not always associated with climatic characteristics.

The act of concealment of structure was not in itself new or an issue for most architects, but it did open the door to variable specifications and, of course, variable costs. Even without economic constraints, and assuming appropriate specification relative to differing climatic stresses and strains, and while taking into account all the other aspects cited above, there is no escaping the fact that the 'international style' of 1927 was intrinsically more risky than traditional practice. Risk is an inherent part of the *modus operandi* of any entrepreneur who drives through radical changes. However, the problem was, and still is, that the financing of buildings often tends to be underwritten by very conservative institutions. Accordingly, individual wealthy clients have been recognised as invaluable in fostering the pioneering experiments of the Modern Movement.

Notwithstanding financial barriers, ideologically driven movements tend to meet equally ideological opposition. Openly confronting the ethos of an 'international style' and taking other kinds of risks, was the man who saw himself as a genius as well as the best modern architect around. Frank Lloyd Wright was given to flowery, but also scathing, oratory which would forcefully 'set out his stall'. Projections were an essential part of his vocabulary, as were the visible textures of stone, brick and timber. Furthermore, even though he often resorted to hiding components such as steel beams to enable large cantilevers in his roofs, the smooth, enigmatic and minimalist aesthetic of the 'international style' was an anathema to him.

Partly in recognition of the constructional fragility of smooth surfaces, it wasn't long before the European stars such as Le Corbusier also began to re-embrace explicit materiality and texture. Thus the comparison in 1927 between the positions of various protagonists is not about smooth versus rough, or modernism versus regionalism, or van Doesburg's *de stijl* versus Wright's *organic simplicity*. It is about interfaces from air to surface and surface to surface, and the role played by the respective thermal properties of materials, particularly at these boundaries. It recognises that the two constructional cultures, one essentially mono-material and the other multi-material, continued to maintain distinct presences. The latter may have become increasingly dominant, but, in today's more ecologically conscious architectural scene, the former is starting to reassert itself. One example is that of rammed earth walls. Nevertheless, relatively slim multi-layer, multi-material construction will always have a strong place. After so many years of dealing with this issue, it should be surprising that architects are still coming to grips with its inherent areas of risk. For example, it is remarkable how often one comes across the 'vapour control layer' on the wrong side of the insulation, sometimes on original working drawings, and sometimes on redrawn versions appearing in architectural periodicals. It does not follow that the construction of the 1920s and 1930s will provide an explanation for current errors; but it does help to support the case for bringing scientific theory and architectural practice together with a greater level of inquiry over a greater time-span than is the current norm. Did buildings of the Modern Movement have 'vapour control layers'? If not why not, and was the omission causal in relation to deterioration? Was there consistency in the relative placing of materials of high and low thermal and vapour resistivities? Where are the greatest risks? Are there as yet unexplored techniques? For example, can we enable the thermal characteristics of a multi-layer wall or roof to vary over daily and/or seasonal cycles – the opaque equivalent of 'intelligent' or 'smart' glass?

Protagonists – aesthetic and tectonic attitude CHAPTER 2

How then do these architectural signposts in 1927 set the scene for an exploration of the multi-layer phenomenon? To start with, one of the most important players, Wright, explicitly extolled mono-materialism as part of his long-standing advocacy of 'organic' and 'simplicity' in an essay commissioned for the *Architectural Record* in 1928:[16]

> *Mono-Material building.* The more simple the materials used, the more the building tends towards a mono-material building, the more nearly will 'perfect style' reward an organic plan and ease of execution economize results. Not only the more logical will the whole become, but all will emerge with the countenance of simplicity.

The last three words also imply positive attributes such as truth and honesty. It is difficult to imagine that a 'countenance of simplicity' could ever be host to deception. Since Wright tended to repeat the same message over many years, it is quite possible that this was not his first association of mono-material building with organic simplicity. For example, when using the term 'organic architecture' in 1910, it is with respect to his entire portfolio of work published in a celebrated monograph in Berlin.[17] Certainly his mono-material message was to be emphasised later in a seminal lecture entitled 'The Cardboard House' (fourth in the series of Princeton Lectures, 1930[18]): 'in favour of mono-material as far as possible'; and the Princeton lectures in turn include his famous Hull House Lecture of 1901,[19] 'The Art and Craft of the Machine'. This monologue also relates to the 'countenance of simplicity' in that it emphasises the virtues of connecting materials together with the help of machines in an open and honestly expressed manner.

His Princeton espousal of 'mono-material' is the sixth of nine principles associated with 'organic simplicity'. Given the title, and following his initial attack on the thin white homogenous appearance of European modernism through his pejorative simile of cardboard houses – 'this superficial new *surface-and-mass* aesthetic falsely claiming French painting as a parent' – his position seems somewhat paradoxical. The European 'box-like forms', which Wright so derides here, usually comprised several layers, some to resist weather, and others to resist heat loss; whereas a typical wall by Wright is either one layer of one material, or two or three layers of the same material. A commonality with the so-called 'cardboard' walls was the equality of outside and inside surfaces.

Wright, however, brought indoors materials that were traditionally thought of as external ones. This also suited the new transparency of entire window-walls, but was also ironically a common factor with the hated 'cardboard houses'. Thus the sameness of the inner and outer surfaces was not the sole concern. For Wright, the issue was the nature of the respective textures and their integrity right through from one to the other.

An example is his concrete-filled, hollow concrete blocks, used in the Millard house, 1923.[20] In describing this house he is complacent about its thermal attributes, asserting 'so the house would be cool in summer, warm in winter and dry always'. This might not be far from the truth in California's soft Mediterranean climate, but transferring the technique to the Biltmore Hotel in Arizona, 1929, was surely folly. His autobiography acknowledges the continental climate, very cold in winter[21] and very hot in summer.[22] However, the concrete wall has a U-value of almost 2.0 W/m²K, so that rooms would gain or lose heat at roughly twice the rate of, for example, a traditional log cabin, which might be said to typify *organic simplicity*. It would also gain or lose heat at a significantly greater rate than many examples of multi-layer modern construction – the target of Wright's 'cardboard' ire.

Having criticised Wright's block construction in this way, it must also be said that the U-value, or coefficient of thermal transmittance, is only one indicator. Overheating is also partly regulated by thermal diffusivity. This is the ratio of thermal conductivity (W/mK) to volumetric heat capacity (J/m³K). The denominator is in turn the product of density (kg/m³) and specific heat capacity (J/kgK). It is the square root of the inverse of thermal diffusivity that regulates both time-lag and thermal damping. Both are important when there are large differences in temperature between night and day. For example, if the heat at the hottest part of the day in mid-afternoon is delayed until the coldest part of the night, this can be beneficial to the interior. Similarly, the greater the thermal damping, the less the temperature will fluctuate inside a building. Working out the time-lag and damping for a mono-layer, mono-material construction is very easy, providing the basic thermal properties are known. But once there is more than one layer, the algorithms become much more complex, and the combination of light and heavy layers is quite subtle.

If the mathematics were to be tackled for a typical multi-layer cavity wall with insulation and then compared with a mono-material cavity wall without insulation, such as that at Biltmore, the Wright specification would not be as effective as the former for a continental climate. The addition of 25 mm of insulation would lengthen the time-lag by about an hour and increase the damping effect by about 10%. The thermal resistance or insulative value would also improve by well over 100%. However, the comparison between Wright's cavity blockwork with a concrete wall lined with insulation, say woodwool, and plaster would not be so clear cut. For example 150 mm dense concrete, lined with 50 mm woodwool and plaster, would have a time-lag of about one hour less than Wright's cavity blockwork and its damping effect would also reduce by some 20%. On the other hand its thermal resistance would be approximately 66% better. It is unlikely that architects of this period would have paid too much heed to such detailed scientific characteristics even if they had had access to the data. But it did not stop strong personalities from coming out with strong statements to justify their aspirations and decisions.

Regardless of how well Wright may have understood the relevance of the dynamic aspects of damping and time-lag, he remained dismissive of the need for insulating walls.[23] Using the Millard House as a bench-mark, his later three-layer, mono-material, 65 mm thick timber Usonian construction[24] did improve its insulation value by 25%. However, this simply reflected the chosen material relative to structural minimalism. Meanwhile in Germany in 1927, while Wright specified dense concrete walls in Arizona, Gropius built an experimental house at Stuttgart[25] which would have fitted Wright's 'cardboard' epithet. But although it was slender, its layers and materials insulated to a level five times that of the Millard walls and, although steel-framed, it obviated cold-bridging by means of timber battens.

Thus it would appear that Wright was concerned with ideas of solidity and regional appropriateness, and was hostile to European modernism which he saw as insubstantial. But such notions related more to myth than fact. His mono-material walls were not always suited to the climates in which they were built, whereas the thin white aesthetic of European modernism revealed, or perhaps concealed, a multi-layer approach that recognised thermal realities. Yorke's seminal book, *The Modern House*[26] also confirms that the 'dry' construction chosen by Gropius was not what drove the multi-layerism. There are many examples of 'wet' constructions that adopt the same thermally conscious approach. For example, Fig. 2.1 illustrates a house by Adolf Bens in Prague built in 1932[27] where a 30 mm layer of Olcedyt insulation* is sandwiched between 150 mm hollow tiles externally and 140 mm cellular bricks internally. In 1931 in Gablonz, Germany,[28] in the Haus Hasek by Heinrich Lauterbach, we find a wall where the structural material is hollow concrete block which was lined internally with woodwool to insulate twice as well as Wright's concrete block buildings. In a house for a doctor in Oslo[29] by Gudolf Blaksted and Herman Munthe-Kaas, a reinforced concrete loadbearing outer wall is backed with cork slabs and pumice concrete, and supports a timber structure above – i.e. a mixture of 'wet' and 'dry' construction and also traditional and modernist aesthetics. In a seaside house in Sweden in 1930[30] by Alfred Roth and Ingrid Walberg, we have a house which is modernist in appearance, but with a

---

*One can only guess at the origins of some of the trade names used. It may be that the 'ol' related to oil as a foaming agent for the 'cedyt', a slight corruption of the Czech word 'cedit' meaning 'percolate' or 'trickle through'. At any rate this does give a rationale for a lightweight aerated material.

2.1 *House by Adolf Bens, Prague, 1932, with Olcedyt insulation*

regional multi-layer timber construction, overall thickness 135 mm (U-value 0.85 W/m²K). Hence, although this Swedish house might well have been deemed by Wright to be a 'cardboard box', it perhaps also deserved the term 'organic simplicity' used by him in the same lecture in 1930 to promote his own ideals.

Of course Wright's hostility and inflexibility with respect to others is widely known. The question is whether or not this aspect of his character has been subjected adequately to critical architectural review. Has his arrogance or greatness or both, tended to eclipse important underlying flaws? It is suggested that the answer is 'yes', but then architectural arrogance was not exclusive to Wright.

Le Corbusier appears to be a notable exception to a European multi-layer norm with respect to walls. However, he does not altogether ignore thermal considerations. Generally his non-loadbearing infill walls are of hollow blockwork, often with a light pumice aggregate as in the houses at Weissenhofsiedlung.[31] He also had a history of involvement with light-weight concrete blocks, starting to manufacture them in 1917,[32] using ash from power station furnaces as the aggregate. His attitude to non-loadbearing walls is clearly expressed in his second lecture in a series given in Buenos Aires in 1929:[33] 'for we shall not build walls but partitions – in cork, in cinderblock, in straw, in wood chips, in anything you like'.

Interestingly, Albert Frey came first to the east coast of America in 1930 fresh from engaging with the working drawings for Villa Savoye. The following year, in a partnership with Laurence Kocher who was already in the USA, the walls of their Aluminaire House[34] achieved a U-value two-thirds more efficient than Wright's Millard House. In form the Aluminaire House owes much to Frey's experience in Le Corbusier's atelier, although it is a much more compact building than Villa Savoye. The construction also might seem to conform to Le Corbusier's 'anything you like' maxim with respect to the slim non-loadbearing walls. But the reality of Frey's layering is not so casual. One might say it is *anything you like*, which will yield the essence of skin or clothing. In other words, the combination must provide adequate strength, durability and thermal resistance in order to mediate between the internal comfort required of a dwelling and the forces of nature. Steel angles simply strengthen 50 mm square timber framing, which is lined on each side with 12.5 mm insulation board and clad externally with finely corrugated aluminium sheeting. The last stiffens the structure, but also has a thermal purpose. During warm days up to 95% of short-wave solar radiation is reflected, while during cool nights, only 5% of outgoing long-wave radiation is emitted. This reflectiveness together with ventilation is then the strategy for avoidance of overheating, since the thermal damping and time-lag for such a lightweight structure would have been minimal.

This pursuit of a slim skin is taken a stage further one year later with Kocher and Frey's canvas-covered stressed ply panelling for their 'week-end house',[35] this time employing aluminium foil as an interstitial reflective radiant insulant. Formalistically, these little units were again redolent of Le Corbusier, adhering to all of his Five Points or Principles which will be discussed in more depth in Part 2. However, the reinforced timber framing in each case also relates strongly to the traditional North American predilection for this technique, only in a refined form which reflected modern technology and mass production. It was also well suited to dwellings with an intermittent occupancy since they would be able to respond rapidly to an input of heat, and could also be easily cooled by means of ventilation.

Returning to Villa Savoye and its construction based on concrete, which is certainly perceived as the dominant material of the Modern Movement, it is not possible to be precise about thermal performance. However, we know that regardless of the thermal resistance of the breeze-block infill, the structural frame afforded major cold-bridging, with U-values of about $2.6\,W/m^2K$. In addition, the plan and section generated a very large area of built surface exposed to the external elements. For wealthy clients, able to buy large quantities of heat over a regular daily cycle, a rapid rate of loss is not necessarily a serious drawback. Also the heavy construction is able to store heat to some extent and may be useful in avoidance of overheating in summer. However, in this case, the initially mooted electric underfloor heating system was impractical due to the size of transformer that would have been required. Further, the oil-fired 'wet' radiator system that was first installed was undersized. It had to be upgraded after the first winter of occupation, 1930–1.[36] Further still, the house was dogged by leaks in wet weather, due more to difficult junctions between walls and roof, and roof and roof windows than to the layering of materials in general. In short, Villa Savoye was damp and hard to heat, terms that still have significant negative currency today for the same underlying reasons – shortcomings not only associated with heating systems, but also with the layering of the external envelope, together with ill-considered junctions.

In 1930, concrete was still a virtually untried walling material for the USA. When Laurence Kocher and Gerhard Ziegler built a house in Connecticut[37] just prior to the former starting his partnership with Albert Frey, they devised an in-situ concrete cavity system that bears comparison with Wright's precast blocks. Assuming a dense mix, this heavyweight, mono-material wall would have had a similar U-value, time lag and thermal damping. Thus thermally and materially, if not formally, at least one American modernist (Kocher was born in California) seems in tune with Wright, but not on the next two projects where the multi-material influence of Frey appears strong. Then again, having moved to California and Frey having had contact with Mies van der Rohe, a Frey and Kocher commission reverted to concrete in a courtyard house in Palm Springs.[38] Here a mix of uninsulated in-situ concrete and reinforced hollow concrete block walls may well have suited the climate reasonably well, with 38 mm insulation incorporated in the roof to deal with summer overheating as well as excessive loss of heat in winter. Thus, although at first sight there appears to be a tectonic inconsistency or randomness, this is not necessarily the case.

Other modernist architects working in America at this time, and qualifying for Wright's 'cardboard house' slight, achieved better standards in multi-material mode. The 38 mm cork lining the concrete shell of a house, again in Connecticut and built in 1932[39] by Howe and Lescaze, reduces heat loss to half that of the Millard bench-mark. But in England one year later,[40] the same team built a house in Devon with cavity brick walls and a 40% higher U-value. The reason for the switch in construction may have been connected to price, but it suggests that, for some architects at least, the hidden materiality of construction was quite subservient to form and surface. However, it is risky to extrapolate this aspect to a view that construction was simply an expedient means to an end for all architects, even if it was a relatively frequent reality. There is ample evidence, and some already suggested, that in many instances the precise make-up of the opaque components mediating between inside and outside was very carefully considered, not only in terms of structural fitness, durability and weatherproofing, but also in terms of thermal adequacy.

Still in England in 1933, but back to concrete, the lining of insulation thins to 12.5 mm in Connel and Ward's house at Grayswood.[41] In combination with a slim 100 mm concrete skin, the U-value increases to over 2.0 W/m²K. Lucas built a house in Kent[42] in 1933 using the same construction, as did Chermayeff in Rugby[43] in 1934. Thus here is a modernist aesthetic in the UK with two primary layers and a U-value to match examples of Wright's mono-material 'organic simplicity'. However, other notable architects are more generous with respect to insulation. Maxwell Fry[44] built a house in Surrey in 1935 which was over 50% more efficient due to the thicker cork lining to the structural concrete. In the same year Gibberd[45] used a similar construction at Slough with the thicker 150 mm concrete marginally reducing the U-value; and a year earlier at Bognor in Sussex, Chitty and Tecton[46] lined 100 mm concrete with both 28 mm and 38 mm cork, the latter reducing the U-value to below 1.0 W/m²K. In retrospect the low-insulators seem to have won the day fully supported by statutory instrument. The first thermal regulations for the UK were not introduced until 1963,[47] and then stipulated a liberal maximum value for walls of 1.7 W/m²K. Even now at the beginning of the 21st century, Gropius's 1927 wall at Stuttgart would comply with building standards in the UK which continue to lag behind those of its European neighbours.

The two heroic European architects working in the USA in 1927, Schindler and Neutra, both worked with Wright for a time. Both also collaborated with each other for about five years in the late 1920s. However, the respective houses for Dr Phillip Lovell were distinctly *Schindler* and *Neutra*. Schindler had already used solid precast 'lift-slab' walls[48] in the house for himself, his wife Pauline and Clyde and Marion Chase in 1921–2. He had also had an unhappy experience with solid *in situ* reinforced concrete external walls[49] used in a housing scheme in Pueblo Ribera, although this had much to do with poorly detailed junctions with flat roofs. At any rate he consequently retreated to the traditional stucco and plastered stud walls, which although multi-layer in reality, contrived to look like a single material. In the Beach House, the five robust concrete piloti-frames again clearly defer to Le Corbusier, but Gebhard[50] states: 'The clean, smooth machine surfaces do battle with small passages of agitated Wrightian details.' And Johnson[51] refused to include the house in the 1932 exhibition at the Museum of Modern Art in New York, 'because it did not reflect the International Style as style'. Gebhard[52] reports Schindler's own description of all non-loadbearing vertical elements: 'All walls and partitions are two inches thick. They are made of metal lath and cement plaster, suspended between the concrete frames.' It is respective thicknesses and sometimes colour that distinguish loadbearing from non-loadbearing elements, and it seems that Schindler remained fundamentally an adherent to Wright's mono-material approach, fused with traditional American stud, stucco and plaster techniques.

The Health House for Dr Lovell by Neutra is very different from the Beach House (Fig. 2.2). Here, in place of the robustly expressed concrete cross-frames, we have a mainly discreetly clothed steel skeleton. It is also one that is in part subtly exposed through the medium of integral, structural steel windows – the transparency still giving the perception of non-loadbearing components. With respect to solid parts of the vertical external skin, Spade[53] reports that: 'Its walls were cast *in situ* using ready-mixed concrete pumped through hoses to cover expended-metal reinforcement itself backed by insulating board used as permanent shuttering.' In other words, compared with Schindler's approach, this is a more European construction where a non-loadbearing, solid, weatherproof layer is combined with an insulant. It is also probable that Wright would have regarded this house, completed only one year before the Princeton lectures,[54] as one of 'the cardboard houses of the *modernistic* movement'.

Neutra was an acknowledged experimenter in innovative techniques of construction and materiality,* and also kept track of what was going on in Europe. In the 1920s and 1930s he was keen to exploit diatomaceous earth as a walling material, and introduced the term 'Diatom House'.[55] Diatomaceous material is essentially a silica from the shell-like skeletons of algae. Although Neutra's ideas applied to a walling material

---

*Richard Neutra is rightly regarded as an important innovator and I had always admired his minimalist clarity of detailing compared with that of Wright. I heard him speak at the UIA Congress in Mexico 1963 along with Buckminster Fuller. Each was a radical experimenter, with a special interest in building envelope. While Fuller reached out globally on the broad issues of resources, Neutra was more introspective, and, as one might expect, more occupied with the refinements of architectural aesthetics.

2.2 *Dr Lovell's Health House by Richard Neutra, Los Angeles, 1929*

apparently never came to fruition,[†] he did use it with cement as a waxed floor in the Beard House, designed with Gregory Ain, 1934.[56] In fact the first floor system acted thermally in conjunction with hollow prefabricated metal walls:[‡] 'The diatom cement slab acts as a low temperature radiating panel during the cold season, while a retarded convection carries the air volume of the sub-floor void into the vertical hollows of the cellular steel walls.' Since the sub-floor void was supplied with warm air from the furnace in winter, it is clear that the walls were also allowed to be dynamically enhanced in terms of temperature. Given the high thermal conductivity of steel, this idea seems more than a little suspect, providing the energy in the heated air an easy pathway for escape – unless the walls referred to by Neutra in this quote are the interior walls only. Certainly the external hollow wall seems to make more sense in summer when it is apparently disconnected from the diatom floor: 'On the building fronts which are exposed to direct sun radiation, small intake openings at the foot of the cellular steel elements initiate, simultaneously with the warming up of the exterior surface, an automatic air convection to cool these walls and minimise heat transmission to the interior caloriferic insulation board lining.' Neutra also acknowledges the role of the insulating lining in controlling heat flux in both directions: 'The interior shell is of caloriferic insulation material and keeps conduction of heat in both ways at a minimum.' The steel deck roof was similarly insulated. Thus, in spite of dubiety about the rationale of the hollow diatom floor in conjunction with hollow metal walls in winter, Neutra is undoubtedly thinking 'thermal' in a very imaginative way.

The discussion has so far concentrated on walls. Roofs of course are generally considered to have a more onerous role than walls when it comes to excluding rain, although wind-driven rain can subject walls to a considerable onslaught in exposed maritime or mountainous locations. In southerly latitudes roofs are also subject to significant thermal stress due to solar radiation. This was acknowledged by Le Corbusier[57] who promoted roof gardens partly to negate such stress and partly to replace the green territory supplanted by the building. Eileen Gray also skilfully deals with the daily solar cycle in the villa at Roquebrune.[58] Here there are two roofs, the first a waterproof roof supported on a lightweight clay pot construction, in turn supported on the second, a concrete grid-slab with beams facing upwards (Fig. 2.3). This sophisticated combination ensures a time lag and thermal damping appropriate to the climate.

The apparent massiveness of the flat roof and parapet of Wright's Hollyhock House,[59] constructed for Aline Barnsdall from 1917–20, is

---

[†]It is known that diatomite was used for thermal insulation, if not by Neutra, and that it was much the same, if not identical, to the German *kieselguhr* (also interestingly used as an absorbent of nitro-glycerine in the manufacture of dynamite).

[‡]It would appear that the descriptions by James Ford and Katherine Morrow Ford[56] are direct quotations by Neutra – at least each paragraph starts with quotation marks, unlike the descriptions for other houses in this book.

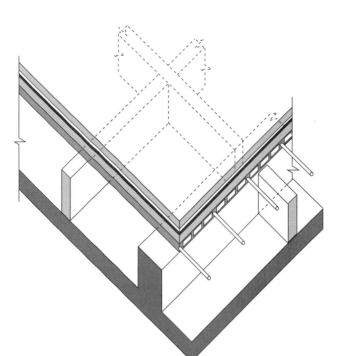

2.3 *Villa by Eileen Gray, Roquebrune, France, 1926–9*

illusory, since it consists of hollow veneered timber framework. Given that the site near Los Angeles will have a Mediterranean climate not dissimilar to that at Roquebrune on the Cote d'Azur, the construction is not thermally appropriate. The detail also appears suspect in terms of waterproofing, and it is no surprise that Wright admits to major conflict with the client and builder.[60] Schindler's roof for the Beach House was also a light timber deck, although honestly expressed, whereas the roofs of most modernist buildings in Europe in the 1920–30s seem to have comprised a combination of heavy and light materials. The roof of Gropius's little house at Weissenhofsiedlung is a particularly good example with three insulating layers, two air spaces and one fairly heavy structural layer – concrete resting on a steel frame (Fig. 2.4). Most of the UK modernists in the 1930s also used a combination of concrete and an insulant, but, as with walls, the picture was quantitatively mixed.

Having already mentioned early 1930s English projects, we come to the interesting point in architectural history when some more influential European protagonists move over to the USA, some having stopped for a productive period in England. In 1931, during his last three years in Germany and the year after Wright's 'cardboard house' lecture, Gropius was involved with a prefabricated copper-clad housing system.[61] In the same way as Kocher and Frey's 'week-end house', the construction relied on radiant insulants with, from outside to inside, copper sheeting, air space, aluminium foil, airspace, aluminium foil, airspace and asbestos cement lining. This represents a U-value in the order of $0.7\,W/m^2K$ or less.

2.4 *Layers of prefabricated house by Walter Gropius, Stuttgart, 1927*

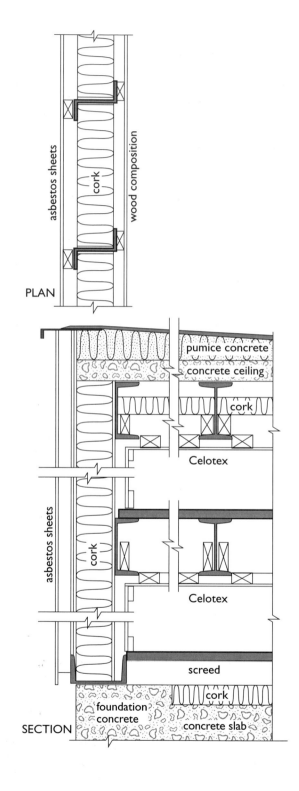

PLAN

asbestos sheets

cork

wood composition

SECTION

asbestos sheets

cork

pumice concrete

concrete ceiling

cork

Celotex

Celotex

screed

foundation concrete

cork

concrete slab

In other words Gropius was continuing to explore lightweight, well-insulated housing systems. However, as one might imagine, a copper-clad house looked very different from that of his Weissenhofsiedlung proto-type. The constructed version in 1931 also sported a low monopitch roof with projecting eaves and verges, resulting in a 'soft' chalet-like appearance. Then Gropius, arriving in England in 1934, collaborated with Maxwell Fry. Their house in Kent of 1936[62] relates strongly to the copper-clad houses, this time walls are finished in horizontal weatherboarding, and it has an almost identical monopitch roof. Walls are more traditionally multi-layer, with plastered woodwool lining internally, breeze-block fill between timber framing, and rough boarding behind cedar 'shiplap' cladding externally. The roof is also multi-layer timber construction with woodwool slabs doubling as decking and insulation. Thus in this collaboration, a brief interlude for Gropius, we have a radical departure from the *international style*, and not only that, but a departure that had much in common with Wright's *Usonian* houses of the late 1930s.

Gropius then moved to the USA, taking up a teaching appointment at Harvard in 1937. He immediately began a four-year long collaboration with Marcel Breuer. Together they reinforced an allegiance to regional conditions and materials, but also a return to other modernist norms – no projecting monopitched roofs during this period. Hence we have Gropius's own Lincoln House in 1937,[63] with brick limited to the eastern fireplace wall and basecourse, and a timber superstructure. This was lined in white-painted redwood sheathing similar to the Roth's Seaside House cited earlier, and it was insulated with a 'Cabot' quilt. It was also quite Corbusian in spirit with its outdoor rooms. A canopy which is more or less detached from the main roof, but nonetheless tied to it on the same plane, provides practical shading to the south façade and further emphasises outdoor space as part of the built domain (more of this in Part 2).

Another outstanding building was the small Chamberlain House in Wayland, Massachusetts, in 1939 where a beautifully detailed timber and glass box, flat-roofed and clad in vertical, v-jointed boarding which was unpainted on this occasion, sails over a rough stone base (Fig. 2.5). According to Berdini:[64] 'particular attention has been paid to the wooden structure in order to guarantee its stability, insulation and durability'. A diagonal layer of bracing is assumed between the outer vertical cladding and the inner horizontal lining. Although smaller, the house in Wayland, generally attributed to Breuer, shares formal characteristics with Gropius's house in Lincoln. Constructionally, the timber-framed parts are much the same, but the expression of materials is different. At Lincoln, the vertically grooved quality is suppressed by the white paint, but not at Wayland. Also at Wayland the roughly hewn stone becomes part of the external skin, a rusticated base, in contrast to Lincoln where it appears at some distance from the house in the landscape – still a base of sorts, depending on the viewpoint, but more muted and diffused. Thus we can say that Gropius is quite pluralistic in his approach to both construction and its appearance, including the consequences of the

2.5 *Chamberlain House by Gropius and Breuer, Wayland, Massachusetts, 1939*

manner in which one element, such as façade, meets another, such as roof. This pluralism probably has much to do with the variety of his collaborations, in these instances Marcel Breuer influencing strongly. In spite of inevitable tensions, and sometimes with competing ideals and ideas, he was happy to work with others in an equal partnership and also to forge constructive relationships with industry. Hence there is a degree of inevitability with respect to the variety of visual outcomes.

Meanwhile, in a very quiet period following his departure from Camp Ocatillo, Wright set up the Taliesin Fellowship Complex where he developed ideas for Broadacre City and the Usonian home. He also published his autobiography in 1932. With only two houses built in the six years from 1929 until 1935, then came the seminal commission by Edgar Kaufmann, Fallingwater, located at Bear Run in West Pennsylvania. Here Wright took the reinforced concrete cantilever to contentious limits. The floor structure is similar to that of Gray's roof on the Côte d'Azur, having a supported veneer of stone flags over a reinforced concrete tray. Edgar Kaufmann jr.[65] relates that although the insulating material was sealed into roofs and floors 'sopping wet' and he later ventilated the voids in order to eliminate 'unsightly condensations', nevertheless the 'captive space allows the stone floors to be well insulated and comfortable even to bare feet'. In spite of the composite nature of the slabs, including timber flooring below the stone veneer and an intention with regard to sound deafening, they remain mono-material in spirit, expressing the solidarity of masonry. Also in the parts of the building where the cantilever is not so pronounced, mainly the higher floors, terraces and roofs, the structure reverts to a single, slender concrete slab, as do the upstands below ribbon windows. Sections of the latter also have an internal veneer in the form of built-in heating units. But although these will inhibit downdraughts, in the absence of adequate insulation the heat loss through the concrete will be considerable. The stone walls at Fallingwater were also of course mono-material, and relatively slender providing capacitance but little resistance.

As an intermittently occupied house, subjected to harsh conditions in winter, Fallingwater only worked for a wealthy client. The Kaufmanns could not only easily afford high fuel bills, but also had servants at hand to make sure the liberally glazed and heavyweight house was warmed up for arrival. In any event, its thermal shortcomings are not generally recognised as an issue. What is recognised, and what is interesting in the context of the 'multi-layer phenomenon', is that it has been acknowledged[66] as formalistically influential in the early design stages of Alvar Aalto's Villa Mairea at Noormarkku in Finland. This important European building was described by Giedion[67] as: 'Architectural chamber music which demands the strictest attention' and so ranks with Fallingwater in terms of historical relevance. It was not the kind of building Wright had in mind in his 'cardboard box' lecture seven years previously. It was regional in character and one would expect Wright to have applauded Aalto's sensitivity towards materials. However, these were employed skilfully by Aalto, not only to limit heat loss in general terms, but also to deal with cold-bridging at critical junctions (Fig. 2.6).

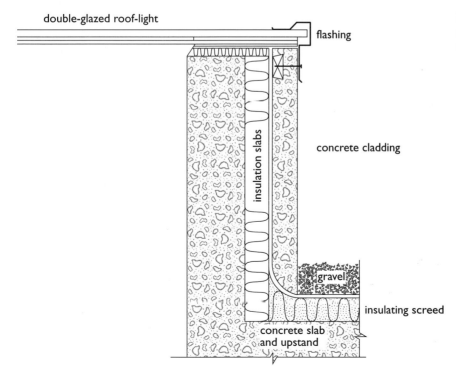

2.6 *Detail: Villa Mairea by Alvar Aalto, Noormarkku, Finland, 1937–9*

Another Scandinavian who is relevant to the cross-fertilisation of ideas between Europe and North America at this time is the Swedish architect, Sven Markelius. In an article about his work, Hamlin[68] asserts: 'Americans have for some time been looking at Sweden with a mixture of wonder and envy.' In particular Markelius collaborated with New York architects, Breines and Pomerance, with respect to the Swedish Pavilion at the 1939 New York World's Fair.[69] The elegant aerofoil roof-canopy, floating above various components of the pavilion, is a fine example of the multi-material, multi-layer construction where the choice of layers assists in thermal performance. The slatted timber soffit enables a continuous cooling draught below the upper weather-layer, thus insulating against the hot summer sun.

Here there is some merging of European multi-layer rationale with a Wrightian roof at least. Also in 1939 the Usonia II project began, with the Goetsch-Winckler residence completed in Okemos, Michigan. In the extended edition of his autobiography published in 1945 Wright[70] describes the laminated system of three 2"×4" joists used to construct the roof of the Goetsch-Winckler residence. Each 2"×4" overlaps the other at the eaves so that: 'The middle offset may be left open at the eaves and fitted with flaps used to ventilate the roofspaces in summer.' He then goes on to confirm that the 2"×4" joists are 'sheathed and

2.7 *Goetsch-Winckler house by F. L. Wright, Okemos, Michigan, 1945*

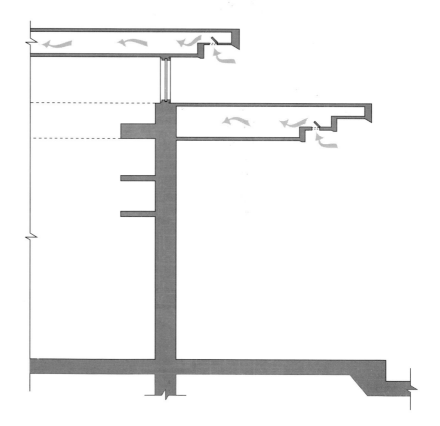

insulated'. Therefore, although copies of the original drawings[71] for this house indicate that the insulation must have been fairly nominal and the appropriateness of its position is challenged below, we have a professedly, thermally conscious, multi-layer construction on the same lines as that of Markelius's pavilion (Fig. 2.7). The deliberate movement of air through a multi-layer structure, be it Neutra and Ain (1934), Wright or Markelius (1939), is very significant. It changes a relatively steady-state thermal situation into a very dynamic one, dependent on the velocity (m/s) and volume flow rate (m^3/s) as well as its temperature.

Condensation factor

Hence we have reached a position 12 years after the chosen starting point in 1927 where we have a number of leading European modernists working in the USA at the onset of a six-year long World War which entailed an inevitable architectural hiatus, particularly within Europe. The war also had an impact in terms of availability of materials and constructional priorities, especially prefabricated techniques to enable rapid completion of large housing programmes. Thus far, the coefficient of thermal transmittance or U-value, and thermal diffusivity, have been used as indicators of performance with respect to mono-material and multi-layer construction. But due to many post-war influences, notably less dependence on solid fuel for heating and greater air-tightness, the risk of surface and interstitial condensation became an increasingly relevant criterion. Hence it is pertinent to look back at pre-war constructions to assess their worth or vulnerability in this respect, and to relate this to subsequent post-war practice.

For example, in terms of heat gain and loss, Wright has been criticised here with respect to his mono-material stance, aired in 1928 and 1930 as a prelude to his Usonian houses. In relation to heat gain, this critique was tempered with respect to thermal diffusivity which controls thermal time-lag and damping. However, mono-material constructions do have other thermal advantages compared with multi-material ones. If there is only one material, there is only one set of thermal properties – density, specific heat capacity, thermal conductivity and vapour permeability. Consequently, there is no risk of interstitial condensation, and if the material is hygroscopic, as with timber, there is also no likelihood of surface condensation. The material simply self-adjusts with respect to moisture content and this sponge effect,[72] as well as inhibiting surface condensation, will also tend to lower relative humidity (RH) within occupied rooms. Also, Simonson[73] has shown that solar radiation reduces the moisture content of timber walls and hence increases their vapour permeability. Therefore the extremely slender all-timber Usonian wall yields some advantages to offset its relatively high U-value. However, it would provide very little in the way of time lag and damping.

The lightweight, aerated nature of Corbusian hollow fuel-ash or pumice blocks would result in fairly similar characteristics in this respect to timber; and it is interesting, jumping forward to the early 1960s, that Ralph Erskine, in his own house and office at Drottningholm, chose Siporex as mono-material wall and roof, protecting the latter with a detached metal 'umbrella'[74] (Fig. 3.1). One might equally well call such an 'umbrella' a horizontal 'rainscreen', but that term, which has a modern history dating to the 1940s,[75] is normally reserved for walls. Essentially the concept was to place a weatherproof material with open joints in front of an insulated structure. Although the screen itself could have a very high vapour resistance, the open joints tended to equalise vapour pressure behind and in front of the screen. Some water was allowed to track down behind the screen, but the air-space that separated it from the insulant was adequate to protect it. In effect this meant that insulation could now be placed on the outside of the structural wall, in contrast to virtually every precedent. Apparently Raphael Soriano did use cork slabs externally on the Noyes house in 1940,[76] but it was reported that they disintegrated. This is not really surprising. It does sometimes rain in California, and cork is extremely absorbent and needs to be well protected from prolonged precipitation once removed from its tree.

At any rate, the attraction of placing weather-protected insulation on the outside of the structure was twofold. First, the structure could now perform as an insulated thermal store within the building (the tea-cosy principle). Second, the relative positions of high and low thermal and vapour resistances was ideal to minimise risk of condensation. The second aspect relied on the drained and back-ventilated rainscreen itself becoming almost thermally irrelevant in this respect. By the early 1950s, the concept had spread from Scandinavia to the USA. For example, the Alcoa tower in Pittsburgh in 1952[75] used storey-high aluminium panels outside the structure and finish, although here there is no mention of insulation other than Perlite plaster on metal lath to a thickness of about 100 mm. This system was repeated by the same architects, Harrison and Abramovitz, in the 1955 Republic National Bank building in Dallas. In the 1960s the concept was refined to a 'pressure equalised' rainscreen,[77] with the initial research again spreading from Scandinavia to North America – to Canada in the first instance.

Returning to Wright, his 1939 Usonian flat roof at Okemos bears some comparison with the technology of rainscreens in the same way that Erskine's later home and office does. It is inevitably multi-material in

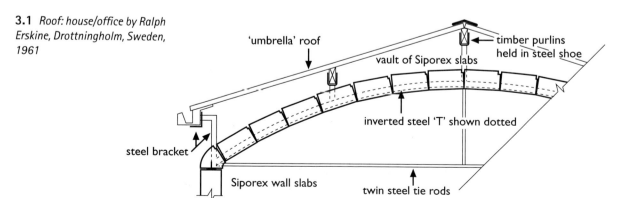

3.1 *Roof: house/office by Ralph Erskine, Drottningholm, Sweden, 1961*

'umbrella' roof

timber purlins held in steel shoe

vault of Siporex slabs

inverted steel 'T' shown dotted

steel bracket

Siporex wall slabs

twin steel tie rods

its make-up. The waterproof layer has entirely different thermal properties compared with timber, in particular a very low vapour permeability, and the layer of insulation will vary again. Hence Wright's decision to ventilate the space in order to cool the roof in summer is equally necessary in winter in order to prevent damaging condensation on the underside of the '3 ply tar and felt' layer, particularly since most windows are then likely to be closed for prolonged periods. On the other hand, the insulation is now in the wrong position with respect to slowing down the rate of heat loss. Wright had specified neither a *warm-deck* nor a *cold-deck* roof,[78] and unlike Markelius's Swedish Pavilion at New York, Wright's houses had to function in all seasons. In winter it could either become an insulated 'umbrella', with the insulation redundant above an uninsulated ceiling, or alternatively, by closing the vent at the eaves, the insulation could come into play, but at the risk of causing severe interstitial condensation.

The concept of 'rainscreens' also carries with it the concept of 'breathing construction'. If an inner leaf of brickwork is protected thermally by an insulant and then from weather by a rainscreen, there is no impedance to water vapour travelling freely from inside to outside. Vapour may also be absorbed and desorbed along the way, depending on how hygroscopic the structural and insulating materials are. This may apply equally to mono-layer and multi-layer construction. In its origins it has grown out of the heroic period of the Modern Movement, apparently without consciously being a concept. For example, Bruce Goff,[79] who set up on his own in the late 1930s designing a number of Usonian-type houses, became more uninhibited during the 1940s. His 1947 Ford House solves the problem of a vapour-resistant, outer layer by externally cladding domed shells, combining wall and roof, in shingles. It is mono-material in essence with diagonal, tongued and grooved timber lining the frame internally. Thus any risk of damage from interstitial condensation due to the presence of insulation between outer and inner linings would have been limited due to its innate breathability. In 1950 his Bavinger house added fresh dimensions or layers to the idea of 'house'. Many rooms became detached saucers within a rough-hewn, mono-layer stone enclosing spiral, which also has ancillary pods attached to it externally. Then in 1962 the Prairie House of one of his students, Herb Greene,[80] exhibits the spirit of Goff's Bavinger House and the technique of his Ford House, this time with rough-hewn shingles inside and out; as well as a close relationship with the work of Scandinavian expressionists.[81] An example is the 1949 Portør House in Norway by Knut Knutsen, and the same architectural dynamic is present in Erskine's contemporaneous Ski Hotel at Borgafjäll – a bolder building tectonically, with its supporting structure separated out from its envelope.

As indicated above, Erskine separates the roof layers in a different way at Drottningholm. The structural vault and insulant are one, with the addition of minimal steel tying and support which does not result in cold-bridging. Condensation is prevented by generous cross-ventilation between the insulated structural mass and its waterproof lid, which in turn works equally well in all seasons in terms of inhibiting radiant losses and gains. Hence in Erskine we have a British architect working mainly in Scandinavia who develops a climate-sensitive, regional attitude to the constructional envelope which tangibly draws on Wright's ascetic mono-materialism in at least one notable project, as well as his more general references to Aalto, Markelius and others. However, not all Erskine's envelopes were so successful. In the mid-1950s his steel-domed weekend/summer house on the Lisö peninsula south of Stockholm[82] was a multi-layer recipe for interstitial condensation with an almost infinite vapour resistance (the steel shell) on the 'cold' side of the insulant.* In fact it constituted the inverse of the 'rainscreen' or 'breathing' construction.

If a radically experimental architect such as Erskine made a more fundamental mistake at Lisö in the mid-1950s, compared with Wright's Usonian roofs in the 1930s, the next question to pose is whether any of the early European multi-layerists fared any better in this respect. Returning to Gropius at Stuttgart in 1927, the roof performs rather well (see Fig. 2.4, p. 18). The two air spaces on either side of the cork insulant were not deliberately ventilated, but fortuitous leakage would tend to reduce the amount of water vapour reaching the underside of the waterproof layer. Then any condensate below this layer would be absorbed by the pumice screed on top of the concrete slab; and the air space below the slab provides an opportunity for the moisture to breathe out harmlessly, downwards rather than upwards. The risk of breaking down the adhesion of the waterproof material is hence reduced. Also, if dewpoint occurred within the layer of cork, its hygroscopic nature would prevent damage. Overall, the most vulnerable components would have been the steel beams, but even these are thermally protected by the pumice screed.

Most of the modernist flat roofs in Europe were based on concrete rather than timber, the exceptions tending to be located in Scandinavia. In general, there undoubtedly was a high probability of dewpoint being above structural temperature from the underside of the waterproof material back into one or more layers below it. However, also in general, the materials such as clay, concrete and cork were able to sustain variations in moisture content. Also in many cases, a layer of protective material above the waterproof layer was specified to reduce thermal expansion and contraction, and hence the likelihood of rapid failure. Taking the example of Roth and Walberg's Swedish House, described earlier as having combined regional construction with a modernist aesthetic, we

---

*My own visit in 1992 confirmed the resulting moisture ingress around rooflights, the condensate on the underside of the steel shell tracking down until it found a pathway inwards at these junctions. In addition, the house is prone to overheating in summer. This is firstly because condensate dropping from the inside of the steel on to the quilted insulation will have resulted in matting and reduced thermal performance, and secondly because voids below the steel shell are unventilated.

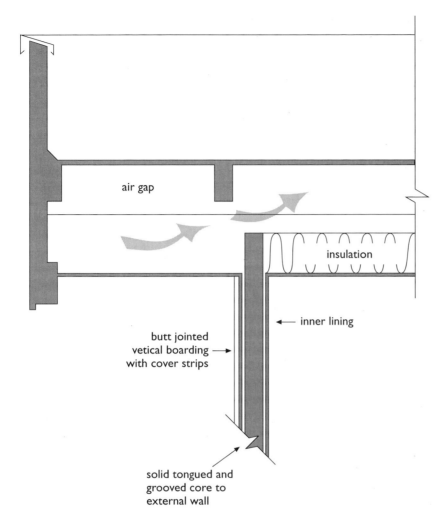

3.2 *Seaside house by Alfred Roth and Ingrid Walberg, Sweden, 1930*

air gap

insulation

← inner lining

butt jointed
vetical boarding →
with cover strips

solid tongued and
grooved core to
external wall

find a cold-deck construction with an ample roof void above the insulated ceiling (Fig. 3.2). Here the opportunity to ventilate the void would avoid the risk of condensate rotting the structural decking, but without compromising a low U-value.

Multi-layer walls tend to be intrinsically less problematic than flat roofs, since there is no need for an outer layer with a very high vapour resistance. Nonetheless, the tendency to use the insulant on the inside face of dense concrete would result in structural temperatures below dewpoint over a significant proportion of the concrete. Therefore, in the same way as roofs, the choice of a hygroscopic insulant, such as cork or compressed peat, was essential to the viability of the construction. Had the order been reversed by placing stuccoed insulation as permanent shuttering on the outside of the reinforced concrete, the construction would have been inherently less subject to interstitial condensation. The

3.3 *Multi-layer wall of Bens house, 1932 – low risk of condensation*

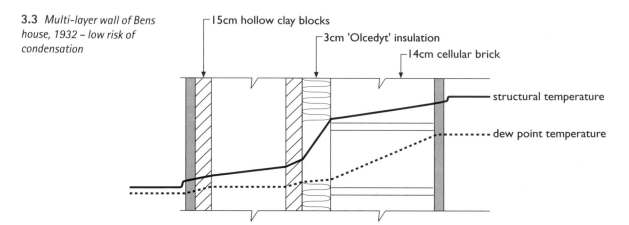

15cm hollow clay blocks

3cm 'Olcedyt' insulation

14cm cellular brick

structural temperature

dew point temperature

Czecho-Slovakian sandwich illustrated earlier (see Fig. 2.1, p. 10) is interesting in terms of the relative positioning of thermal resistance and vapour resistance. It is a generally vapour-permeable construction where the layers with the greater thermal resistance and lower vapour resistance are located outside the main structural layer of brick, which has a comparatively low thermal resistance, but somewhat higher vapour resistance. Hence there is less likelihood of structural temperatures falling below dewpoint (see Fig. 3.3).

CHAPTER 4

Using a specific date, 1927, as a starting point for this topic, suggests a complementary stopping or pausing point which is also not arbitrary. The early 1960s have specific relevance. In particular, 1963 is the date of the introduction of the first national building regulations in the UK, and these initiated a thermal requirement for the external envelope. There is also a pleasing symmetry about 1927 and 1963 since the half-way point between these dates is the end of the Second World War. Further, having used Fuller as one of the markers for 1927, 1963 happens to be the date of Fuller's Carbondale publication. This sets out a challenge to architects to redeploy the world's chemical and energy resources to serve a great deal more than 44% of humankind (at that time). Presented to delegates of the second half of the 1963 UIA Congress held in Mexico City,[83] it was then appraised in the final issue of *Architectural Design* that year. Fuller emphasises that 'all in the universe is in constant transformative complex motion and all transform in the patterns of least resistance'. He implicitly takes a neutral position in terms of the make-up of walls and roofs, rather challenging architects to specify required properties so that technologists are able to find materials to match their specification.

Fuller would undoubtedly have approved of the tectonic ingenuity of Jean Prouvé's houses and schools, also published in 1963, and praised by Le Corbusier:[84] 'Everything that he touches and conceives immediately takes on an elegant plastic form, while at the same time he achieves brilliant solutions to the problems of resistance and assembly.' It is not clear if *resistance* refers to resistance to wind, degradation to the forces of weather or acoustic and/or thermal resistance. However, the various composite sealed-sandwich walls and the open multi-layer, cold-deck roofs do tackle thermal resistance very well for the period. The so-called Rousseau panel (Fig. 4.1), which forms a structural ceiling below a layer of insulation and the corrugated aluminium lid, is simply a horizontal version of the Usonian wall, but with the addition of insulation coping admirably with cold weather. It is perhaps ironic, given the praise of Le Corbusier, that Prouvé's designs conform so closely to a thermally improved Usonian paradigm. It is also noteworthy that the roof of Albert Frey's own second Californian House, started in 1963 and completed in 1964,[85] conformed to the principle of a corrugated metal canopy and ventilated airspace above an insulated 'cassette'. However, in this case there is no timber 'Rousseau' panel to prevent cold-bridging through the structural steel which is on the same plane as the layer of insulation.

4.1 *System by Jean Prouvé, 1950s – low risk of condensation in roof*

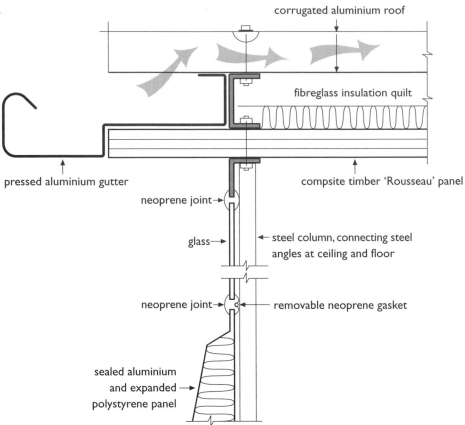

corrugated aluminium roof

fibreglass insulation quilt

pressed aluminium gutter

compsite timber 'Rousseau' panel

neoprene joint→

glass→   ←steel column, connecting steel angles at ceiling and floor

neoprene joint→   ←removable neoprene gasket

sealed aluminium and expanded → polystyrene panel

There was also much more tailored, site-specific assembly in Frey's 1963–4 house than was promised by the Aluminaire prototype, or even his first Californian House of 1941,[86] where the influence of both Mies van der Rohe and Neutra is evident.

In general, although by the 1960s the initial temporary post-war building period had moved on to an apparently more secure phase in terms of investment, it is paradoxical that building technology was so shy of sophisticated prefabrication. Rather it regressed to a more traditional plateau, from which there have been few advances in spite of the microchip, petro-chemicals and research related to space exploration.

Other landmarks of the early 1960s, such as the publication of the work of Tcam 10 in 1960,[87] with its strong connections to the heroic modernists – Wright had just died and Le Corbusier had not long to go – impacted more on the formal issues of architecture, rather than aspects of a building's external envelope. For example, this is exemplified by van Eyck's orphanage in Amsterdam and Kahn's house designs for Philadelphia and New York. However, there is a requirement for an extremely well-insulated envelope which is implicit in Erskine's design for an arctic city. More significantly in relation to the issue of multi-layer construction, the book *Supports* by N. J. Habraken[88] published one year later in 1961 strongly relates to Le Corbusier's Unité concept[89] where internal layers comprise light factory-made 'drawers' nesting in a heavy framework – or 'bottles in a wine-bin' as he put it. *Supports* proposed a more user-friendly approach to mass housing. It differentiated between permanent structure plus essential servicing, and shorter-term, fit-out components where the occupant was much more in control. Back in 1963, rapidly erected, large-scale prefabrication, with or without any user-participation, also had critical socio-economic relevance for some developing countries.* Retrospectively, most mass housing, in many cases influenced by the Unité, has been widely acknowledged as disastrous. For all that, a 'supports' dimension to the 'multi-layer' phenomenon, that of different life-spans or choices for some constructional layers, has intermittently gained currency along with political moves to facilitate stake-holding by users.

Still pursuing the notion of detaching the layers of construction from each other, it is worth returning to Erskine. An example has already been cited of his unsuccessful multi-layer construction in the 1950s, where a major rethink and rebuild would be necessary to resolve the problem; and a successful and intrinsically mono-layer one in the 1960s, which looked almost new in the early 1990s. Two years earlier than the construction of his own house and studio, Erskine[90] detaches balconies and canopies from the façade of Villa Ström. Here some 'bottles' stand outside a closed 'bin', and their independent support has a thermal function in the avoidance of cold-bridging. Again this makes a case for different constructional approaches for discrete components. The walls of the 'bin' are composite and insulated, and the 'bottles', balconies and their supports, are of homogenous reinforced concrete. However, Erskine's own mix of thermal success and failure raises the question of just how generally random or consistent was the tectonic and environmental performance of the *skin* of much earlier buildings of the Modern Movement.

In other words, has the construction of external floors, walls and roofs evolved through the decades in a climate of ignorance or one of knowledge gained through experience and research? The answer may well be a mixture of both, given the evidence. But the prevalence of poor construction supports the former contention and reinforces the case for shifting the emphasis of our published material. Constructional and spatial interpretation and analysis of buildings are required in equal measures. Then, in

*The first half of the UIA Congress held in Havana in 1963, with its impassioned speeches by Fidel Castro and Che Guevara on the politics of architectural education and the problems of building for education, health and housing in revolutionary Cuba, made me much more aware of the political dimension embodied in architecture, including its construction. I saw six-storey-high prefabricated frames for students' hostels, and lift-slabs for the academic blocks erected as a very rapid support system for the subsequent skin of these buildings, a major precasting plant having been set up on site.

terms of this appraisal, is it possible to identify post-war trends or characteristics arising from the Modern Movement? It has been shown that the main advantage offered by a multi-layer construction is a fairly high thermal resistance for a fairly modest thickness. However, due to inherent vulnerability to interstitial condensation, specification of materials and ventilation of any air gaps becomes very important. In the pre-war period, the types of insulant and other relatively porous materials tended to limit damage in this respect, but the dominance of post-war problems suggests that the principles were not generally well understood by architects. Although Aalto continued to demonstrate sound thermal principles, as in his ventilated, cold-deck roof over the council chamber at Säynätsalo in 1951[91] (Fig. 4.2), others apparently did not.

The initial post-war emphasis on light, prefabricated structures resulted in buildings that were rather poorly insulated and prone to interstitial condensation. These owed allegiance to a mix of influences – proprietary systems developed in the inter-war period,[92] the pioneering work of architects such as Gropius, global thinkers such as Fuller, and the Californian case-study houses in the late 1940s.[93] Not all were sound role models. For instance, Breuer[94] accepted a link between de-laminating plywood ceilings and insulation at the Chamberlain cottage, his last project while in partnership with Gropius. He implied a condensation problem caused by the relative locations of insulation and other layers in the roof. Then in terms of protection against the Californian sun, or even worse if translated to cold climates, the $\frac{1}{2}$" insulation board over the steel roof-deck of the famous 1949 house by Charles and Ray Eames was just too skimpy.

4.2 *Wall-head: Town Hall by Alvar Aalto, Säynätsalo, Finland, 1951*

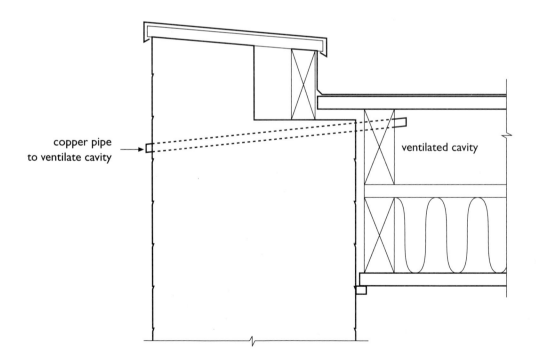

copper pipe
to ventilate cavity →

ventilated cavity

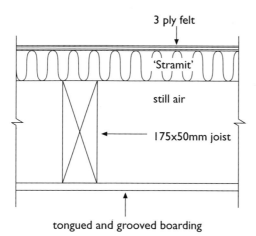

4.3a *No vapour check on warm side of insulation, and still air in voids*

3 ply felt

'Stramit'

still air

175x50mm joist

tongued and grooved boarding

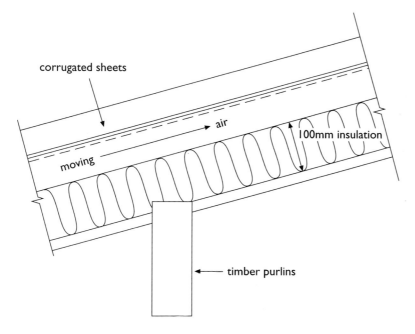

4.3b *Moving air inhibits condensation*

corrugated sheets

moving air

100mm insulation

timber purlins

By 1960, there is evidence of the UK/North European divide with respect to standards of insulation which continues to the present. For instance an architect's own house in the UK[95] (Fig. 4.3a) had three layers of bituminous felt over Stramit straw boards, used as structural decking over 7" × 2" joists with a ceiling of redwood lining. Not only is this not very well insulated, it is highly vulnerable to condensation.† In contrast a

† As a student in 1962 I specified this particular warm-deck specification for a new ambulance station in Edinburgh. The idea of an insulant that doubled-up as the structural deck was appealing. As above it was without a vapour control layer. Moreover it was above toilets, showers and canteen, an area of high moisture production, and it was built with, in hindsight, predictably drastic consequences.

typical holiday home in Denmark, also built in 1960,[96] not only had twice as much insulation, but its construction (Fig. 4.3b) allowed for generous ventilation of the space above 100 mm mineral wool, thus negating the incidence of interstitial condensation. It is tempting to regard this kind of construction as a norm in Continental Europe, or at least in Scandinavian countries. However, details of a similarly insulated, cold-deck, flat roof over the 1950s houses in Oslo,[97] mentioned in the preface, indicate no means of ventilating the air space; and details of a similarly constructed house to the 1960 Danish example, this time in Switzerland[98] and again dated 1960, finds the insulation reduced to 45 mm.

In the case of Fuller,[99] whose prefabrication related strongly to the production of terrestrial vehicles and aircraft, the single skin example of casein-based plastic for Dymaxion's walls, windows and ceilings neglected insulation. Again, although the 1945–6 Wichita House is known to have insulated Duralumin panels and a foil vapour check above the ceiling,[100] the insulation was probably minimal since it is also known that Fuller expected the aerodynamic circular form to reduce both heating and cooling loads.[101] The logic here is, to say the least, questionable. In winter, the form would slightly reduce thermal resistance, but might inhibit infiltration of air; while in summer the cooling impact of reduced drag would be insignificant compared with a well-insulated shell combined with the building's unique central roof extractor.[102] Fuller's strand of streamlined, curvilinear prefabrication later began to simultaneously associate itself with both natural forms and space technology. Arthur Quarmby dubbed his 1963 proposal for free-form pods attached to a polygonal tower a 'Corn on the Cob'.[103] The pods invoke Dymaxion and Wichita as well as bubble cars of the 1960s; and while the overall 'corn cob' might conjure up some kind of space station, it was the forerunner of a decade of unbuilt 'plug-in cities' and 'living pods'.

There is no reason why relatively short-life cells, pods or capsules should not be adequately insulated, taking the cue from Prouvé rather than Fuller. The fact that such ideas did not find a market is a quirk of economic history rather than the consequence of technical barriers. In 1941, the American Technical Society[104] listed 166 proprietary insulating materials. Moreover, most of these would now be labelled 'green'. In the 1950s lesser-known advocates of prefabrication such as Carl Koch[105] were not only foreseeing structural insulation as a logical progression from foamed stressed-skin panels, but also phase-change thermal storage walls as a natural extension of the passive solar techniques of that time. Thus we see a growing, if patchy, sophistication to the knowledge-base that supports multi-layer design from the birth of The New Architecture onwards. Opening up the understanding and the debate around any such aspects of modernism that were side-lined or forgotten, and which remain relevant today, inevitably places a focus on light versus heavy, thin versus thick, and multi-material versus mono-material.

It does seem that van Doesburg's maxim 'bad construction leads to bad surface' holds true. Interstitial condensation may break down surfaces on the inside or on the outside, just as inadequate attention may be paid to the manner in which junctions between external materials affect the flow of water over them, and hence their weathered appearance and prospect for longevity. Vulnerability to oxidisation or other chemical action or interaction, and degradation caused by the action of the sun, are other aspects that support van Doesburg's premise, but often remain underestimated. What does not hold true is using this notion to support the universal applicability of his 'de stijl' and to attack well tried and tested regional detailing. Indeed, to give a specific example that proves van Doesburg's point, Rietveld's Schröder House exemplifies the problems associated with aligning traditional brick and timber construction with a 'de stijl' aesthetic. Then again, for Rietveld, this was intended to be a short-term experiment.

Looked at from the angle of statutory regulation, our thermal standards in the UK have not yet reached the level achieved by Gropius in 1927, and our techniques for multi-layer construction are often extremely suspect. As indicated in relation to the Schröder House, it would be foolish to suggest that all modernist construction worked well. However, this overview does support certain propositions. It appears that the external envelopes of buildings in the 1920s and 1930s were indeed more complex than is generally perceived through the medium of text or illustrations in most books and periodicals published then or since. Further, among a small band of leading figures, there were competing ideals regarding the nature of the envelope. These merit re-examination, particularly in terms of the following two aspects.

The first is the separation of layers with different functions. For example, a detached metal 'rainscreen' made permeable with slots or perforations, outside an insulated structural wall, makes more sense than ceramic tiles bonded on to masonry, with insulation in a cavity or as an internal lining. Apart from vapour pressure, dewpoint and frost acting to remove the bond, the rainscreen is easier to replace after a life-span that is probably less than the rest of the wall. As well as working with climate and function, the idea accords with a flexible life-cycle approach where different owners and users may be responsible for different layers. The second is that a vapour-permeable, 'breathing' construction, using hygroscopic materials, has advantages in terms of the indoor environment. The Prouvé roof described above exploits both principles. It is essentially a horizontal external rainscreen, and the glue holding the layers of the timber Rousseau panels together should provide adequate vapour resistance, given the free cross circulation of air above. However, many architects seem to have become too used to standards or norms where multi-layer construction is sealed with a vapour control layer of plastic or metal foil. They are conservatively reluctant to endorse a looser approach that relies on modest, relative contrasts in thermal properties.

This implies a need to get back to first principles, and to analyse and classify. Thermal analysis can be simple or complex depending on the level of examination required or wanted. But modern software can cope easily with the most advanced dynamic analysis. Classification is simply a matter of logical ordering rather than instinctive serendipity. For instance, we can classify envelopes that are 'dynamic by design', as well as by 'behaviour' examined in short time-steps. If air is pulled through an insulant, the wall, roof or floor this would be dynamic by design. The Beard House by Neutra and Ain is such an example. The commonality between 'rainscreens' and 'breathing construction' has been identified. Grouping these types is logical classification, but within the latter, mono-layer construction would be a different sub-set compared with a multi-layer version. Multi-layer systems would have further sub-sets depending on the relative placing of insulation and dense materials, in turn possibly dependent on whether a rainscreen is involved or not. 'Sealed sandwich' construction may deserve its own category. Although three layers and two materials are commonly involved, such a panel behaves as one material – an insulant with an almost infinite vapour resistance, which is also waterproof. Sealed sandwiches may also be used with further layers, for example, in order to conceal the structure that supports the panels. It is such an approach, in conjunction sometimes with new products, that is most likely to lead laterally into untried innovation.

In other words architects should build systematically, imaginatively and courageously on the knowledge and experience of the past. This supports the case for looking deeper than the most publicised passions of the main players which were, more often than not, formalistically focussed and challengingly expressed. Tectonic ambitions were also present, and even if the realisation of such ambitions failed to endure, this does not invalidate the intention. At any rate, a tectonic investigation of the past to inform the future is a more rewarding approach than timidly and unquestioningly accepting the presented 'deemed to satisfy' specifications of others. This implies being open to accepting a degree of control over scientific analysis, which will in turn help to reduce the factor of risk, otherwise tending to inhibit clients and their financiers. Reduced risk equates to increased trust – a 'win-win' situation in modern managerial terms.

References to Part One

1   Le Corbusier (trans. Etchells 1927), *Towards a New Architecture*, The Architectural Press, London, and Frederick A. Praeger, New York.

2   Yorke F. R. S. (1934), *The Modern House*, The Architectural Press, London, 76–7.

3   Ibid. 72–5 and 202–3.

4   Droste M. (1990), *Bauhaus*, Bauhaus-Archiv Museum für Gestaltung, Berlin, 135.

5   Molema J. (1989), *Jan Duiker*, Editorial Gustavo Gili, S.A., Barcelona, 114–27.

6   Hecker S. and Müller C. F. (1993), *Eileen Gray*, Editorial Gustavo Gili, S.A., Barcelona, 60–113.

7   Frampton K. (1983), *Modern Architecture 1920–1945*, GA Document, Special Issue 3, A.D.A. EDITA, Tokyo Co. Ltd., January. 1983, 302–5.

8   Ibid. 298–9.

9   van Doesburg T. (trans. Loeb and Loeb 1990), *Theo van Doesburg on European Architecture, Complete Essays from Het Bouwbedrift 1924–1931*, Birkhauser Verlag, Basel, 167 (Het Bouwbedrift Vol. 4, No. 24, November 1927, 556–9).

10 Wright F. L. (1945), Book 4 Freedom. In *An Autobiography*, Faber & Faber, London, 267.

11 Persitz A. (1946), *Richard J. Neutra, Architect*, l'Architecture d'Aujourd'hui, No. 6, May–June.

12 Gebhard D. (1971), Ch. 6 The making of a personal style. In *Schindler*, Thames & Hudson, London, 80–9.

13 Pawley M. (1990), The Year of Silence. In *Buckminster Fuller*, Trefoil Publications, London, 36–7.

14 Ibid. 39–56.

15 (1927), *Building Educator*, Vols. I–III, Ed. R. Greenhalgh, Pitman, London.

16 Wright F. L. (1941), In the Cause of Architecture: The Logic of the Plan (from The Architectural Record, January 1928) In *Frank Lloyd Wright on Architecture, Selected Writings 1894–1940*, Ed. F Gutheim, Duell, Sloan and Pearce, New York, 107–9.

17 Ibid. 1910: Studies and Executed Buildings (from Ausgeführte Bauten und Entwürfe, Berlin), 59–76.

18 Wright F. L. (1953), Modern Architecture (The Princeton Lectures)

4 The Cardboard House. In *The Future of Architecture*, Horizon Press Inc. (and Mentor Books, 1963, 144–5 and 156).

19   Wright F. L. (1941), 1901: The Art and Craft of the Machine (lecture at Hull House, Chicago) In *Frank Lloyd Wright on Architecture, Selected Writings 1894–1940*, Ed. F.Gutheim, Duell, Sloan and Pearce, New York, 23–24; and (1953), Modern Architecture (The Princeton Lectures) 1 Machinery, Materials and Men, The Art and Craft of the Machine. In *The Future of Architecture*, Horizon Press Inc. (and Mentor Books, 1963, 84–102).

20   Wright F. L. (1945), Book 3 Work. In *An Autobiography*, Faber & Faber, London, 216.

21   Ibid. Book 4 Freedom, 269.

22   Ibid. Book 4 Freedom, 272.

23   Wright F. L. (1955), *An American Architecture*, Ed. E. Kaufmann, Horizon Press, New York, 174.

24   Patterson T. L. (1994), Ch. 2 Wood. In *Frank Lloyd Wright and the Meaning of Materials*, Van Nostrand Reinhold, 23.

25   Yorke F. R. S. (1934), *The Modern House*, The Architectural Press, London, 202–3.

26   Ibid. 46–54.

27   Ibid. 146.

28   Ibid. 83.

29   Ibid. 110–11.

30   Ibid. 118–19.

31   Ibid. 72–5.

32   Lowman J. (1976), *Corb as structural rationalist*, The Architectural Review, 956, 229–33.

33   Le Corbusier (1930, trans. Aujame 1991), 2nd Lecture 5th October 1929. In *Precisions on the Present State of Architecture and City Planning*, The MIT Press, 42.

34   Yorke F. R. S. (1934), *The Modern House*, The Architectural Press, London, 197–9.

35   Ibid. 211.

36   Sbriglio J. (1999, trans. Parsons), *Le Corbusier: La Villa Savoye*, Fondation Le Corbusier, Paris, Birkhauser Basel·Boston·Berlin, 138–49.

37   Yorke F. R. S. (1934), *The Modern House*, The Architectural Press, London, 108–9.

38   Ford J. and Ford K. M. (1940), *The Modern House in America*, Architectural Book Publishing Co. Inc., New York, 69–70.

39   Yorke F. R. S. (1934), *The Modern House*, The Architectural Press, London, 150–2.

40   Ibid. 160–1.

41   Ibid. 162–3.

42   Ibid. 166.

43   Ibid. 164–5.

44   Ibid. 167.

45   Ibid. 168–9.

46   Ibid. 170–1.

47   Statutory Instruments (1963) No. 1987 (S. 102), Part IX Resistance to the Transmission of Heat. In *Building and Buildings The Building Standards (Scotland) Regulations 1963*, HMSO, 66.

48   Gebhard D. (1971), Ch. 4 Opportunity: California in the twenties. In *Schindler*, Thames and Hudson Ltd., London, 50–1.

49   Ibid. 69–72.

50   Ibid. 88.

51   Ibid. 82.

52   Ibid. 86.

53   Spade R. (1971), *Richard Neutra*, Thames and Hudson Ltd., London, 13.

54   Wright F. L. (1953), Modern Architecture (The Princeton Lectures) 4 The Cardboard House. In *The Future of Architecture*, Horizon Press Inc. (and Mentor Books 1963), 144.

55   Hines T. S. (1989), Case Study Trouvé, Sources and Precedents Southern California, 1920–1942. In *Blueprints for Modern Living: History and Legacy of the Case Study Houses*, Ed. E. A. T. Smith, MIT Press, Cambridge, Massachusetts, 94.

56   Ford J. and Ford K. M. (1940), *The Modern House in America*, Architectural Book Publishing Co. Inc., New York, 84–6.

57   Le Corbusier (1930, trans. Aujame 1991), 2nd Lecture 5th October 1929. In *Precisions on the Present State of Architecture and City Planning*, The MIT Press, 40.

58   Hecker S. and Müller C. F. (1993), *Eileen Gray*, Editorial Gustavo Gili, S.A., Barcelona, 100.

59   Patterson T. L. (1994), Ch. 7 Concrete. In *Frank Lloyd Wright and the Meaning of Materials*, Van Nostrand Reinhold, 192.

60   Wright F. L. (1945), Book 3 Work. In *An Autobiography*, Faber & Faber, London, 203–6.

61   Berdini P. (1994), *Walter Gropius*, Editorial Gustavo Gili, S.A., Barcelona, 128–9.

62   Ibid. 151.

63   Ford J. and Ford K. M. (1940), *The Modern House in America*, Architectural Book Publishing Co. Inc., New York, 41–3.

64   Berdini P. (1994), *Walter Gropius*, Editorial Gustavo Gili, S.A., Barcelona, 174.

65   Kaufmann E. (1962), Twenty-five Years of the House on the Waterfall in *Frank Lloyd Wright's Falling Water*, ETAS/KOMPASS, Milan 1963, reprinted from *l'Architettura* No. 82, August 1962.

66   Weston R. (1992), *Villa Mairea*, Phaidon Press Ltd, London.

67   Cantacuzino S. (1964), *Modern Houses of the World*, Studio Vista Ltd., London, 101.

68   Hamlin T. F. (1939), *Sven Markelius*, Pencil Points, June 1939, 357.

69   Op. cit. 364–6.

70   Wright F. L. (1945), Book 5 Form. In *An Autobiography*, Faber & Faber, London, 426.

71   Kresge Art Museum Bulletin, Special Issue (1991), Ed. S. J. Bandes, *Affordable Dreams, the Goetsch-Winckler House and Frank Lloyd Wright*, Vol. VI, Michigan State University.

72   Garratt J. and Nowak F. (1991), *Tackling Condensation*, BRE Report BR 174, 22–3.

73   Simonson C. J. (1994), *Effect of Solar Radiation on the Moisture Content of Insulated Log Houses.* In proceedings North Sun '94, Glasgow, James & James Ltd., London, 361–6.

74   Collymore P. (1982), *The Architecture of Ralph Erskine*, Granada Publishing, London, 101–2.

75   Anderson J. M. and Gill J. R. (1988), Appendix A: A review of the origins and development of rainscreen cladding. In *Rainscreen Cladding, A Guide to Design Principles and Practice*, CIRIA/Butterworths, London, 74.

76   McCoy E. (1989), Arts & Architecture Case Study Houses. In *Blueprints for Modern Living: History and Legacy of the Case Study Houses*, Ed. E. A. T. Smith, MIT Press, Massachusetts, 29.

77   Anderson J. M. and Gill J. R. (1988), Ch. 2 Historical Perspective. In *Rainscreen Cladding, A Guide to Design Principles and Practice*, CIRIA/Butterworths, London, 3–4.

78   Porteous C. and Markus T. (1991/1995), *Condensation Culture: Cause and Cure*, Mackintosh School of Architecture, Glasgow G3 6RQ, 30–1.

79   (1995), *The Architecture of Bruce Goff, 1904–82, Design for the Continuous Present*, Eds P. Saliga and M. Woolever, Prestel-Verlag, Munich and New York, 49–54, 72–3 and 76–7.

80   Greene H. (1976), *Mind and Image*, University Press of Kentucky (Granada 1980), 28–9 and 124.

81   Grønvold U. (trans. Almaas 1996), *Summer House*, Architectural Review, 1194, August, 73–7.

82   Collymore P. (1982), *The Architecture of Ralph Erskine*, Granada Publishing, London, 68–9.

83   (1963), *UIA Cuba-Mexico – Buckminster Fuller* (News), Architectural Design, December, 557.

84   (1963), *The Work of Jean Prouvé*, Architectural Design, November, 512.

85   Golub J. (1998), *Albert Frey/Houses 1 + 2*, Princeton Architectural Press, New York, 47–69.

86   Ibid. 15–27.

87   (1960), *CIAM Team 10* Ed. A. Smithson, Architectural Design, May, 179–205.

88   Habraken N. J. (1961, trans. Valkenburg 1972), *Supports, an Alternative to Mass Housing*, Scheltema and Holkema N.V. (pb Architectural Press 1972), 59–69.

89   Le Corbusier (trans. Sainsbury 1953), *The Marseilles Block*, The Harvill Press, London, 42–4.

90   Collymore P. (1982), *The Architecture of Ralph Erskine*, Granada Publishing, London, 88–9.

91   Weston R. (1993), *Town Hall, Säynätsalo*, Phaidon Press Ltd, London.

92   Scottish Office Building Directorate (1987), *A Guide to Non-traditional and Temporary Housing in Scotland*, 1923–55, HMSO Edinburgh, 53–97.

93   Steele J. (1994), *Eames House*, Charles and Ray Eames, Phaidon Press Ltd, London.

94   Driller J. (2000), *Breuer Houses*, Phaidon Press Ltd, London, 143.

95   (1960), *Houses: Architect's own house Ipswich*, Architectural Design, November, 436–7.

96   (1960), *Et Sommerhus*, Arkitektur 1, 37–40 and A 28.

97   (1956), *The Modern House: Architects' own houses at Oslo*, Architectural Design, March, 69–72.

98   (1960), *Houses: Architect's own house in Gockhausen*, Architectural Design, November, 459–62.

99   Pawley M. (1990), The Year of Silence. In *Buckminster Fuller*, Trefoil Publications, London, 56.

100   Ibid. House of the Century, 106–7.

101   McHale J. (1960), *Commentary on 'Universal Requirements Check List' by Buckminster Fuller*, Architectural Design, March, 105.

102   Pawley M. (1990), House of the Century. In *Buckminster Fuller*, Trefoil Publications, London, 93.

103   Dahinden J. (1971, trans. Onn 1972), Projects. In *Urban Structures for the Future*, Pall Mall Press, London, 68.

104   Close P. D. (1941), Ch. II Types of Thermal Building Insulations. In *Building Insulation*, American Technical Society, USA, and The Technical Press Ltd, London, 9–44D.

105   Koch C. And Lewis A. (1958), 4. The Designer and his Kicks. In *At Home with Tomorrow*, Rinehart & Co. Inc, New York/Toronto, 70–5.

The glass is greener . . .

Frank Lloyd Wright's Five Resources	Le Corbusier's Five Points
1. sense of 'within' . . . growing into light . . . dissolve inside–outside barriers	1. piloti . . . continuity of view . . . no basement . . . freeing the building from the ground
2. glass . . . the enabler of 1st resource	2. roof garden . . . giving back ground in air
3. continuity . . . plasticity (of structure)	3. free plan . . . enabled by structural continuity
4. nature of materials . . . honest expression	4. free façade . . . multiple options of materiality
5. pattern as natural–integral ornament	5. horizontal windows . . . even/abundant light

What is green?

CHAPTER 5

This second part deliberately widens the scope of the first which concerned itself with different approaches to the opaque skin of buildings in the period 1927–63. The specificity of this time-span was a device to suit the relatively narrow focus of that topic – the make-up of opaque walls and roofs – albeit impacting significantly on buildings as a whole, and including thermal comfort and running costs as well as aesthetic aspects. Here, although influences arising from the particular period of the Modern Movement from the 1920s to 1940s are still very much in the frame, there is a correspondence between the widening of the subject matter and the chronology. Whole buildings are discussed in relationship to a broader set of 'green' issues and, as a particular aspect of the main theme demands, the period is extended backwards and forwards to include the start, and to move tentatively towards the latter end, of the 20th century. The introduction discussed the close relationship between the topical words 'green' and 'sustainability'. They also embrace or at least engage with other terms that post-date the period most under scrutiny – passive solar design, bioclimatic design, bio-regionalism and so forth. The proposition is that although such terms gained currency during the 1980s and 1990s, the precepts have a much longer history, and merit discussion in relation to the main players of the Modern Movement or New Architecture. The consistent objective is not simply to post-rationalise but to illuminate today's debate on green architecture from the pragmatic sagacity of Brenda and Robert Valc[1] to the 'quirkily mannerist form-making' of Thomas Spiegelhalter.[2] In other words, the contention is that if a 'green' architectural language or syntax does exist, it is very pluralistic and inclusive. This may seem surprising to some who associate 'green' either with add-on engineering gadgets, or with an extreme strand that might come under the term 'deep ecology' and has a visual connotation that might conjure up 'organic' in a visually literal way. Hence it is necessary to make a further effort to define what is meant by 'green' as applied here, and also to place some limits on the range of issues to be tackled within such a definition.

The problem with many generic terms is that definitions tend to be illusive, varying from one author to another. Also the word 'green' as applied to architecture has enormous scope. At one end issues include fundamental planning strategies, policies and dilemmas such as 'greenfield' versus 'brownfield' development, suburban versus urban housing, mixed versus zoned development. All these have profound influences on vehicular generation, and hence intake of fuel and release of gases, as well as other related matters which belong in the realms of social and economic sustainability. Suburbs tend to work for the relatively well-off with young families, but can be a hopeless model for the poor with young families. Also urban housing is often close to heavy traffic and its pollutants such as benzene invade and lodge inside homes. However, these wider issues will be more or less set aside here. At the purely architectural end, the scope of 'green' includes: the size and shape of buildings; their usefulness; their materiality; their embodied and recurring energy-loads; their embodied and recurring output of pollution; their longevity and vulnerability to disrepair; their recyclability and reusability; and their contribution or disruption to microclimate and biodiversity. Several of these aspects have sub-sets such as the type of fuel used to meet the annual demand for fuel, whether it is renewable, and how much the loads have been offset in the first place by free solar energy. Energy conservation versus health and environmental well-being is another issue. This is because there is an energy penalty to the frequency with which air inside buildings is replenished with fresh air from outside. 'Green' design can address this penalty in more than one way.

It is not the intention to move systematically through all these aspects, but the first part has already engaged with some of them. Others will be addressed in the following chapters, but always within the framework of design, and following on in a logical sequence from the *multi-layer phenomenon*.

Attitude is also an issue touched on above. Some perceive green design as worthy but dull, whereas others are opportunistic to the point that outcomes are vulnerable to the criticism of merely paying lip-service to important global ecological concerns. Designing in an environmentally responsible or sustainable manner also tends to become harder the larger the building and the more urban the context, although generation of transport to and from a building can offset deficits in the latter situation. It can be argued that some overtly green design is too bland, or too unadventurous, to do justice to its cause. One might be equally critical of 'green dressing' which adds some piquancy, but which does not stand up to objective scrutiny. The bottom line is that architects who dare to shift experiential boundaries often also offer potential for conversion to sincere green opportunism. This is harder to criticise, and it has much to offer future generations of architects.

The green architectural spectrum is then a relatively wide and overlapping one. The debate on materiality is contentious and is frequently aired in the architectural media, including talks, lectures, seminars and exhibitions. For example, for some who see themselves as participating in 'green' practice, the use of very energy-intensive materials such as aluminium is an anathema. However, this is not the case for others who argue its merits in terms of a favourable strength to mass ratio and recyclability. In fact there are adherents and detractors for most common building materials, including reinforced concrete which played such an important part in modernism. Although its embodied energy per unit of mass may be low, the value for cement in isolation is high and its production is very polluting. Moreover, the quarrying of aggregate is now a major environmental concern, with sites quite likely to be subjected to a public inquiry.

Moving out from materials to contrasting views involving the overall design of the external skin, it may be argued that a highly insulated building with small windows is more energy efficient, and therefore more ecologically desirable, than a passive solar one with large areas of glass. In terms of servicing, the same argument may be used to support an air-conditioned building compared with one that is naturally ventilated and so on. Different members of the teams who procure buildings vigorously justify particular positions with respect to 'green' credentials and the debate is sure to run on. Sick building syndrome[3] has become an important indicator of lack of greenness, while the promotion of health and well-being by design had a strong relationship with the Modern Movement. However, this issue is again too complex, with a large number of interrelated variables, to pursue at more than a basic conceptual level here.

The material that has had the most consistent impact in terms of the architectural skin over the past century has been glass. The technology continues to be refined and offers architects more and more in the way of environmental control, but its unique role as a transparent and robust mediator between inside and outside is a constant. Also glass is probably the least contentious material in terms of a 'green' agenda. Its basic ingredients such as sand and soda are not seen as anti-green, and it is readily accepted that the energy required for production can be paid back within a reasonable period due to the ability of glass to trap short-wave solar radiation – the benign small-scale 'greenhouse effect'. Better still, in doing so it can offset the need for other fuels, and in turn it can reduce the non-benign global 'greenhouse effect' or 'global warming'. Moreover glass is not only an inherent attribute of modernism that influences environmental impacts quantitatively, it is also associated qualitatively with heightened sensory impacts. Thus the use of glass, and what the main protagonists said about it, is the logical follow-on from the opaque envelope. This leads naturally to the early modern development of passive solar design, and how such techniques meshed with other 'lifestyle' and design priorities. That discourse then moves on to other 'green' issues, using the term 'eco-footprint' as a vehicle. An underlying aim throughout is to explore where greenness by today's terms of reference may have been deliberate, or may have occurred by default at the time of building. A further aim is to identify any apparent common ground or paradoxes between main players, the latter aspect turning primarily on 'organic simplicity' and 'a house is a machine for living in'. The respective influences of Wright and Le Corbusier are hard to ignore, but with so much still written about them, it is surprising how little acknowledgement there is of their strong 'green' relevance.

Liberating transparency **CHAPTER 6**

Increased transparency and luminance epitomised the New Architecture of the Modern Movement. Glass was liberated partly by new structural frames of reinforced concrete and steel and partly by advances in the techniques of production. Although his negative phrasing makes one wonder if he entirely approved, van Doesburg[4] wrote in 1924: 'The new architecture has disrupted the wall and in doing so destroyed the division between inside and outside.' A much more recent quotation by Chris Smith[5] (Heritage Secretary in the New Labour Government brought to power in 1997) provides an insight into glass as a liberator. Speaking of the Finsbury Health Centre, he said: 'It's a wonderful, wonderful building, full of light and space and air.' By their nature buildings require to enclose space and air. What is meant here is that buildings that exploit the quality of daylight and sunlight feel spacious and airy, almost regardless of how easy or convenient it is for users to physically open windows, or how well a mechanical system operates. The phrase might equally apply to Duiker's Zonnestraal sanatorium (1927–32), or that of Aalto in Paimio (1929–33), with its cross section manipulated specifically to maximise natural light. Of course linkages between modernism and health were not confined to buildings concerned with care and cure. In the 1920s and 1930s diseases such as tuberculosis originated predominantly in homes and workplaces. Clean Air Acts (UK)[6,7] were still some decades away, while cramped, disease-ridden urban slums inherited from the Industrial Revolution remained the norm throughout the developed world. The Modern Movement represented a systematic approach to a better way of life in keeping with the spirit of the age.

Le Corbusier

The words of Chris Smith in 1997 echo those of Le Corbusier[8] in the 1920s. The Manual of the Dwelling in *Towards a New Architecture* (published in English in 1927, translated from *Vers une Architecture*, 1923) includes: 'Demand ventilating panes to the windows in every room' and 'Teach your children that a house is only habitable when it is full of light and air, and when the floors and walls are clear.' Such dictates are specifically directed at improved health. Moreover, clear floors are still relevant today when carpets and other soft materials tend to harbour too many allergens in rather poorly ventilated rooms.

Paradoxically the drive of the 1980s and 1990s towards greater energy efficiency and more tightly sealed dwellings, coupled with the earlier move away from heating by open fires, has resulted in relatively poor quality of air and higher levels of humidity. In turn there are correspondingly increased populations of dust mites and aggravated incidence of respiratory ailments such as asthma. This irony has an important general application. Due largely to specialisations, the typical architect of today apparently no longer feels as confident as Le Corbusier or as in control of the aspects of design that have a significant influence on the interaction of occupants with a building. In this respect, sunlight, daylight and the quality of air are still at the top of the agenda, but apparently not well understood or acted upon by most of the profession.

In 1926,[9] the third and fourth of Le Corbusier's Five Points for a New Architecture related to glazing in terms of the *free plan* and *free façade* afforded by a columnar structure, which in turn enabled maximum ventilation and light. This was reinforced by the fifth point which extolled the use of long horizontal windows (*la fenêtre en longueur*). Expounding on the Five Points in the second of his ten lectures in Buenos Aires in 1929[10] (Techniques are the Very Basis of Poetry), Le Corbusier stated: 'I am going to announce an outrageous fundamental principle: *architecture consists of lighted floors*. Why? You can easily guess: you do something in a house if there is light; if it is dark, you are sleeping.' Later in the same lecture, acknowledging that not all façades should be glazed, he sketched his four categories: the window wall (*le pan de verre*), the ribbon window (*la fenêtre en longueur*), the mixed wall (*le mur mixte*) and non-loadbearing masonry or masonry cladding (*le pan de pierre*).

In the fifth lecture in the same series[11] (The Plan of the Modern House), he extended the subject of light to sunlight in his description of the proposed Villa Savoye (occupied mid-1930, but remedying faults continued beyond 1931). Here he was dealing with a situation where the entrance was to the south while the main view lay to the north (Fig. 6.1). He stated: 'It is on the hanging garden that the sliding plate glass walls of the salon and the other rooms of the house open freely: thus the sun is everywhere, in the very heart of the house.' The link between lightness and airiness is again made: 'To finish, look at the section: air circulates everywhere, there is light at every point, it penetrates everywhere.'*

It has to be said that many of the illustrations in *Towards a New Architecture* lack north points, and one has to make logical assumptions as to orientation. An exception is the scheme by Le Corbusier and Pierre Jeanneret in 1924 for housing at Cité Audincourt. In this case,

---

*The shortcomings of Villa Savoye in terms of its high heating load and lack of weathertightness are cited in Part 1. However, Le Corbusier did succeed with respect to 'lightness and airiness'. I visited the building in March 2000 on a sparklingly sunny day. The building has at last been made weathertight (for now), and it looked and felt pristine – everything that Corb intended. The main salon was slightly too hot due to solar gain, in spite of the heavy mass of the floor. But this could be easily remedied by using modern thermostatic valves on radiators and by allowing windows to open.

6.1 *Villa Savoye and orientation*

6.2 *Student housing proposal*

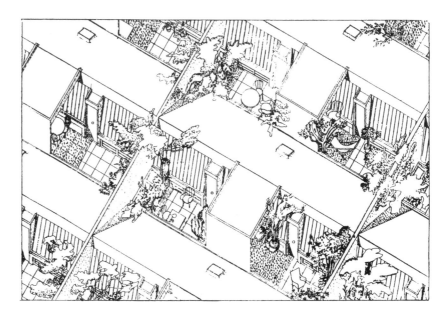

well-spaced parallel blocks have the main rooms facing somewhat west of south. Again it is fairly safe to assume that the tilted glazing with which it was proposed to toplight the compact carpet of student housing faced the sun (Fig. 6.2). The principal spaces in the Villa de Monzie at Garches face south, with most of the serving spaces along the north edge, and the important kitchen having a generous east-facing window. Both north and south edges have *la fenêtre en longueur*, but the band is much narrower on the north than the south, while the latter has nicely integrated external shutters to facilitate shading (Fig. 6.3a). Although not

6.3a *Villa Stein at Garches – pre-1934 photo with shutters down*

evident in all early photos (Fig. 6.3b), respective hard and soft shading
suggests that usage of shutters corresponded to climatic need. The
arrangement thus acknowledges the basic criteria for *direct passive solar
gain* as defined in the 1980s.[12]

Shading in the form of the *brise-soleil* and *baldequin* were soon to
become hallmarks of Le Corbusier's work, but the device of the outdoor
room, exemplified in the south-west corner at Garches, 1927, is a preoccupation from an early stage. The proposal for *freehold maisonettes* in
1922 (Fig. 6.4a) is one example, eventually manifested as a prototype in
the Pavillon de L'Esprit Nouveau at Paris in 1925. The proposed housing

6.4a *Freehold maisonettes
proposal, 1922*

6.4b *Roof gardens at Bordeaux-Pessac, 1924*

scheme on the honeycomb principle in 1925 is another. The roof gardens at Bordeaux-Pessac fulfilled the same purpose (Fig. 6.4b) as did those planned for the student housing. In 1926 one quarter of the top floor of Maison Cook at Boulogne-sur-Seine is again a protected loggia, bounded by two glazed walls, one solid wall and a partial canopy. The *hanging garden* at Poissy is similarly partially enclosed, the ribbon of window openings in the outer walls continuing around it. The proposed Villa Baizeau in Carthage, 1928 (Fig. 6.5a), protects a split level roof terrace with a canopy or *baldequin*, providing partly double-height and partly single-height spaces similar to those realised a year earlier at Garches. This also echoed the spatial idea first exploited internally in Maison Citrohan, the intended mass production house, 1920–1 (Fig. 6.5b), and then the artisan's dwellings and freehold maisonettes of 1924.

The doubling of height above all fulfils his dictum that 'a house is only habitable when it is full of light and air'. The volume promotes routes for natural thermo-circulation and also permits generous exploitation of *pan de verre*, and hence deep penetration of light. The outdoor spaces of later buildings such as the Maison Curutchet in La Plata, Argentina designed in 1949 (Fig. 6.6), and the Villa Shodhan in Ahmadabad in 1956, are further developments used in conjunction with the *brise-soleil* and *baldequin*.

Le Corbusier's architectural control over microclimate both broke down visual and environmental barriers between inside and outside, and became a vital constituent part of the *promenade architecturale*. His allegiance to the picturesque route is discussed very fully by Etlin.[13] Further, it was strongly stated by Le Corbusier[14] in relation to the outdoor room or hanging garden of the Pavillon de L'Esprit Nouveau that it has a physiological, environmental role.

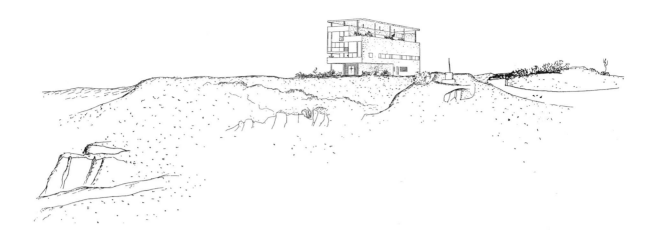

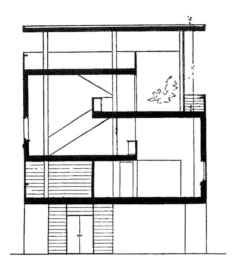

6.5a *Villa Baizeau, Carthage, 1928*

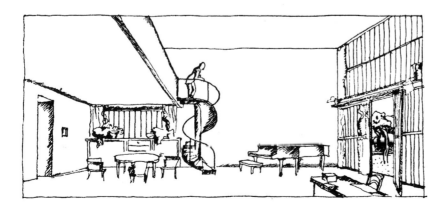

6.5b *Mass production Citrohan House, 1921*

6.6 *Maison Curutchet, designed 1949*

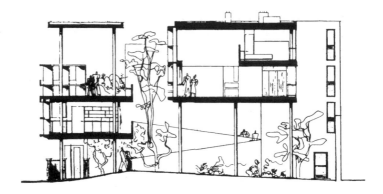

> I insist: the hanging garden seems to me the modern formula for a practical intake of fresh air, close to the centre of family life; one walks on it with dry feet, avoiding rheumatism, sheltered from the vertical sun and from rain ... This garden for taking in air, multiplied along vast blocks of buildings, is in fact a real sponge for air.

Moreover, Lapunzina[15] in his description of the commissioning and building of Maison Curutchet, draws attention to Le Corbusier's interest dating from his first visit to South America in 1929 in the verdant patios of *casa chorizo* and acknowledges the vertical equivalent in Maison Curutchet as the building's 'respiratory system' as well as having a strong poetic role – the park within the dwelling and the contribution to the *promenade architecturale*. We have seen that it may often be difficult to discern architects' intention, or lack of it, with respect to the layering of construction – a purely technical matter, but one with environmental consequences to both thermal comfort and health. We know that Le Corbusier had a fairly cavalier attitude to materiality hidden from sight. However, with respect to this arguably more subtle aspect of microclimatic design, there is no doubt that he wished to exert specific control and felt confident about the outcome. Indeed he was as passionate about these environmental, health-giving characteristics as he was about the spatial poetry of the route.

Le Corbusier's application of solar geometry with respect to the *brise-soleil* is more controversial. Mackenzie[16] points out that his knowledge of solar geometry was lacking. Le Corbusier had criticised the use of movable horizontal panels of *brise-soleil* at the Ministry of Education and Public Health in Rio, 1936, saying: 'The real principle is this: it is the sun that does the moving, never occupying the same place in the sky for 365 days.' Setting aside the fact that solar geometry is symmetrical between the solstices (with the period from December 22nd forward to June 22nd matching the period from December 22nd back to June 22nd), Mackenzie suggested that 'moveable *brise-soleils* may be the only way to achieve "at least two hours of sunlight per day at the winter solstice" (Charter of Athens 1951) and protection from sunlight during the warmer months'. He also reports the lack of logic in the orientation of the Marseilles block relative to the design of the *brise-soleils*, with an analysis by Olgyay and Olgyay showing that the long west elevation permits two hours of solar penetration in summer, but only about twenty minutes in winter. On the other hand, the short south elevation has up to eight hours penetration in winter and none between April and September. Similar criticisms are levelled at the buildings by Le Corbusier in Ahmadabad. Charles Correa is reported as describing the *brise-soleils* as 'dust-catching, pigeon-infested contrivances, which gather heat all day, and then radiate it back into the building at night causing indescribable anguish to the occupants'. There seems to be a case that the success of the *brise-soleil* is more as a visual component which sets up a strong dialectic with what lies behind it – glazed *pan de verre* at Maison Curutchet, and curved walls at the Mill Owners' Association Building in Ahmadabad.

The negative words of Correa carry some authority. Although his work, particularly in the 1960s, contains many references to Le Corbusier, he does engage more thoughtfully with the need for passive modification of the climate by buildings. He uses double volumes and outdoor rooms, at ground level, intermediate level and on roofs, but he modulates volume more carefully to exploit natural ventilation by means of wind and thermal buoyancy. He also recognises that different sections are appropriate for different seasons – the 'winter section', which widens towards the roof to admit as much sunlight as possible, and the reversed 'summer section' to minimise solar gains and promote the exhaust of air. The Parekh House, 1967–8 and his own house, 1968, in Ahmadabad both exploited this technique, and also employed a horizontal form of *brise-soleil* to shade roofs, other terraces and courts, without inhibiting free flow of air.

Returning to Le Corbusier, other research indicates quite thorough investigation when designing, as well as successful performance despite apparent paradoxes of geometry. At Maison Curutchet nearly identical *brise-soleils* are employed for orientations which differ by some 30°. Although it is known that Curutchet complained about excessive glare, recent analysis by Evans and de Schiller[17] demonstrates that the shades work well, allowing 'excellent penetration of winter sun in the dwelling (orientation 45° west of north) and the consulting rooms and terrace (12° east* of north [*author's note: should read west]) while providing almost complete shade in summer'. They also find partial shading at the equinoxes for both orientations, but point out that the climate of La Plata gives a greater requirement for cooling in March than in September.

Similarly, basing conclusions on her own measurements, observations and interviews with occupants, Ali[18] is quite complimentary about the performance of the *brise-soleils* at Chandigarh. With respect to the Assembly Building she states: 'Use of the brise soleil cuts direct radiation from coming inside the building. Glare protection is also good with adequate natural light in the offices. Monsoon and early summer are comfortable in the offices inside the building. On very hot humid days it is sufficiently comfortable with the help of fans in these spaces.' However, in support of Correa's reported comment, she acknowledges that concrete as a material is not ideal since it re-radiates absorbed heat into the buildings.

Baldequins or parasol roofs are less controversial in that in any location with high solar altitudes they will provide shade. According to Ali, the one over the High Court has also had some success in catching and funnelling prevailing winds, and so assisting the cooling of the top storey. Both the research by Ali and that by Evans and de Schiller acknowledge the solar analysis carried out by Le Corbusier's atelier. In the latter case the *baldequin* was also found to shade the terrace very well from midday onwards in summer. But was Le Corbusier the first to apply such techniques? Aronin[19] asserts: 'The *brise-soleil*, as it is known today, can be attributed to the inspiration of Stamo Papadiki.' He refers to his chapel of 1928 which employed a horizontal brise-soleil. Then there is a design for a surgical pavilion on the Suez Canal by Paul Nelson.[20] This was drawn up and a model made in 1934–5 some six to seven years after Villa Baizeau's *baldequin* and at much the same time as the inception of the *brise-soleil* in Rio. It exploits both techniques in a thoughtful manner. It also confirms an awareness of much older precedents (Fig. 6.7).

With respect to windows themselves, Yorke[21] informs that those at Weissenhofsiedlung in Stuttgart, 1927, are double-glazed, horizontally sliding timber, and so also were the ribbon windows of Villa Savoye, 1930–31. (The same details are attributed to both.) However, the south

6.7 *Nelson's surgical pavilion, Suez cf ancient precedent*

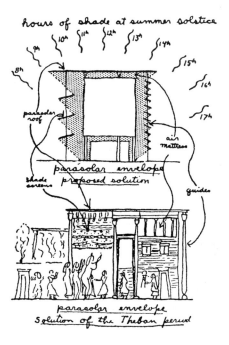

facing windows of the Pavillon Suisse at Cité Universitaire in Paris, 1933, were single-glazed in steel frames and lacked external shutters (Fig. 6.8). While the earlier villa at Garches had included shutters, these were a much later addition to the Pavillon Suisse, indicating that the initial omission here may have been due to cost constraints. The original elegant steel and glass curtain wall of the Salvation Army Rest Centre in Paris (Cité de Refuge), 1929–33, was fully sealed with no window openings and relied on 'conditioned air'. Cost cutting was definitely relevant here. The intention at the outset was to have a double-skin neutralising wall (*mur neutralisant*) as described in his 1929[22] lecture in Buenos Aires. The proposed system employed two air-conditioning circuits. The first was to keep the temperature between the two outer layers at 18°C, and the second to condition the air in the occupied part of the building. This concept – 'hot air is pushed (into the cavity) if in Moscow, cold air if at Dakar' – compares starkly with the natural controlled ventilation of Aalto's wards in the Paimio Sanatorium (1929–33), a twin-skin baffle system; as well as the 'green' regionalism evident in some of Le Corbusier's work at that time (e.g. the Errazuris house in Chile, 1930). It also did not make sense in terms of energy consumption, and historians such as Banham[23] have been rightly critical. In any event, the double system was not built, and the dormitories overheated in summer,

6.8 *South façade, Pavillon Suisse, Cité Universitaire, 1933*

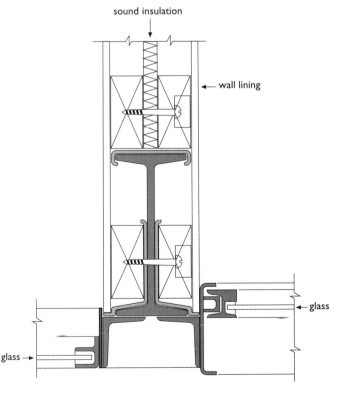

indicating that the solar loads were too much for the mechanical ventilation system. Both openings and *brise-soleils* were later provided. Similarly, discomfort was reported in his Tsentrosoyuz Building in Moscow, 1929–36.[24] Here the twin-skin was built, but apparently the air-conditioning was not installed.

Are there then contradictory facets to Le Corbusier's concepts and resolutions? This section started with a demand in 1923 for openable windows in every room in pursuit of light and air – a very 'passive' way of controlling the internal environment. Then a few years later we have the *mur neutralisant* – a very 'active' system of control, and the statement 'a window is made for lighting, not for ventilation'.[25] But perhaps there is no conflict in these positions. We know that Le Corbusier was just as enthusiastic about modern technology in 1923 as in 1929. It could be argued to be partly a matter of scale, larger buildings affording more expensive 'active' solutions, and partly a matter of priorities. With respect to the latter, if costs are cut, the visual concept should not be compromised, even if it is almost inevitable that ensuing problems will require to be dealt with at some stage. In any case, then as now, energy loads did not represent a significant financial burden for corporate clients. The consumed units of energy may be considerable, but as a proportion of the turnover of a business or institution, the cost tends to be fairly insignificant.

Hence it has always been difficult to steer the managers of such buildings towards energy efficiency. This might also explain the difference in approach between the villas of the late 1920s and larger institutional buildings (Pavillion Suisse and Cité de Refuge, Paris) and flats (Nungesser et Coli, Paris), all of the early 1930s. Heating such buildings is likely to have been deemed a routine on-cost. Another important work of this time, the Clarté flats in Geneva, 1932,[26] is either the exception or conforms to the notion that energy-efficiency only suffers when capital costs are constrained. Here, double glazing, external blinds, awnings and shutters reflect a generous budget for the accommodation and client group: 'two-room to nine-room studio flats for professional class, particularly doctors, writers and painters'. It is also worth emphasising with respect to these flats, that the occupants are fully in control of their means of moderating the climate. They can slide open windows, open french doors to balconies, and adjust both shutters and blinds. As a model for east and west façades, Clarté provides much more than a fixed *brise-soleil*.

The contrast between two distinct strands in his work from an early date is more difficult to rationalise. One strand, which more obviously leans towards 'green' in today's terms, does not observe his Five Points of 1926 and normally has low Catelonian-style vaults or monopitched roofs. Examples are: the Monol Houses, 1919; Maison de Mandrot, 1929–32; the Errazuris House, 1930; the Celle-St-Cloud Weekend House, 1935; Vacation House, Les Mathes, 1935; Les Murondins during the Second World War; Villa Sarabhai, 1951–5; Maison Jaoul, 1956. Although the vault dates back to Monol, Etlin[27] argues that: 'From the

1930s Le Corbusier developed a secondary type of architectural system that reflected his new interest in rough natural forms.' He also sees it as another aspect of Le Corbusier's maxim of 1923: 'Architecture is the skillful, accurate, and magnificent play of volumes seen in light;' corresponding to the *brise-soleil* as a development of the *free façade* and *la fenêtre en longueur*. Etlin's reasoning that an interest in rough natural forms drove a secondary system seems suspect or over-simplified. The Pavillion Suisse, 1933, the apartments at 24 rue Nungesser et Coli, 1932–4, and the Unité at Marseilles, 1952, are all essentially Five Points prototypes. The first exploits a manicured, but definitely textured, stone wall to enclose the single-storey wing; the second takes this a stage further by selectively exposing a rough stone party wall internally; while the last has a roughly textured structure with smooth-finished non-structural inserts. Thus rough natural forms were not confined to the Monol derivatives. In turn, textural aspects of such derivatives often align with later examples of the Five Points typology. For instance, although Maison Jaoul does not have the same structural to non-structural dialectic as the Unité, nevertheless it does have smooth internal finishes inside a much rougher external shell.

Curtis[28] simply rationalises: 'Le Corbusier characterised the Citrohan descendants as "male" architecture, standing square and rigid against the landscape. On the other hand, the Monol image was "female", with low vaulted spaces blending into the setting.' This seems a more likely explanation, with the interest in rougher textures applied in some measure to both lines. Curtis also recognises that while some of the 'female' houses were driven by regionalism, in terms of available materials and building ability, others such as the Celle-St-Cloud Weekend House had another ideological agenda. He also posits that Le Corbusier's interest in rough materials was in part due to the problems of maintenance associated with smooth stucco. In his apartment block in rue Nungesser et Coli, six floors have a 'free plan' and 'free façade' enabled by concrete columns, while the freedom of his own seventh floor is structured by cross-vaults, with his studio terminating on the rough stone wall (Fig. 6.9). One might say then that this is not a secondary type of architectural system, but the spirit of Citrohan with Monol overtones – or a masculine spirit with feminine overtones. In any event, added texture occurred down both 'family trees'. The introduction of glass blocks in the spandrels eliminates stucco, adds an aesthetic ripple, combines the free façade's *fenêtre en longueur* with *pan de verre* and ensures maximum penetration of daylight to the floor plate – '*architecture consists of lighted floors*'. Hence we return to the theme of this chapter.

The footprint of this gap site is typical with the depth approximately twice the width. However, the planning, with two lightwells separated by a central bridge of hallways, lifts, stairs and some servicing accommodation, means that the depth of the principal spaces is quite shallow. Also every room, including kitchens and bathrooms, has access to some natural light and ventilation. It is generally acknowledged that Le

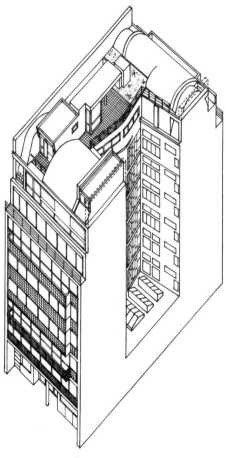

6.9 *24 rue Nungesser et Coli, 1933 – Citrohan and Monol*

Corbusier's use of glass blocks in this building was influenced by Pierre Chareau's famous *Maison de Verre* built for Dr Dalsace from 1928–31. Its notion of a wall, rather than window, that offers transparency in terms of light, but some visual seclusion, endures to this day. Maximising diffuse, rather than direct, daylight in tandem with privacy was a composite priority in relation to Chareau's ground floor consulting suite. The walls of 'the house of glass' are of glass blocks occasionally punctuated by strips of window, unlike the spandrels of 24 rue Nungesser et Coli with sliding *fenêtres en longueur* above (Fig. 6.10a, b). Despite this essential difference, in 1933 in Athens, Le Corbusier[29] himself referred to the façade as a single unit of illumination between floor plates: '. . . in each apartment there is a glass façade running from the ceiling right down to the floor, enabling light to be lured inside and captured'. This statement could equally apply to the Clarté block in Geneva. There are no glass blocks here, but there is a *pan de verre* over the entire extent of east and west façades. The only interruptions to a continuous surface of glass are the projecting floor plates, the housing for shutters and awnings, and

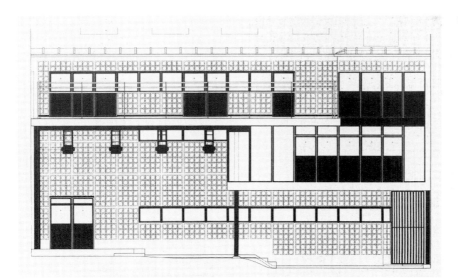

6.10a *Chareau's Maison de Verre, 1928–31*

6.10b *24 rue Nungesser et Coli, 1933*

framing. Clarté has six apartments per floor, ingeniously served by two staircases and two lifts, and each with an area of about 200 m², some 19 m deep by 10.5 m wide. This is about 25% less than the overall dimensions at Nungesser et Coli, but about the same proportionately. The solution at Clarté is to use maisonettes with west-facing double-height spaces to illuminate deep into the floor plate, and the two wells, within which the stairs are set, also allow some borrowed light and ventilation inside the core of the block. The design of the Clarté block slightly predates that of rue Nungesser et Coli, and therefore one may regard the use of glass block in the latter as a refinement in his thinking, albeit to some extent influenced by Chareau.

The issue of ventilation was not so easily resolved in the case of the Maison de Verre, the size of which was determined to a large extent by the existing building above. This was approximately 15.7 m wide by 13 m deep, but Chareau made it deeper still by thrusting the main façade out some 2 m beyond the original building line. Although the windows can open individually or separately when in a series, Taylor[30] points out that the municipal authorities were concerned about ventilation of the interior, and Dr Dalsace himself had to give a written assurance that the mechanical system provided by means of ducts under the floors would satisfy norms. Taylor also refers to Chareau's allegiance to 'an ideological trend in French architectural thinking that emphasised physical and mental hygiene', a concern also strongly held and expressed by Le Corbusier. However, regardless of the need to augment natural ventilation at the Maison de Verre, and the appeal of glass blocks in terms of light and hygiene, it would be considered poor today in terms of its thermal balance for the external skin of most buildings. U-values are approximately 3.0 W/m²K and the heat gain factor is relatively low at about 0.5. Thus in cool, cloudy weather the thermal loss from a glass-block wall will be much greater than its passive solar gain.

Accepting then that in general terms there are two parallel systems, one freed from the ground in contrast to the other and expressed by Le Corbusier as essentially male and female, a critical commonality lies with 'the skillful, accurate, and magnificent play of volumes seen in light'. In terms of windows, the Monol-rooted system yields *le pan de verre* and *le mur mixte*, but not *la fenêtre en longueur*, and loadbearing walls, piers and columns move back to the external skin. The *pan de verre* as at Celle-St-Cloud (Fig. 6.11), or a pivoting screen at Villa Sarabhai, both still permit the dissolution of boundaries between inside and outside, with outdoor spaces a second aspect of male–female commonality.

An explanation that is not explicitly driven by gender, but which is bound up with the transparency of boundaries, is that the Citrohan or Five Points model owed much to the raised 'piano nobile'. This was prevalent in urban Europe as a technique for achieving adequate visual protection from the street for the principal rooms of dwellings, while at the same time providing daylight and ventilation to the servicing floor below. In contrast, in rural areas, where horizontal space was not at a

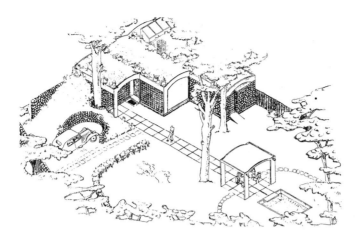

6.11 *Pan de verre, La Celle-St-Cloud, 1935*

premium, living spaces could be located close to the ground without compromising privacy. Hence the transparent dissolution between inside and outside at ground level could flourish in the wide open spaces of the United States. The Monol descendants of Le Corbusier do adhere to the principle of sufficient territory to provide a suitable degree of seclusion. The weekend house at Celle-St-Cloud is an example of this. On the other hand Villa Savoye had a similar suburban to rural locus. However, it can be posited that Savoye was actually an urban manifesto, despite its site; and in turn, the weekend house conformed to a rural one – perhaps not totally at ease with its context. Then the logic of a difference that was not simply male to female holds good. Similarly his apartment at Nungesser et Coli could well be regarded as a rural model atop an urban one.

Of course one can also align this theory with gender, rurality signifying mother earth, while urbanity symbolises predominantly male achievement through commerce and conquest. At any rate, regardless of the thinking that underpinned Le Corbusier's two paradigms, it is a generic reality that transparency at ground level does not tend to work well for dense urban housing, but does for commercial urban centres. Glass at pavement level both allows the display of goods and enlivens the sense of city as a magnet for social interaction. On the other hand, dwellings demand either a degree of opacity or an appropriate combination of horizontal and vertical separation between public and private domains.

In terms of energy efficiency, the relative dimensions deemed appropriate for this balance will also relate to solar access, but with the needs of housing and commercial buildings being quite different. Basically, within a close-knit urban grain, the notion of a raised domestic 'piano nobile' increases the opportunity for desirable sunlight and daylight. This contrasts with street-level shop windows, which may often be beneficially shaded by means of architectural devices such as arcaded pavements or movable awnings.

In summary, returning specifically to Le Corbusier, it would appear that his use of fenestration was associated with airiness and health, usually adhered to the logic of orienting large windows to the south and smaller windows to the north, respected the benefits of double-glazing where affordable, and increasingly tackled the need for shading. However, such practical aspects were vulnerable to relegation in his pursuit of visual poetry. The extent to which this may be justified remains at the nub of today's green debate. For example, various comments with respect to the *brise-soleils* at Chandigarh have been quoted, but the more controversial poetic statement was the placing of the buildings so far apart in such a climate. Today, with architects attempting to design green skyscrapers in the centres of cities, a corresponding issue is whether very tall buildings can be environmentally appropriate under any circumstances, and how such a form intrinsically compares with its competitor, a low-rise block in an out-of-town commercial park. Here of course any poetry inherent in the architectural statement or image is also deeply bound up with the short-term economics of the client as well as the aspirations of both client and architect. In this fundamental planning respect, as in others, there are well-known differences between Le Corbusier and Wright – Ville Radieuse cf. Broadacre City. But at the same time, there are more commonalities than either would readily acknowledge during their respective overlapping careers.

Frank Lloyd Wright

This 'economics and image' aspect comes more clearly to the fore with two of Frank Lloyd Wright's major commercial buildings, the Larkin Building and the Johnson Administration Building. However, in order to gain insight into Wright's attitude to the sun and glass in particular, relative to the commentary on Le Corbusier, his intentions with respect to a less site-constrained complex is a good starting point. Speaking about the 'San Marcos in the Desert' Hotel, 1928, in his autobiography[31] he says: 'The plan of this far-flung, long-drawn-out building, owing to the placing of the levels of the sun-lit terraces, is such that each room, each bathroom, each closet, each corridor even, has direct sunlight. Every portion of the building to be lived in is free to the sun and also to magnificent views. The whole building has the warm southern exposure every winter resort so covets.'

He also specifically eulogises[32] about what glass has to offer as a material and makes a connection between glass and air as well as light: 'This super-material GLASS as we now use it is a miracle. Air in air to keep air out or keep it in. Light itself in light, to diffuse and reflect, or refract light itself.' In other words, for Wright, the glass itself is air and light. Like Le Corbusier, he is fascinated by the dissolution of the boundary between inside and outside: 'By means of glass, then, the first great integrity may find prime means of realisation. Open reaches of ground may enter as the building and the building interior may reach out and associate with these vistas of the ground'; and 'Walls themselves because of glass will become windows and windows as we used to know them as holes in walls will be seen no more. Ceilings will often become as window-walls, too.' He also associates glass with the potential for greater well-being: 'Perhaps more important than all beside, it is by way of glass that the sunlit space as a reality becomes the most useful servant of a higher order of the human spirit. It is first aid to the sense of cleanliness of form and idea when directly related to free living in air and sunlight.'

The idea of ceilings as window-walls which enhanced well-being was exploited in Unity Temple as early as 1906:[33] 'I flooded these side alcoves with light from above to get a sense of a happy cloudless day into the room. And with this feeling for light the centre ceiling between the four great posts became skylight, daylight sifting through between the intersecting concrete beams, filtering through amber glass ceiling lights.' Again when talking about schools[34] he advocates: 'a building no more than one storey high – with some light overhead, the school building should regard the children as a garden in the sun'.

In the Usonian menu of five materials, glass had special status:[35] 'Yes, we must have polished plate glass. It is one of the things we have at hand to gratify the designer of the truly modern house and bless its occupants.' The others were wood, brick, cement and paper (e.g. paper between layers of wooden boards). Speaking of the first Usonian house for Mr and Mrs Jacobs he states: 'The way the windows are used is naturally a most useful resource to achieve the new characteristic sense of space. All this fenestration can be made ready at the factory and set up as the walls. But there is no longer sense of speaking of doors and windows. These walls are largely a system of fenestration having its own part in the building scheme – the system being as much part of the design as eyes are part of the face.' Therefore, although Wright's Usonian glass wall is loadbearing while the *pan de verre* of Le Corbusier is not, effectively the end is the same in terms of visual continuity from inside to outside and vice versa.

Wright[36] tells us that his preoccupation with redefining the concept of windows as holes punched in walls dates back to just after the building of the Winslow House in 1893. In converting the window into a lengthy screen which went right up to the ceiling and soffit of a generous overhang, he both sheltered the windows and strove to enhance the quality of light reaching the interior: 'Overhangs had double value: shelter and preservation for the walls of the house, as well as this diffusion of reflected light for the upper storey through the 'light screens' that took the place of walls and were now often the windows in long series.' This sense of shelter provided by the generous overhang was very important to Wright. It was a recognition of the primitive survival instinct for simultaneous prospect and sanctuary which was referred to above in the discussion of 'piano nobile' and private domain relative to Le Corbusier. Wright clearly sought to justify it at every level. While it did provide physical as well as psychological shelter, and also valuable shade for south-facing façades in summer, the idea of reflecting light into the interior is very dependent on the albedo of the adjacent ground as well as the soffit of the overhang. There is an irony here in that Wright's horizontal ribbons of window limited overheating, but cut down on light transmission, while those of Le Corbusier maximised light transmission, but could overheat the interior.

The other aspect of Wright's Spartan pallet of materials in his Usonian houses is that it appears to play a part in a wave of 'direct gain' passive solar designs throughout the USA during the 1940s and 1950s. The polished concrete floor was ideal for thermal mass in radiant view of the sun as were masonry walls and the core around the hearth which was so essential to Wright's dwellings. Timber on the other hand provided a rapid thermal response as a counterpoint to the dense material. This combination has a well-known precedent – a log cabin around a masonry core accommodating the flues from stoves and ovens.

The Suntop Homes or Ardmore Experiment, 1939, suggest a passive solar intent. However, the pinwheel plan of the four apartments (Fig. 6.12) denies equity of solar access through the double-height corner window, and the slight overhang from the shiplap balustrade to the roof terrace provides scant protection from the sun in summer to the double-storey windows with a southerly orientation. By way of contrast, the Herbert Jacobs Residence II, 1943–8, with its northern earth-berming, its convex, double-height south-facing glass wall and generous roof

6.12 *Suntop Homes, Ardmore, 1939*

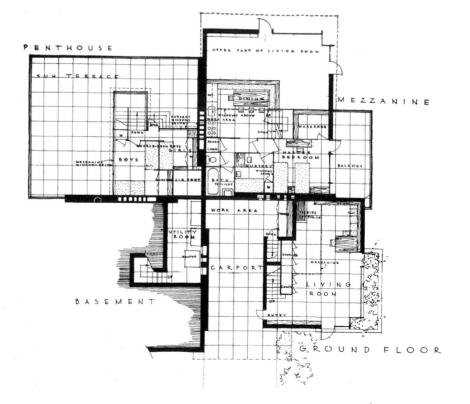

6.13 *'Solar hemicycle', Jacobs No. 2, designed 1943*

overhang is very explicitly a solar house, termed 'solar hemicycle' by Wright. Here the curvature (Fig. 6.13) allows all parts of the house to enjoy some sun at some time of the day for most of the year, even the rooms along the convex northern edge. Herbert Jacobs[37] confirms that Wright saw the house as a 'first' and also praises its solar performance: 'Usually by nine o'clock on a sunny morning, even in below-zero weather, the heating system stopped, and did not resume until late afternoon. The sun even reached the back wall below the mezzanine.' Then the Robert Levin Residence, 1948, and the Quentin Blair Residence, 1952, use mono-pitches to increase the height of glazing offered up to the sun, while the roofs oversail to provide shading in summer (Fig. 6.14a, b). This profile

6.14a *Robert Levin Residence, Kalamazoo, Michigan, 1948*

6.14b *Quentin Blair Residence,*
Cody, Wyoming, 1952

was to be repeated by later passive solar pioneers such as Emslie Morgan in the Wallasey School, 1961, and by Felix Trombe and Jacques Michel in the solar house at Odeillo in the Pyrenees, 1967 (Fig. 6.15a, b). The solar hemicycle might also be regarded as the model for a recent unit at Bellsdyke Hospital in Scotland by Foster and Partners, where day-rooms are on the concave edge and bedrooms on the convex one.

In spite of such precedents, it is retrospectively difficult to be certain as to who gave the initial lead. These houses by Wright were built in parallel to, or post-dated, many others with solar, bioclimatic or healthy-living credentials such as those by George Keck, Richard Neutra and Louis Khan. Although the Usonian paradigm was influential in the 1930s and 1940s, one building of Neutra's, the Lovell House of 1927–9, had a competing impact with respect to evolving transparency. According to Drexler[38] it 'became for a while indispensable to the iconology of modern architecture'. Therefore, this European dimension will precede the work of other American architects with a solar bent, firstly through Rudolph Schindler and Richard Neutra, and then through the second wave of immigrant modernists before the Second World War.

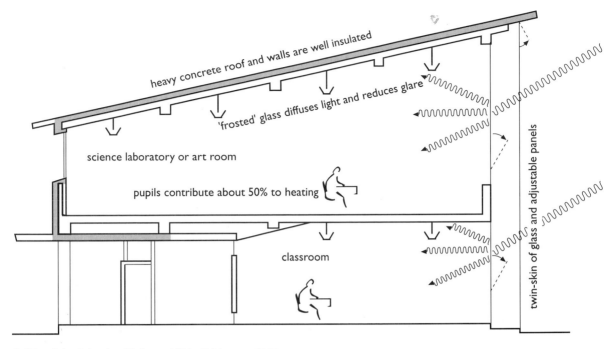

heavy concrete roof and walls are well insulated

'frosted' glass diffuses light and reduces glare

science laboratory or art room

pupils contribute about 50% to heating

classroom

twin-skin of glass and adjustable panels

6.15a *Solar School at Wallasey, UK, by E. Morgan, 1961*

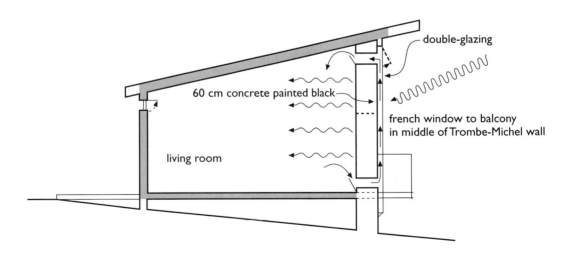

double-glazing

60 cm concrete painted black

french window to balcony
in middle of Trombe-Michel wall

living room

6.15b *Trombe-Michel Solar Wall at Odeillo, France, 1967*

Rudolph Schindler and Richard Neutra

Schindler and Neutra first met in the studio-salon of Adolf Loos in Vienna in 1912. Thereafter Schindler went to the USA just before the First World War followed by Neutra almost a decade later. Both worked briefly for Wright and they also collaborated for a short period in the mid-1920s in Los Angeles. The commission for the house for Dr Lovell, known as the Health House, which went to Neutra in 1927, established Neutra as an important figure, but is thought to have begun a rift with Schindler. Although friendly contact continued for several years thereafter, their respective careers diverged from this point.

Schindler expressed the same enthusiasm as Wright and Dr Lovell with respect to the merging of exterior and interior afforded by glass as well as the benefits of sunlight. In a series of articles published in 1926[39] for Dr Lovell's 'Care of the Body' column in the *Los Angeles Times* he enthuses: 'Our rooms will descend close to the ground and the garden will become an integral part of the house.' The following year his design for a new house for Aline Barnsdall was labelled The Translucent House. Here the upper zone of the battered or steeply tilted walls of the house were clad in panels of translucent glass which folded over to form the first 45 cm of the flat roof. Hence Schindler has followed Wright in terms of exploiting the additional light available from the upper part of the sky-vault. In turn, ten years later, Wright potently returned to this notion with his continuous clerestory of Pyrex tubes at the Johnson Administration Building (although it was not without problems in terms of dealing with excessive glare).

Schindler's progressive and persistent adherence to the tenets of European de Stijl, sets him apart from Wright in architectural language. Projects such as the Elliot House by Schindler in 1930 would surely have been derided by Wright as a 'cardboard box'. On the other hand Wright must have applauded the skilful way in which Schindler allows daylight and sunlight to flood into the double-height stairwell in the heart of the compact, deep-plan hillside home (Fig. 6.16). However, as well as these full-height south-east facing windows, there is a generous north-west facing window between the living room and the upper patio. Gebhard[40] asserts that Schindler designed for California's climate in terms of averages and ignored extremes. In particular, large areas of glass facing away from the sun will lose heat in damp, cold weather. Therefore although Schindler exploited glazing to introduce sunlight and daylight deep into his buildings, often in a visually dramatic way, and was undeniably concerned with radical solutions to healthy living, Gebhard implies that he was a 'fair-weather' bioclimatic designer who ignored certain practicalities.

Exactly the same issues arise with Neutra. There is an overt agenda about health linked to a European modernist architectural aesthetic, and glazing is a major contributor to this aesthetic. The fundamental characteristic of transparent glazing is its multi-functionality as an intermediary

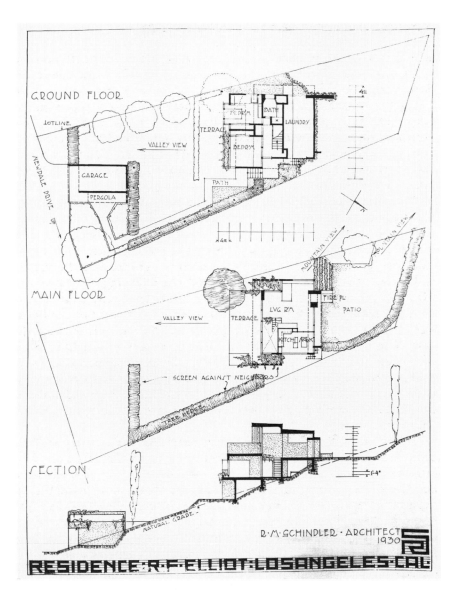

between inside and outside. It admits light and captures radiant energy – sometimes too much of both. In the other direction it permits view and releases energy by conduction. A weighting accorded to such factors is evident in the work of Neutra, as with Schindler, Wright and Le Corbusier. Just as inconsistencies are apparent in Le Corbusier's work, so are they with that of Neutra. At least it appears so in that there is a lack of consistency in the orientation of the main living rooms in his dwellings, almost all of which include a roof-canopy extended well beyond the line of glazing. However, there is consistency in that view is afforded priority over orientation. It would appear then that Neutra's pallet of canopies and pergolas had more to do with poetically blurring the edge between inside and outside and enhancing prospect from within, than with providing a prosaic rationale for solar shading.

The preoccupation with transparency and view, irrespective of orientation, resulted in some criticism from clients, even those who were generally ecstatic about their houses. For example, with respect to the Brown residence of 1938 located on Fisher's Island off the Connecticut coast, Hines[41] quotes Ann Brown: '. . . because of the immense amount of light, the view windows had to be fitted with sunproof glass'. However, where view and sun coincided, Neutra did produce dwellings with an apparent bioclimatic intention. For example, in the Miller House of 1937 (Fig. 6.17) Neutra protected the living room along the south edge with a combination of screened porch and canopy, the latter located above the pool at the south-east corner. The kitchen and maid's room further west along the south façade also have their windows shaded by a cantilevered

6.17 *Miller House, Palm Springs, California, 1937. Photos courtesy of Dion Neutra, architect*

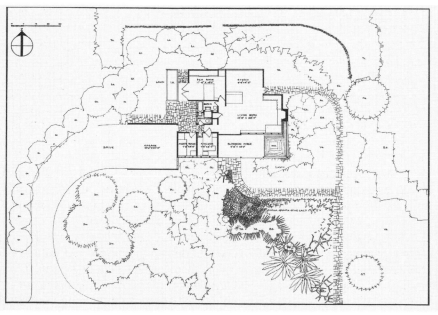

section of roof; while 'screened ventilation soffits' incorporated in the canopies allowed fresh air to circulate between ceiling and roof. In this case, Hines[42] reports that Grace Miller was very appreciative of these devices, both in terms of environmental control and aesthetic enhancement. For instance, the dynamic reflections from pond to ceilings as well as its functionality in permitting evaporatively cooled air to enter the interior. The Maynard Lyndon plywood house of 1936 and the timber-clad houses for H. G. McKintosh and Philip Gill in 1939 are other such examples. In all these cases the best aspects coincide with south and west orientation, and glazing is set well back from the line of the roof.

Other projects of the 1930s, such as Neutra's own home (1931–2) facing north to Silverlake reservoir and the Landfair apartments, 1937, had substantial amounts of north-facing glazing in order to secure a view. The tendency to overglaze is of course offset by the mainly benign climate of California, home to most of his houses, but the point made with respect to Schindler working optimistically on averages, also holds for Neutra. The dichotomy with respect to orientation is maintained in his work through the 1940s and into the 1950s. For example, the dining–living room in the Nesbitt House faces north-north-west and east-north-east; while that of the Bailey Case Study House, 1946, faces south and west. In the 1950s several houses conform to a direct passive solar gain model with south-facing windows, cantilevered roofs, and exposed dense floor finishes to act as thermal storage. The Kesler House, 1953, the Serulnic and Kronish Houses, 1955, all adhere to these principles. In contrast, the living room in the famous Moore House, 1952, faces north to mountains, and the one in the Hall House, 1953, faces north to Newport Beach.

Friedman[43] also comments that Neutra's 'formal manner and air of intellectual superiority' did not necessarily mean that he would not immerse himself very fully in the needs and aspirations of a client. In the case of the small house completed in 1955 for the academic, Constance Perkins, she acknowledges that the very positive relationship that established itself from the outset in 1952 endured until Neutra's death. Friedman also tells us that Perkins was seen as 'affected, superior and contentious' by colleagues, and that this may have resulted in a recognition of 'kindred spirits in one another'. At any rate, Neutra's longstanding interest in the workings of the mind, through his friendship with Freud's son and his own neuroses, was probably what led him to take more than a passing interest in the psychological profile of his clients. He would ask them to submit an autobiography which included likes and dislikes. In the case of the Perkins House, this constituted a strong component of the briefing process. The dialogue led to devices such as the pool blurring distinction between inside and outside in a small and quite highly glazed dwelling. Further, the unifying generosity of an open-plan space to house the functions of cooking, eating, relaxing and entertaining, is complemented by compartmentalised private areas – her studio where she also slept, a guest bedroom and the service spaces. In addition she was able to influence the texture and colour of the finishes, as well as have many other detailed practical requirements taken into account.

This then is an important aspect of Neutra's work. Glass will only be liberating for a client, if the client is completely in tune with it and if there are adequate devices to maintain a sense of sanctuary. Such devices involved subtle interplay between plan, section and landscaping – a forte of Neutra in much of his work.

Walter Gropius, Marcel Breuer, Ludwig Mies van der Rohe and Serge Chermayeff

For America, Schindler and Neutra were the first 'bridgehead' of Europe's light, airy modernism, and both kept in touch with its main architectural players. Then, resulting from the rise of Fascism in the 1930s and the imminence of another world war, another exodus of Europe's talent landed on this safer cosmopolitan scene. Gropius was in the vanguard. A decade beforehand, his dramatic Bauhaus curtain wall of 1926 epitomised 'liberating transparency'. At a much smaller scale, the first part described his prefabricated, lightweight, well-insulated envelopes. Modest, but not without glass, the copper-clad prototype of 1931, designed by Gropius for Hirsch Kupfer, included a greenhouse along one full wall (Fig. 6.18a). Some 12–14 years later, his Packaged House System for the USA's General Panel Corporation translates this feature into a sun-porch buffering one side of the main living space

6.18a *Hirsch Kupfer prototype, 1931*

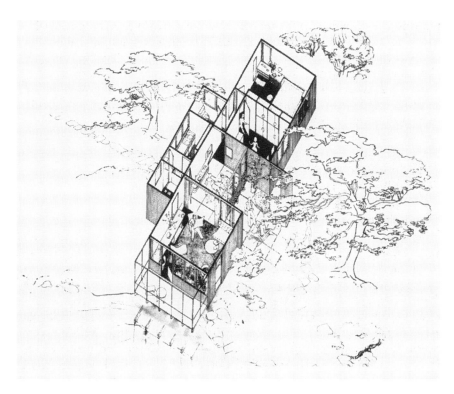

(Fig. 6.18b). In between, we have the glazed porches of his own New England house in Lincoln, 1937, and the Chamberlain House in Wayland, 1939, both in collaboration with Marcel Breuer. Also just before Gropius crossed the Atlantic, he worked with Maxwell Fry on the Village College, Impington (1936). This has a south-east facing terrace of classrooms which are fully glazed and openable. It is an almost identical approach to that of Neutra's Carona Avenue School of 1935. Thus both Gropius and Neutra were using glazing to temper climate next to a heated space, and also to break down the inside–outside divide, simultaneously displacing electric lighting.

In another example of related thinking, the Doldertal apartments in Zurich, 1934–6, designed by Breuer with Albert and Emil Roth, followed Le Corbusier's Five Points closely. Its movable awnings and shutters also provided its ribbon windows with the same flexible control of light and shade as the Clarté apartments, completed a year or two earlier. Shortly after, in his English stop-over, Breuer and Yorke's Bristol Pavilion used the device of an outdoor room and walls of glass between walls of stone in a manner that suggests the influence of Le Corbusier's Petite Maison de Weekend at Celle-St-Cloud, 1935. Thereafter, the collaboration with Gropius from 1937–41, continuing into his own practice in the 1940s, yielded several houses where ribbon windows were shaded by fixed pergolas. Notable here is the south-shading of the house for James and Katherine Ford in Lincoln, 1938–9. However, the east-shading of his own home in New Canaan, 1947, with its dramatically cantilevered outdoor deck, is less convincing.

In the case of Mies van der Rohe, the Barcelona Pavilion in 1929 used refined sweeps of floor-to-ceiling glass to merge indoor and outdoor spaces. This was later developed as a housing model in the Berlin Building Exposition, 1931, and in the somewhat softer brick and glass court-yard form of the Lemcke House, in Berlin, 1932, as well as several unbuilt projects of this period. The Tugendhat House, completed in 1930, does not adopt outdoor rooms in the form of enclosed courts. However, the south-east and south-west facing terraces, respectively on upper and lower floors and each partly protected by the building, offer defined outdoor spaces with their own particular microclimate. They are sun-traps depending on weather and time of day. Then on the main floor, walls of glass were constructed to disappear downwards into the basement, converting the living space to a south-facing loggia at the touch of a switch (Fig. 6.19).

This then is a remarkable building in terms of its ability to opportunistically take advantage of fine weather. Moreover, the glazing is concentrated on the south and east façades, with only the hall and one bathroom facing north, and the entire main floor below ground along this edge. The south façade can be flexibly shaded by means of awnings to avoid discomfort from overheating, say in sunny but windy conditions which would preclude completely lowering the windows. The east façade is thermally buffered by a glazed winter-garden, giving the potential to function as a source of prewarmed and freshly oxygenated air for the main living zone. Also, whereas the glazing offers the opportunity to reduce the energy needed for heating and can also open up or be shaded to avoid overheating, brick walls are designed to conserve heat. These are

6.19 *Tugendhat House, Brno, Czechoslovakia, 1930*

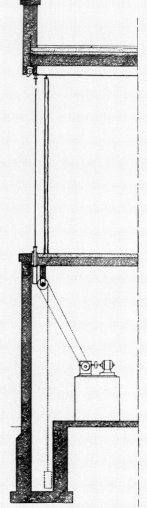

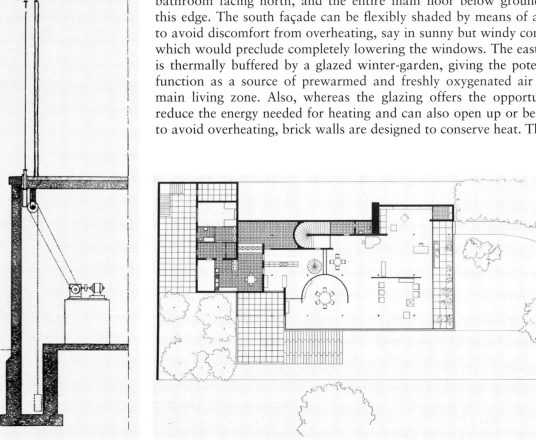

insulated with loosely compressed slabs of peat, a product called Tor-foleum. Therefore, although one might complain that the large Fenesta steel-framed windows are single-glazed, this is nevertheless an early passive solar paradigm.

It is also a dwelling that one feels has dealt with the programmatic needs of the client rather than being simply a promotional vehicle for the architect. The discrete suites of bedrooms, the service wing, the hierarchy within the open plan of the main floor and the manipulation of public and private realms all attest to this. According to Friedman,[44] the Miesian minimalism is also taken on board positively by Grete Tugendhat. She praises the austerity of preventing just 'letting oneself go', and claims 'being forced to do something else' is what 'people, exhausted and drained by their professional work, require and sense as a liberation'.

However, Mies van der Rohe's preoccupation with transparency and maintenance of purity of an idea led to the abandonment of such an apparently energy-conscious approach in one of the century's most famous buildings. Twenty years after the completion of Tugendhat, the house for Dr Edith Farnsworth in Plano, Illinois, consisted of three horizontal planes, a threshold, a floor and a roof. The latter two were separated only by glass, other than four pairs of slender steel columns and even more slender mullions. Although trees were available to partly shade the sun-facing surfaces in summer, one mature maple in particular, only money and many joules of energy could compensate for the loss of heat in winter. The single-glazing will have also contributed to discomfort with quite complex stratification of temperatures between ceiling and floor. It is almost as if the inclusion of warm-water coils below the travertine floor finish[45] was intended to render the single-glazing thermally irrelevant, on the basis that occupants would be radiantly heated by the floor. In reality, during cold weather, the floor and the large sweep of glass together would set up very asymmetric radiant conditions, gaining from the floor and losing to the glass. The warm floor would also drive a convection loop, warmed air moving up to the ceiling, before cooling on the cold glass, and hence incurring a down-draught which would move towards the centre of the room at low level before rising again. Further, the large rate of heat loss by conduction through the glass calls into question the ability of the heating system to meet its thermal load in cold weather. It certainly did not prevent surface condensation[45] as a continuing problem in winter, and the interior also got far too hot in summer.

In terms of multi-layer construction, both roof and floor were well designed, the covered terrace neatly dealing with drainage of storm water within the same thickness as the internal floor, which was insulated and incorporated the heating coils. Although this might be taken to support the contention that the glass was not viewed as a thermal priority, the overriding factor may simply have been the technical difficulty and high cost of producing double-glazed units of these dimensions. It also bears comparison with the Tugendhat house. Here a combination of heated rails at the base of the window and blown warm air apparently worked to Grete Tugendhat's satisfaction.[46,47] (The air inlet was located towards the rear of the living room, and close to the stairwell.) In this instance, the heated rails would adequately combat down-draughts, and the blown warm air would tend to provide good mixing within this generous space.

Returning to Edith Farnsworth, her use of roller blinds rather than silk curtains was probably more for privacy and seclusion than for thermal moderation. However, they would have provided extra shading to exposed parts of the glass in hot weather, as well as improving comfort in cold weather, especially on the north side. This would not be so much by lowering the U-value, but by moderating the thermal 'surface factor', much in the manner of tapestries covering cold stone walls in a medieval castle. She also insisted on fly screens around the covered terrace to make this usable as a cool, ventilated space in summer.

Lack of an adequate facility for ventilating the dwelling was the other serious environmental consequence of the architectural manifesto of Mies van der Rohe. The maximised transparency, with large fixed floor-to-ceiling panes of glass and minimal mullions inhibited natural ventilation. There were only two low-level hoppers on the east gable and the west-facing doors to the terrace which could be opened, and if they were, they allowed invasion by mosquitoes and other insects. This then was another major contributor to overheating in warm weather, and eventually resulted in the next owner, Peter Palumbo, resorting to the use of mechanical aids. Just as Neutra's adherence to prospect sometimes compromised energy-consciousness, so also did Mies van der Rohe's adher-ence to concept – *his* concept which completely overruled any programmatic agenda of the client in this case.

What is surprising is that Edith Farnsworth apparently willingly col-luded in all aspects of the design over the five-year long period of gesta-tion. It was only after she moved in in December 1950 to a leaking roof and condensation misting her windows, followed in 1951 by unexpectedly high bills for the construction not to mention architect's fees, that the rela-tionship with Mies deteriorated. The resulting litigation and publicity only made matters worse. In interviews of the period[48] she apparently said the lack of privacy meant that she felt 'like a prowling animal, always on the alert' and she used medical metaphors such as X-rays pejoratively to allude to the exposure of the transparency which had been the very essence of the project from the outset. On the other hand, she did use the house for a significant time. So it may be fair to conclude that, with the addition of roller blinds and fly-screens, she came to terms with the build-ing. One should also bear in mind that the transparency of glass, whether from inside to outside or vice versa, is relative. Glass and light together do a substantial amount of editing. One of the photographs taken in 1955, from the inside of the south façade, shows the glass, or at least its reflec-tion, slicing west across the terrace. Another shot taken of the outside from the north-west, presumably as visible from the public road, shows only dark obscurity through the portions not covered by blinds.

Mies van der Rohe's 'Fifty-by-fifty' project in 1951 refined the visual and constructional purity of the Farnsworth House a stage further – only four columns, and mullions between glass sheets replaced by butt joints – while further negating natural ventilation. However, in this instance there was no patron found to take it forward to built reality.

Of this group, it was probably Serge Chermayeff that came closest to an archetypal passive solar design. His house at Halland in Sussex, 1938,[49] had all the main rooms facing due south, the ground floor able to open on to a slabbed terrace which was continued inside as thermal mass, and had a pergola to shade the bedrooms on the first floor (Fig. 6.20). There is also a series of service rooms, with a lower demand in terms of temperature, along the north edge on each floor. It is possible that this design was influenced by a study of solar geometry published by the RIBA[50] in 1932. However, the conjunction of the means of thermal storage for solar energy that is captured in the main living spaces, and the means of central heating and its controls, is frequently problematic. The house at Halland is no exception.

The radiant heating with warm water coils below the strip of paving was well-intentioned, and probably required to avoid down-draughts in cold weather, even though the windows here were double-glazed. But solar displacement of the fossil-fuel energy for central heating is inevitably compromised. There is a time-lag between the boiler shutting down in response to solar capture by the slabs, and this gain of energy actually becoming useful. This would especially be the case in intermittently sunny weather. It would also have been necessary to have had a separate circuit for the coil below the slab, with its own suitably placed thermostat. The complementary radiant heating, with a coil embedded in the ceiling directly above the slab, would not have had the same problems. First, it was lighter. Second, it could never have a direct radiant view of the sun. It might be that the heated ceiling would have been adequate on its own. It would have radiantly heated the slabs in dull weather in the same way as solar radiation; but when the slabs were solar-warmed, the ceiling's circuit of warm water could have rapidly switched to a cooler setting.

It is also noteworthy as one of the best insulated buildings of this period. Not only were windows double-glazed, the timber-frame construction together with insulation endowed the walls with a U-value in the order of 0.8 W/m²K. This denotes a thermal resistance more than twice as much as that required by the statutory national building regulations which came into force more than 25 years later. Frustratingly, in spite of the historical importance of this house, there is no information available as to its performance. Also, there is no substantial continuing opus of work with which to follow through on Chermayeff's passive solar aspirations since his career tended towards academia after his arrival in the USA in 1940.

6.20 *Chermayeff House,*
Halland, Sussex, 1938

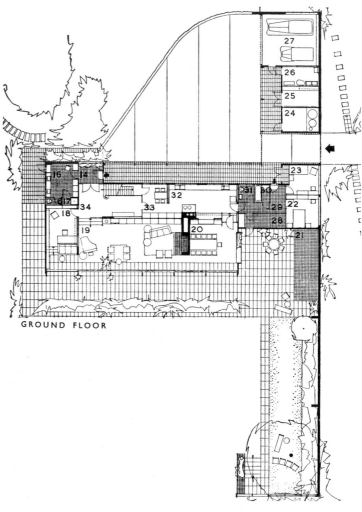

GROUND FLOOR

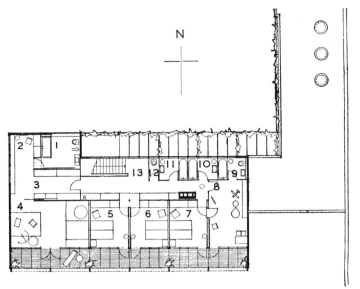

FIRST FLOOR

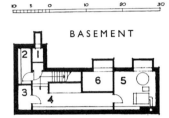

BASEMENT

1. Fuel store
2. Wine cellar
3. Trunk store
4. Corridor
5. Boiler room
6. Fuel store

USA's development of passive solar design from the 1930s

George Fred Keck first gained prominence in 1933 with his twelve-sided House of Tomorrow, rapidly followed by his Crystal House in 1934. He noted both the capture of heat due to the greenhouse effect and the relatively rapid loss of heat after nightfall due to conduction. Indeed the Crystal House was air-conditioned to cope with excessive thermal gains and losses. By 1935, in his design for the Cahn House (Fig. 6.21) he was experimenting with fixed overhangs to reduce solar gain in summer while accepting it in winter; as well as with movable shading in the form of external venetian blinds. By 1939 this sectional concept manifested itself more strongly in the Kellet House. Boyce[51] also tells us that in 1935 the Libby-Owens-Ford Glass Company started to manufacture sealed double-glazing. Hence Keck was able to improve the thermal balance through south-facing windows, although at that time the failure rate of the organic seals was fairly high. In addition, the aesthetic expression of a roof tilted upwards to the south and with a strong overhanging 'cornice' started to assert passive solar design in a new way, more for example, than did the restrained geometry and shading louvres of Chermayeff's house at Halland. However, Keck was not entirely consistent. The Duncan House, 1941, the second Sloan House, 1942, and his experimental Rockford prototype, 1945, are all visually more of the Halland mould.

Returning to the technology, Keck also began to disaggregate the function of ventilation from windows with a variety of louvred panels.

6.21 *Cahn House, Lake Forest, Illinois, 1935*

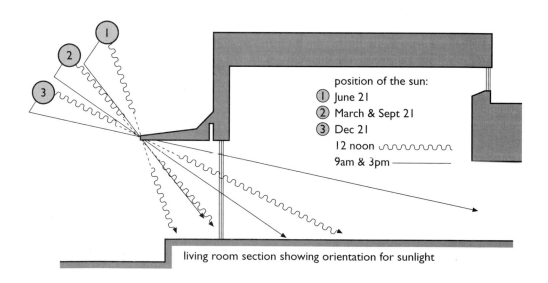

position of the sun:
① June 21
② March & Sept 21
③ Dec 21
12 noon
9am & 3pm

living room section showing orientation for sunlight

For example, in his 1942 house for Howard Sloan, fixed spandrels of louvres regulate ventilation below unopenable windows, contrasting with the opening casements in the first house constructed two years earlier. There was also a recognition at this time that not enough was known about the performance of passive solar dwellings. Keck's Duncan House completed in 1941 (Fig. 6.22a) was monitored for a year, commencing in the autumn of 1941. Boyce[52] gives details of this test, the findings of which were summed up in cautious terms. It was conceded that the energy gained through the large area of glazing at least balanced the losses. One identified problem was excessively air-leaky construction. Another was the time lag between receipt of insolation (solar radiation) and the output from the concrete floor slab. Much of this was attributable to heating by warm water coils rather than solar energy. This is exactly the same issue as cited above with regard to Chermayeff's strategy in 1938. Although the effect was advantageous in summer in ironing out excessive swings in temperature between day and night, in winter it meant that potentially useful solar energy was displaced by the purchased fuel.

Keck addressed this problem in tandem with a perceived need for cheap prefabricated dwellings. By 1944 a lightweight, hollow, vitrified

6.22a *Duncan House, Flossmoor, Illinois, 1941*

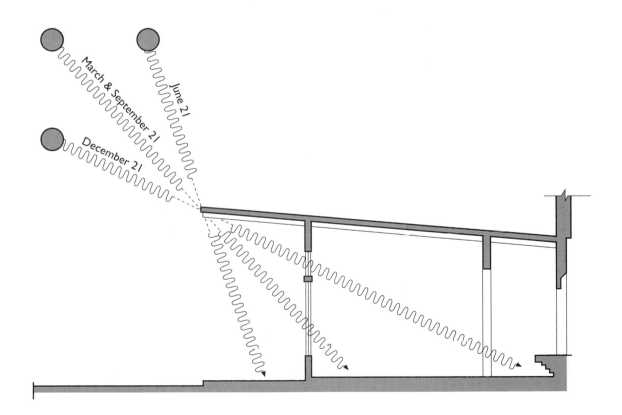

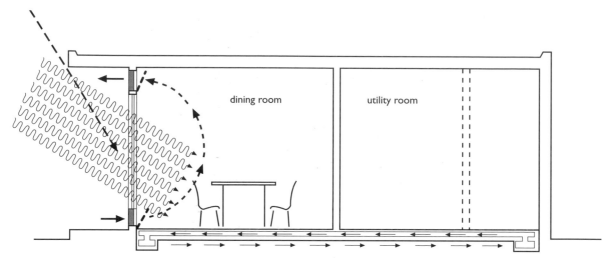

Hypocaust floor: main duct on North side supplied by gas boiler in utility room.
Solar gain helps to reduce cooling before start of return loop below hollow floor tiles.

6.22b *G. Keck's Prototype Solar House, Rockford, Illinois, 1945*

Radian Tile was patented (Fig 6.22b). It was a 20th century version of the Roman hypocaust floor, and since the tile constituted the finished floor, with a slender thickness between the channels of warm air and the surface, the lag in time was significantly reduced. Adjustable canvas awnings also came into use in America in the 1940s, increasing the scope for flexible shading, and Keck continued to design what would now be termed 'direct gain' passive solar houses through to the 1970s.

It was another American architect, Arthur Brown, that experimented with an 'indirect gain' solution in his house in Tucson, 1945. Here he introduced the notion of a solar buffer space, backed with a dense wall that would collect solar heat during the day and deliver it to north-facing rooms at night (Fig. 6.23). Butti and Perlin[53] tell us that Brown estimated heat flow at the rate of one inch per hour, and hence made the dividing wall eight inches thick. However, the system was never measured and this house again raises both scientific and aesthetic issues. A wall painted black as a solar absorber is functional as long as there is enough short-wave solar radiation to charge it. At night, and on overcast days, it is simply a rather gloomy surface of an uninsulated wall that is able to 'leak' heat outwards. Visually, whereas the outer glazing and the shading louvres to the living room do carry some authority, the perfectly functional and sensible small shuttered windows on the north side give the same kind of nondescript message as any mundane speculative suburban scheme.

The American House Today, 1951, by Ford and Creighton[54] illustrates a series of houses from the 1940s that share the enthusiasm of both Keck and Brown for essentially passive solar and/or climate-sensitive design, which in turn owes much to the visual pallet of Neutra, Schindler and Wright. In particular, Harwell Harris, who was strongly impressed

6.23 *Brown House, Tucson, Arizona, 1945*

summer sun excluded

winter sun

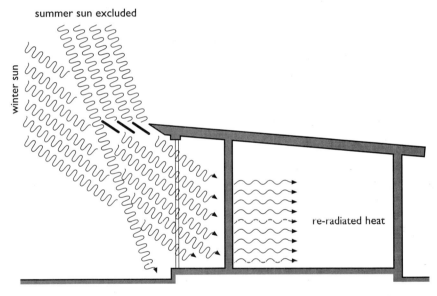

re-radiated heat

in 1925 by Wright's Hollyhock House for Aline Barnsdall, entered the domain of both Schindler and Neutra in 1928 at Kings Road. At that first meeting, Neutra opportunistically asked Harris to work for him for a brief period on the Lovell House. According to Germany[55] in her biography of Harris: 'The sudden encounter with Neutra would hit him like a much-needed and very bracing blast of twentieth century air.' By 1932 Harris had his first commission, a house for an old friend, Clive Delbridge and his wife, Pauline Lowe. Known as the Lowe House, the plan owes allegiance to both Mies van der Rohe's Barcelona Pavilion of 1929 and Schindler's house at Kings Road. The outdoor rooms, two bedroom

6.24 *Havens House, Berkeley, California, 1940–1*

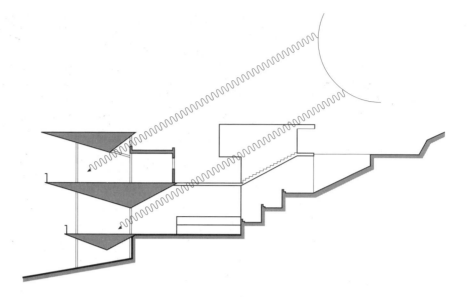

courts, an entrance court and a living terrace share equal status with internal rooms, and glazed screens are overtly Japanese in quality. The bedroom wing faces somewhat south of east and the living room somewhat west of south. The hipped roofs resulted from pressure by the lender, but also refer back to Wright and forward to many, but by no means all, of Harris's later projects.

Indeed Harris's attitude to the section was such that roofs contributed to the admission and exclusion of sunlight through clerestories and walls of glass according to time of day and year. For example in the Havens House of 1940–1, an inverted pitched roof (i.e. flat top and sloping soffit) welcomed low-angle sunlight in mornings and evenings (Fig. 6.24); and the cantilevered roof with sunholes of the Birtcher House a year later, employs the same technique as Keck's Kellet House of 1939. Thus Harris was quite eclectic in terms of his solar syntax, but nevertheless his designs had a degree of potency.

Another Californian house included in *The American House Today* epitomises the merging of inside and outside afforded by glass, without sacrifice of view, privacy or solar gain (Fig. 6.25). Designed by Henry Hill for himself and his wife, and located in Carmel, the garden within this house also adds a green dimension that extends the scope of this review beyond the gifts of glass to wider green issues. With the threat of global warming, these are increasingly topical today in tandem with the narrower techniques of improving energy efficiency such as passive solar design.

It is interesting to note that the early American interest in passive solar design petered out in the 1950s with falling fuel costs, apparently only to be revived architecturally by events in the Middle East, notably in 1967, 1973 and 1979. However, some physicists and engineers were still

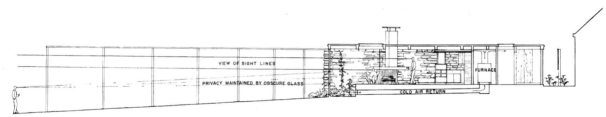

committed to solar potential for the built environment during the 1950s. In fact the period marked the beginnings of a more science-based or 'active' approach which was still not without its architectural followers. It has been mentioned that by 1958 architects such as Carl Koch were publicising the opportunities for phase-change materials embedded within prefabricated building components. By 1959 the Association for the Advancement of Solar Energy (AFASE) was constituted. Members included notable non-architects such as Felix Trombe and George Löf, but also included Frank Lloyd Wright in the last year of his life. AFASE was the embryonic International Solar Energy Society (ISES), fully established by the early 1960s. Although it was biased to sunny climes such as Australia, it had national sections around the world, including the UK. (UK-ISES was inaugurated in 1964.) It is today a flourishing learned society with a growing influence on architecture. It should also be seen in parallel with the rising influence of 'green' political parties, and charitable organisations such as Greenpeace and Friends of the Earth, together with a recognition of global warming as a phenomenon, some 50% of which is building related. The Brundtland Commission and the 1992 Rio

6.25 *Hill House, Carmel, California, 1940s*

Earth Summit's ensuing commitment to Agenda 21, followed by Kyoto in 1997, have all helped to maintain an ecological dimension in the sights of architects and other building enablers. Understandably, for the latter group in all of this ongoing process, the use of glass continues to be pivotal.

Eco-footprint

In the same way as the word 'green', the notion of an 'eco-footprint' is subject to variability depending on the author and context. It is used here to acknowledge four aspects: first, a share of the area of the Earth that is tied up in the building process; second, a share of energy, pollution and desecration of natural assets that is embodied in the production and transportation of materials from source to building; third, a building's consumption of energy and output of pollution during its life, including its dismantling; and fourth, a building's ability to promote the health and well-being of its occupants and surrounding fauna and flora, with minimum disruption to the last two. The critical word in the first two aspects is 'share'. Although it is very difficult to quantify such a concept, there are underlying principles that are quite easy to rationalise. For example, it makes sense to ship redwood from a managed forest in California some way down the western seaboard to another Californian location, but not to lay waste a rainforest in South America and transport the spoils northwards by a combination of road and rail.

In terms of the impact of housing once built, van Doesburg[56] early on drew attention to the problem of individual suburban dwellings incurring greater fuel consumption and pollution through transport compared with a collective urban model:

> It is curious that with frequent application of modern materials and modern building methods, the small separate dwelling, the so-called 'minimal dwelling', can still be considered indispensable. According to modern insights, and taking into account traffic, including that to the suburbs, it was rather to be expected that collective centralised construction would be a radical solution to the problem.

It was also van Doesburg[57] who asserted that the essential differences between French and German architecture corresponded to climatic characteristics: 'A more equable climate, the smaller transitions, in short, a milder atmosphere is the reason that in France construction can be lighter than in Germany, where seasonal contrasts necessitate a completely different system of shelter.'

However, van Doesburg[58] did not respond favourably to overtly climate-sensitive design. Seven years after his 1919 visit to a school of architecture in Vienna, when he spoke with Peter Behrens, he was sharply critical of the 'painterly' designs. Alexander Popp[59] wrote a strong rebuttal the following year. His published drawings of the students' work in question confirm a strong climatic and regional flavour in terms of the form, the structure and the local materials, but one that did not compromise a sense of remarkable architectural adventure for the time in the juxtaposed monopitches and catenary curves of shingle-clad roofs. Unrepentant, van Doesburg[60] rejoined that the drawings were 'whimsical and arbitrary' and moreover he challenged: 'Although it is self-evident that the Austrian Alps impose different requirements on architecture than do flat countryside or the cities, I can in no way understand why a modern, strict architecture would not be applicable, *particularly in contrast to the fanciful scenery*.' He goes on: 'In modern architecture the exterior aspect is the result of *function* and *dimensions* and [is] based on a clear arrangement of space and plane.' In other words van Doesburg is saying that he sees no reason why a modern international aesthetic cannot take account of regional climatic variations.

This then sets the polemical green scene for this chapter, which returns initially to where the preceding one left off – the house in Carmel by Henry Hill – before looking again to the more influential figures, and concluding with Wright and Le Corbusier. Hill's design belongs to the same 'natural' genre as the later work of Neutra, adhering to modern European rationalism, but with local sensitivity ... as in the work of masters such as Aalto. Would van Doesburg have approved? The roofing grid of timber beams supports a structural tongued and grooved timber deck, and rests on a combination of timber posts, timber stud walls, and walls of stone. The stone was native to Carmel and the timber is most probably Californian redwood. Part of the floor is stone-paved and part appears to be polished concrete with occasional rush matting. Fig. 6.25 p. 91) shows that the garden extends well into the living room behind the west and south-facing glazing. This device not only assists eco-performance in providing thermal capacitance in radiant view of the sun, but also has a further environmental function in oxygenating the diurnal supply of air to the boiler and hence to the circulating warm air within the dwelling. During the nocturnal period one would expect the boiler to be off or at least set-back so that circulation of CO_2 from the plants would not be problematic. Outdoor rooms also suggest a healthy lifestyle and flourishing biodiversity.

Kahn's Weiss House of 1948–9 expresses much the same spirit as Hill's house in Carmel (Fig. 7.1). In this case local Pennsylvanian stone is much in evidence in walls and floors, and an exposed timber post, beam and deck structure is juxtaposed with the masonry. Outdoor rooms feature again, both in recessed form to separate the realms of day and night, public and private, and by means of solid elements projected outwards. An internal hearth corresponds to one outside, a 'standing stone' within the park. The 'butterfly' roof, tilted up to the south over the living room and main bedroom to maximise glazing for solar gain, also results in internal drainage. This technique, also advocated by Ralph Erskine in Sweden, means that downpipes are not vulnerable to freezing in the cold

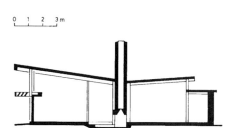

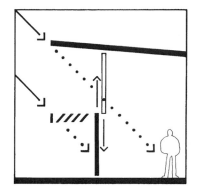

Pennsylvanian winter, and snow does not melt on to the heads of occupants as they enter and leave. Returning to the walls, Kahn devised an ingenious reversible double-hung sash to enable alternative arrangements of transparent and opaque panels. Thus intake of light and energy as well as loss of heat may be tailored to suit ambient conditions. This device and this building has not been given the historical prominence that it deserves, and in general such omissions lend support to the case made here for re-examining quite humble buildings of the past.

In his contemporaneous pavilion for Gerald Loeb in Connecticut, Harwell Harris utilised three types of interchangeable removable panels – glass to admit sun in winter, translucent plastic to partially exclude sun during some sunny days, and insect-proof mesh to admit cooling breezes, say during hot nights. Similar ecological awareness was evident as far back as the mid-1930s in his own Fellowship Park House. The dominant characteristics here were a lightness of touch on the site, and an elegant minimalism of structure and materials. Germany[61] reports that he even hosed down a bed of mint in order to freshen the air before visitors arrived. But apart from general site-sensitivity in these examples by Kahn and Harris, the most interesting common denominator is the idea of a flexible, climate-controlling window-kit. This offers not only improved performance, but also opportunities with respect to prefabrication for relatively small dwellings, a major post-war preoccupation, given the scarcity of resources.

The Great War had ensured that this same shortage of materials, coupled with a large demand, also had the attention of figures like Gropius and Neutra during the 1920s and 1930s. In 1927, Gropius's prefabricated contribution to the Weissenhofsiedlung was not only remarkably well insulated, it was very compact and his adherence to a 3' 6" grid minimised waste. His copper-clad houses for the Hirsch Kupfer company in 1931 introduced the notion of a small starter-kit that could be extended in stages with the heating and plumbing core unchanged. Gropius[62] was very clear about his advocacy of prefabrication from 1910 onwards. He also specifically associated this with criteria that involved more efficient use of resources together with higher tectonic standards, physical well-being – again in terms of air, daylight and sunlight – and a light touch in terms of a building's impact on its site:

> Dry assembly offers the best prospects because (to take only one of its advantages) moisture in one form or another is the principal obstacle to economy in masonry or brick construction (mortar joints). . . . Moreover the use of reliable modern materials enables the stability and insulation of a building to be increased and its weight and bulk decreased. A prefabricated house can be loaded on to a couple of lorries at the factory – walls, floor, fittings and all – conveyed to the site, and put together in next to no time regardless of the season of the year. . . . The New Architecture throws open its wall like curtains to admit a plenitude of fresh air, daylight and sunshine. Instead of anchoring buildings ponderously into the ground with massive foundations, it poises them lightly, yet firmly, upon the face of the earth.

Gropius was thus concerned with most of the aspects that have been included here to formulate the concept of 'eco-footprint'. He also associates the physical with the psychological. Still referring to air, light, sunlight and the manner of touching the ground, he goes on: 'Thus its aesthetic meets our material and psychological requirements alike.' Neutra also engaged with the associations that space, colour, light, texture and so forth had on the psyche. Moreover, although Neutra gained fame in California with his large house for Dr Lovell, which was a model for healthy living but not so much for total prefabrication, his own preoccupation with this latter aspect was soon applied to houses with a much smaller footprint. The steel-framed Beard House, 1934 (see Chapter 2), was not only tightly planned within a modest budget of $5,000, but also its cellular walls (Fig. 7.2) functioned as a system of passive environmental control, in summer taking in fresh air that had been evaporatively cooled by water sprinkled on adjacent bushes.

Thus we have a useful principle in that small prefabricated components can have a green relationship with the immediate micro-climate set up by the architect. Also the thermal capacitance of water can be a useful counterpoint to lightweight structures. Neutra's use of a pond to promote evaporative cooling has already been mentioned with respect to the Miller House. In his Kaufmann House set in the desert landscape of Palm Springs, 1946, a swimming pool is sited south-east of the living areas. While Neutra acknowledges the imported nature of the house, he considers it contextually appropriate:[63] 'While not grown there or rooted there, the building nevertheless fuses with its setting, partakes in its events, emphasises its character.' In the tightly planned Hansch House of 1955, Neutra sites a roof pond over bedrooms – the timber posts and beams can take this load. This is not only estimated to reduce the internal temperature by about 4 K, it also acts as a reflector to increase daylight into the living room while the overhanging roof protects it from direct

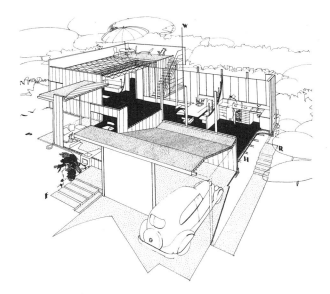

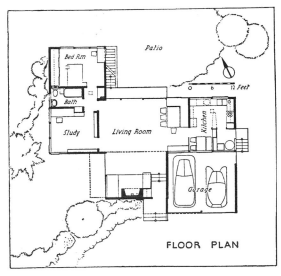

FLOOR PLAN

sunlight. An uninterrupted view from the living room to the mountains lies to the west, with the glazed screen protected from most direct sunlight by an even more generous overhang.

Hence, accepting that Neutra's passive solar models occur only when view and sunlight coincide, there are aspects of 'greenness' and climatic sensitivity in most of his work. Turning to Schindler, we find early 'green' impact, but less enduring consistency. The shared dwellings at Kings Road represented an early *alternative* experiment, with which Neutra engaged for a period. The stretching of social norms in terms of shared facilities also conserves resources, as does the abandonment of bedrooms in favour of open-air sleeping porches on the roof and the supplementing of daytime space with several layers of outdoor rooms. However, it is hard to find many clients who are prepared to be so experimental, and even at Kings Road there were aspects of the design that were over-committing for at least some of its adventurous bohemian occupants. Nevertheless, in terms of its materiality, Kings Road was Usonially minimalist, marking at least some lasting reciprocity of thinking with others, notably Wright.

'Organic simplicity'

Wright, while deprecating 'international-style' modernism, adhered to 'a sense of cleanliness directly related to living in sunlight';[64] and while aligning himself with (perhaps claiming authorship of) other trends such as passive solar design, appears not to waver from his tenet of *organic simplicity* from the early years of his own practice. As early as 1894[65] he talks about simplicity as 'something with graceful sense of beauty in its

7.2 *Beard House, Altadena, California, 1934. Photos courtesy of Dion Neutra, architect.*

utility from which discord and all that is meaningless has been eliminated'. In 1908[66] he refers to 'organic integrity', 'organic harmony' and he asserts: 'A sense of the organic is indispensable to the architect.' He attributes 'organic simplicity' to his thinking at the time of building his Oak Park studio in 1898, when writing his autobiography[67] at least three decades later. We also know that he thought of this term as natural functionalism. In 1908[66] he states: 'A knowledge of the relations of form and function lies at the root of his [an architect's] practice.'

We may note at this point a set of definitions of 'organic' in a dictionary:[68] 'forming an essential element of a whole, integral; having systematic co-ordination of parts, organised [as in "an organised whole"]; having the characteristics of an organism; developing in the manner of a living plant or animal'. In his autobiography[69] Wright lends spirituality to the *organic simplicity* of nature. He quotes Jesus: 'Consider the lilies of the field.' Hence we find the dichotomy of his buildings for business as ecclesial cathedrals to the ethic of work and functionalism. Thus in the Great Workroom for S. C. Johnson, the lean, engineered pads which cap his *dendriform* columns (Fig. 7.3) are emotive islands in light, or even lilies of a lake.

7.3 *Dendriform column, Johnson Wax Building, Racine, 1936*

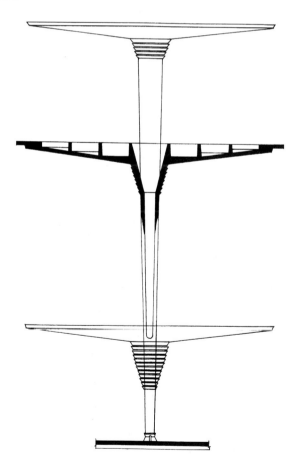

The test in 1937 proved to sceptics the effectiveness of the design in efficiently distributing loads to the ground. But over and above functional purity with its strong spiritual message, Wright did not reject well designed, complementary decoration. The ribbing at the top of the dendriform 'trees' expressed compression in a decorative way. Again in his autobiography[70] he states: 'Plainness is not necessarily simplicity.' He also associates organic simplicity with spatial *plasticity*, which could be accentuated by arguably inessential facings: 'I did make the "trim" plastic, that is to say, light and continuously flowing instead of the prevailing "cut and butt" carpenter work.' However, he sometimes advocates plasticity which runs counter to function, with or without decoration. Compared with the casement, his detested 'guillotine window' demonstrated functional superiority (flexible ventilation and weathertightness).

A similar weakness is evident in the use of Pyrex tubing at the Johnson Wax Building (Fig. 7.4). The tubes were wanted primarily for

7.4 *Pyrex tubing, Johnson Wax Building, Racine, 1936*

visual plasticity. When it was shown that rather than evenly diffusing light, as he had hoped, they would focus light and produce intolerable glare under certain conditions,[71] Wright prioritised visual plasticity over the flawed function. This was ironic in this instance, given the proven functionality of the dendriform columns. Predictably also, the numerous caulked joints suffered with time, giving rise to frequent leaking. The burden of maintenance eventually resulted in replacement of the top layer of tubes with flat sheets of glass fibre in a built-up aluminium frame, and the 1961 addition by Taliesin Associated Architects used corrugated sheets of Plexiglass at the insistence of the Johnson Company.[72] Such a building, undoubtedly one of his finest in spite of technical shortcomings, suggests that Wright tended to justify a particular visual approach by means of an architectural system described with seductive slogans, the logic of which was, at least occasionally, flawed. By contrast in Europe, Aalto, although influenced by Wright's work, appears to adopt 'organic simplicity' with unflawed richness. A question to pose here is how risky is organic simplicity assuming it is relevant to green architecture? Aalto seems to take less risks, using tried and tested local materials alongside modern ones – double-glazed windows with variable solar protection, insulation . . . all at Villa Mairea before 1940.

Interestingly in the Larkin Building, built four decades earlier and boasting significant environmental advances, Wright adheres more rigidly to the tactics of practicality. When describing it in 1906,[73] he confines himself prosaically to its technological merits, as well as those relating to cost. He maintained it was good value for money and justified its appearance in terms of gritty North American functionalism. Then, when defending it in 1909[74] against the strongly critical aesthetic attack by Sturgis[75] the previous year, Wright describes the building as a 'bold buccaneer'. On the topic of innovation, Quinan[76] maintains it was one of the earliest examples of modern air-conditioning, contradicting the quibbles of Banham[77] on that point. Not only that, it was a building where ducts for transporting air were integrated with the structure, and with a relatively high and deep plan, its natural daylighting was of a high order (Fig. 7.5). It was also supremely fire resistant, and excluded both noise and pollution from its aggressive industrial surroundings. What is rather frustrating here is that neither the writings of Banham nor Quinan adequately explain the route by which some of the outgoing air is led between the outer glazing and the laylight of the main atrium, thus helping to keep it clear of snow as well as obviating cold downdraughts.

However, aside from all such physical considerations it was again a building where a level of spiritualism, manifested through light, geared into the ethic of work and provided the client with value for money that seemed to be well understood at the time. Although Wright leaves others to talk about this aspect in 1906, he acknowledges his indebtedness to the transcendentalism of Emerson in his autobiography.[78]

The Larkin–Johnson comparison is illuminating for commonalities and differences, with many more of the former. Did Wright simply grow

7.5 *Larkin Building, Buffalo,*
New York, 1904

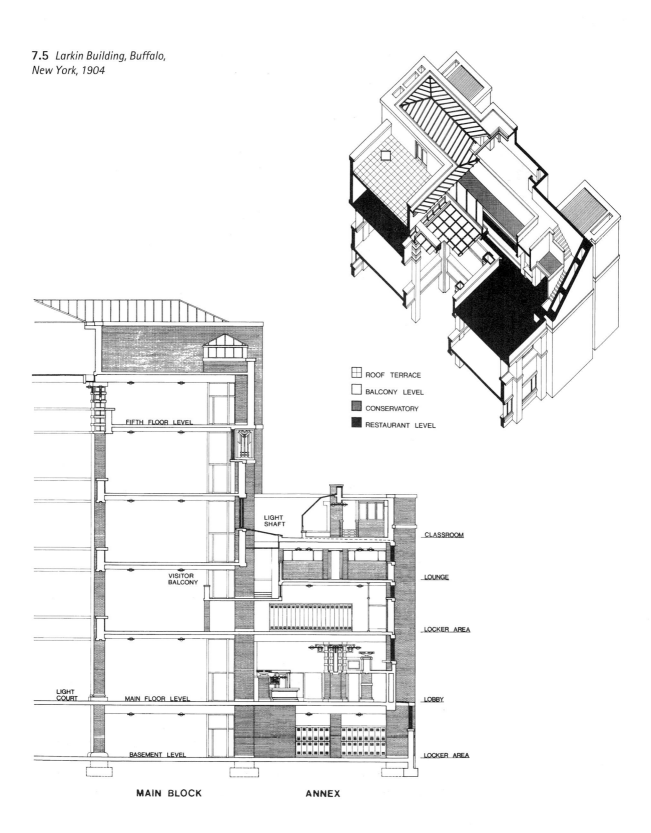

ROOF TERRACE
BALCONY LEVEL
CONSERVATORY
RESTAURANT LEVEL

FIFTH FLOOR LEVEL

LIGHT
SHAFT

CLASSROOM

LOUNGE

VISITOR
BALCONY

LOCKER AREA

LIGHT
COURT

MAIN FLOOR LEVEL

LOBBY

BASEMENT LEVEL

LOCKER AREA

MAIN BLOCK   ANNEX

bolder and bolder with age, taking the kind of risks that could inevitably upset clients? There is the apocryphal 'why not move her chair?' story in connection with a guest at Johnson's house, completed not long after the first phase of the factory. (Reputedly Johnson phoned Wright to complain about the roof leaking on to his guest at a dinner party.) Arguably, the Larkin Building was more controversial. It certainly caused a furore within the architectural establishment. In terms of Wright making the most efficient use of materials, the answer has already been given with respect to the Johnson example – sometimes (the columns), sometimes not (the tubular Pyrex glazing). The Larkin risks, aside from aesthetics, were also embodied in its physics, albeit based on quite well-established 19th century technology. Here the science worked prophetically in terms of the generation of office buildings of the 1980s and 1990s, some of which have seriously addressed environmental issues.

For example, the ING (formerly NMB) Bank headquarters in Bijlmermeer on the south-eastern edge of Amsterdam and designed by Ton Alberts, is acknowledged as a 'green' and energy-efficient exemplar.[79] It also has much in common with Wright's Larkin Building. For a start, the locations for both were hostile. Larkin's industrial context is a counterpoint to the socio-economic desert of Bijlmermeer, only now being slowly turned round by means of structural intervention at governmental level combined with commercial co-operation. In terms of technical detail, both Larkin and ING ventilate mechanically, but neither recirculate air. Both use their buildings to moderate thermal demands. For instance, ING employs solar preheating in the form of black attics as well as mechanical heat recovery by means of thermal wheels; whereas Larkin uses the long intake ducts from roof to basement to lower and raise temperatures of the incoming fresh air, while outgoing warm air passively enhances the dual-skin glass lid in winter. Both use tall, narrow lightwells to great effect. Both also have a literal green dimension. ING uses plants to moderate the quality of air entering from outside as well as that contained inside. Larkin, in its unsympathetic urban setting, uses them on the inside only, with conservatories leading to roof terraces. Then both have social break-out spaces to give relief from work-stations which exploit the green spaces.

Finally, both are imbued with strong, and quite similar, spiritual overtones, ING with Rudolph Steiner's anthroposophy and Larkin with Ralph Emerson's transcendentalism. It may be that the respective architects of these two buildings regarded the spirituality, with its own specific credo, as an essential *organic* ingredient. On the other hand it is widely accepted that physical and emotional states are linked, and that all good architecture has a spiritual dimension since it impacts on people's emotions as well as corporal well-being. To quote van Doesburg[80] again: 'That is where the crux of the matter lies! We function not only physico-organically, but psycho-organically, spiritually, as well. And the future architecture will have to respond to that function also!'

These words embraced Le Corbusier as well as Wright. A strong synthesis of art and architecture arguably satisfied Le Corbusier's emotional–spiritual id; whereas Wright, who lacked a similar artistic insight or desire, sought fulfilment from more craft-based sources. Van Doesburg's acerbic comments about romantic regionalism have been noted. He attacks Le Corbusier's *paquebot* style[81] with the same vigour, deriding his interiors as 'puristic paintings, converted into sculpture'. He goes further: 'In no building is one so much aware of the painter and so little of the constructor as in the dwellings by Le Corbusier.' Van Doesburg's position was that construction was the generator of form: 'There is absolutely no secret in the new construction methods, the problem is sober, clear and business-like, and the correct, logical use of the modern building materials will cause the new form of architecture to emerge quite involuntarily.' The irony or hypocrisy implied in his quotes lies with championing such icons of 'de stijl' as Rietveld's Schröder House of 1924. Its polychromic appearance suggests concrete, when it is mainly constructed in brick and timber.[82]

Also his attack on Le Corbusier appears to be directed specifically at the Citrohan paradigm of the 1920s, rather than that of Monol. Of course van Doesburg, who died suddenly in 1931, did not live to see Le Corbusier's later development in terms of materiality. This is acknowledged to have been partly driven by constructional vulnerability of the smooth stucco surfaces common to most of the earlier modern European buildings. However, he did live long enough to take note of one of Le Corbusier's most famous dictums.

'A house is a machine for living in'

Near the beginning of *Vers Une Architecture*[83] in a section entitled EYES WHICH DO NOT SEE, and at the end of a subsection AIRPLANES, Le Corbusier first states: 'The house is a machine for living in.' On the same page he links materiality and emotions: 'The business of Architecture is to establish emotional relationships by means of raw materials.' Later[84] he says: 'Architecture is a matter of *harmonies*, it is *a pure creation of the spirit*.' He further links harmony to the Wrightian concept of organic simplicity, without using the term:[85] 'Our engineers produce architecture, for they employ a mathematical calculation which derives from natural law, and their works give us the feeling of HARMONY.'

Still talking about the significance of engineers, he states:[86]

Not in pursuit of an architectural idea, but simply guided by the results of calculation (derived from the principles which govern our universe) and the conception of A LIVING ORGANISM, the ENGI-NEERS of today make use of the primary elements and, by co-ordinating them in accordance with the rules, provoke in us architectural emotions and thus make the work of man ring in unison with universal order.

It is this line of thinking, which is very close to that of Wright, that relates to the repetition of his famous quotation:[87] 'A house is a machine for living in.' The sense of this statement is further illuminated towards the end of his book:[88] 'Every man today realises his need of sun, of warmth, of pure air and clean floors'; and of course this sentiment relates to other quotations used earlier which support the view that the physical, and therefore measurable, qualities of the built environment were at least as important to Le Corbusier as the poetic and romantic characteristics that assailed the psyche.

Returning to the first two of his Five Points of 1926, the pilotis and roof gardens signify a small and light *footprint*, with part of the built area potentially natural at ground level, more on the roof and sometimes vertical hanging gardens between these two extremes. Apart from verdure below, within and above his dwellings, he also had practical suggestions for use of the land immediately adjacent, for example the intensive agriculture recommended for his 'garden cities on the *honeycomb* principle' in 1925.[89]

Describing Une Petite Maison built for his parents in 1923, Le Corbusier[90] refers to the 'dwelling machine' in terms of its compact and functional use of space:

Dimensions precisely adapted to individual functions permit maximum exploitation of space. The arrangement is practical and spatially economical. Through a minimum use of space for each function the total surface area was fixed at 50 square metres. The finished plan of the single-storeyed house, including all approaches, covers a surface of 60 square metres.

Here there was also economy of volume, but not at the expense of solar access: 'The height of the house is two and a half metres (the regulation minimum) . . . The rising sun is caught at one end by a slanting skylight and for the rest of the day it passes on its circuit in front of the house [Fig. 7.6a]. Sun, space and greenness – what more could be wanted?' He goes on at some length about 'greenness' over the years, honestly declaring problems as well as benefits – for example, the necessity to trim or remove some trees, partly due to excessive shading and partly due to roots attacking foundations.

He is also both practical and emotional with respect to the green roof terrace and its biodiversity: 'We are in the middle of the dog-days; the grass is parched. What does it matter, for each tiny leaf gives shade and the compact roots insulate from heat and cold. They regulate temperature without costing anything or requiring any upkeep.' Then:

Pay attention! It is towards the end of September. The autumn flowers are blossoming and the roof is green once more, for a thick carpet of wild geraniums has overgrown everything. It is a wonderful sight. In spring the young grass sprouts up with its wild flowers; in

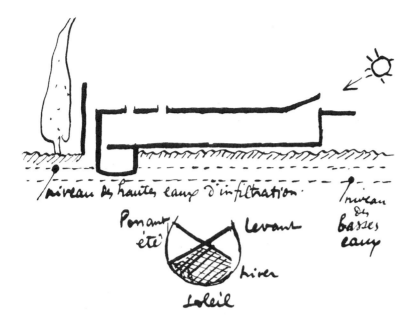

summer it is high and luxuriant. The roof garden lives independently, tended by the sun, the rain, the winds and the birds which bring the seeds. (Latest news, April 1954: the roof is completely blue with forget-me-nots. No one knows how they arrived.)

In terms of the construction and materiality of this modest dwelling, Le Corbusier's account in the 1950s mixes practicality and organic metaphor in the same idiosyncratic way. He describes the inadequacy of the original north wall in terms of thermal loss and weathertightness, leading to the addition of cladding with 'shingles of galvanised iron plate'. He talks about the problems ensuing from Lake Geneva's variable water table in terms of 'rheumatism' and 'whooping cough', the latter causing the watertight cellar to become a 'floating boat', thrusting the superstructure upwards (Fig. 7.6b). The consequent seasonal cracking was eventually countered by means of flexible control joints and more

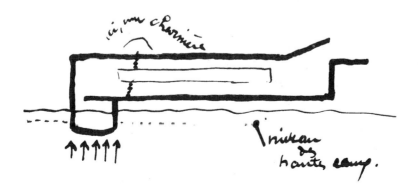

7.6b *Une Petite Maison as a 'floating boat'*

cladding: 'A butt-hinge of pliable copper-plate was constructed on the roof terrace. But in order to avoid the annual excitement of watching an experiment in physics the south elevation was covered with an aluminium facing.'

Sbriglio[91] reports that Le Corbusier shows similar attitudes to both the roof garden and materiality at 24 rue Nungesser et Coli in Paris. Although initially veering to a formal garden, the onset of occupation during the Second World War persuaded him to pragmatically eulogise about nature 'left to its own devices'. In terms of nature interacting with materials he was again pragmatic in deciding in 1948 to replace the steel-framed glass screen on the west side of his own apartment with a new timber and glass assembly constructed by the same joiner who had fabricated seven hundred similar units for the Unité d'habitation in Marseilles. At the same time he was writing to those he saw as responsible for the maintenance of the building as a whole, complaining of 15 years of neglect, and in particular the problems of rust. Finally in 1962, as a result of rotting timber and seepage of moisture between the two layers of glass, he replaced his own screen for the second time, on this occasion with anodised aluminium sliding sashes located over a neoprene guide.

Aside from the roof garden and façade (which address three of the 1926 Five Points), the flats at 24 rue Nungesser et Coli manifest the 'free plan' afforded partly by the columnar structure and partly by the four plumbing zones relative to the two lightwells (Fig. 7.7a). The flexibility of the floor plate relative to multiple dwellings bears comparison with that of the Schröder house for a single dwelling (Fig. 7.7b). In the latter case the first floor of less than 60 m² was designed to close and open on a daily cycle rather like a flower, taking the concept of 'a machine for living in' to another level. Also there is remarkable organisational correspondence. The Schröder roof lantern over the central stairs compares with lift–stair core and lightwells of the flats, and plumbing locates along opposite long walls in each case. Today such flexibility might be espoused in terms of 'lifetime homes', and of course impinges on the *eco-footprint* in terms of resources and energy tied up in a building until demolition. The many variations in number and size of flats per floor proposed at Nungesser et Coli testify to the long-term effectiveness of this pioneering synthesis of structure and services. There is also no doubt that in terms of its access to light and sunlight the apartments were intended to promote the health and well-being of all of its occupants, just as it was in Rietveld's Schröder House. However, there is a wider aspect to well-being in housing that is recognised today in 'green' circles – participation in the procurement and management process by the residents. Le Corbusier was not so altruistic in this respect. In 1934, exercising the unofficial power of his status as architect, he insisted that a fellow co-owner remove the window boxes from her balcony.

There are other less visible characteristics of Le Corbusier's designs which address green issues that are still topical. For example his 'houses of coarse concrete' in 1919[92] tackled mass production in such a way as to

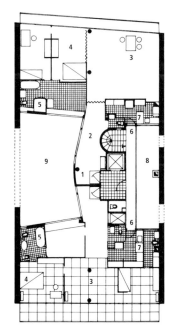

7.7a *Free Plan at 24 rue Nungesser et Coli, Paris, 1933*

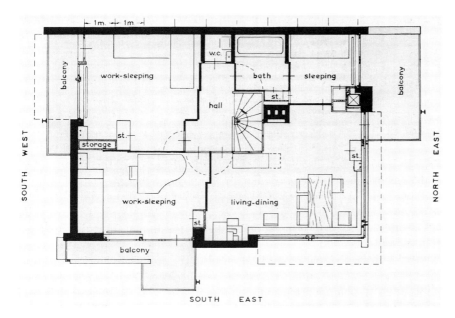

both minimise transport of materials and exploit natural resources: 'The ground consisted of layers of gravel. A quarry was opened on the site; and the gravel was run with lime into a raft 12 inches in thickness.' The Monol proposal of the same year[93] extended this principle to walls, with lime again the binding agent for site-found aggregate held in place with light permanent shuttering. He prefaced this specification with: 'The ordinary house weighs too much and involves the cost of transportation of a quantity of material.' His proposal for mass-produced artisan's dwellings of 1924[94] structurally employed a single hollow central column which doubled as a rainwater downpipe; and had an external skin on non-loadbearing walls of compressed straw, rendered externally and plastered internally.

Just as energy-efficient design has fluctuated with the price and availability of fossil fuels, so also politics and economics relate to the distance materials are transported from origin to building, and the extent of profligacy in terms of numbers and types specified. Thus green industrial concern today is, for example, resulting in ingredients like rennet casein used in early plastics[95] such as Bakelite making a come-back in materials such as casein-lime plaster. It is accepted that some green attributes of modernism occurred by default. For example, early insulating materials predated the oil-based chemical industry. However, the importance given to mass and transport by Le Corbusier, and the lengths undertaken by Wright both to exploit local materials and minimise the number of materials used, underscore a deliberate environmental concern, albeit sometimes influenced by shortages brought about by war and economic recession.

An apparent paradox is that Wright and Le Corbusier applied much of this degree of rigour to clients with some wealth. They could afford not to skimp on resources, whereas today's avowedly green architects are more likely to direct limitations of this kind at the poorer sections of society than the rich. However, this is all relative, and architects have always had to 'go with the flow' of clients. Not only that, wealthy clients have a respectable history in terms of sponsoring innovation and the consequent risk.

Another possible paradox is that there are apparently more common green denominators between Wright and Le Corbusier than the green radicals of today. We are used to the two masters being compared on the basis of differences, whereas we expect a consensus from today's environmentally conscious movement.

Commonality between Le Corbusier and Wright is increasingly being addressed. Doremus[96] in discussing their respective attitudes to a 'machine aesthetic' maintains: 'both architects were really referring to the *art of the machined* rather than the *art of the machine*'. This sense could be applied to the liveability or usability of a space. But Doremus uses these terms to assert that each was concerned with the buildability afforded by industrial processes, although with strong links to Arts and Crafts in Wright's case.

In introducing *Frank Lloyd Wright: Ausgefuhrte Bauten* in 1911, Charles Ashbee[97] acknowledged Wright's 'inner kinship' with 'so-called Arts and Crafts men like Lethaby, Voysey, Lutyens, Ricardo, Wilson, Holden, Blow, Townsend, Baillie, Scott'. Nevertheless, referring to the Unity Temple, he acknowledges: 'he displays a firm determination, which sometimes reaches heroic proportions, to impress machine technology into the service of his goals – through forms and methods that are adaptable to the machine, but without disregarding traditional forms'. Ashbee also quotes Wright from the *Architectural Record* in 1908 reviewing his Prairie Houses: 'The machine is the tool which uniquely characterises our cultural epoch. . . . Adapting a work to the potential of the machine is the content of the modern industrial ideal which we must construct if architecture is not to lose its leading position within the realm of art.' He further quotes Wright from the same text complaining about misuse of the machine:

The machine can no longer be removed from the world; it is here to stay and is the pioneer of democracy, which is the ultimate goal of our hopes and desires. The architect of our time should know no more important task than the deployment of this modern tool as much as possible. But what does he do instead? He misuses this tool for the creation of forms that arose in different times . . . and all this takes place with the help of the machine whose main task it is to precisely destroy these forms.

More than 80 years on, Etlin[98] quotes Wright from the same article: 'These forms were the result of a conscientious study of materials and of the machine which is the real tool, whether we like it or not, that we must use to give shape to our ideals.'

However, unsurprisingly, Ashbee's allegiance to Arts and Crafts results in him expressing some reservations with respect to Wright's work: 'As an architect, I would like to say that individualism in Lloyd Wright's work appears strong and healthy to the core, but I don't always like it.' Also at the end of his introduction to this published series of plans and photographs, he states:

I have in mind particularly certain works of Lloyd Wright that I would like to touch with a magic wand. Their inner structure should remain, but I would adorn them in a gentler more vivid manner. The time for this has yet to come and I would not want to see Wright himself trying his hand at this, for I don't believe he could succeed. For the kind of adornment I am envisioning presupposes the existence of a well developed Arts and Crafts movement, reflecting the indigenous culture of America.

Significantly, Doremus[99] also parallels Le Corbusier's Five Points with Wright's Five Resources for Modern Architecture written for his autobiography in 1932. He compares Wright's first resource, *the sense of the within – space – as reality*, with Le Corbusier's third of the five points, the *free plan*; and in discussing the other four resources – *glass, continuity, understanding of the nature of materials, and pattern as natural–integral ornament* – relative to the Five Points, Doremus raises several of the issues already covered here. In essence, he saw only two significant areas of difference between the two masters: 'the appropriate relation between man and nature and the proper expression of modern construction methods'. Both, of course, are relevant to an 'eco-footprint'.

Although there are clear differences between Le Corbusier's 'male' buildings, at least in their detachment from nature and Wright's earth-rootedness, Etlin,[100] in discussing their respective 'systems', identifies a critical 'man–nature' correspondence. He refers to the 'prospect–refuge' theory of Appleton, and the writings of Hildebrand and Bachelard, on the topic of Wright's Prairie Houses. He notes the same intention with respect to Le Corbusier's design for Une Petite Maison, dating from 1922–3: 'When Le Corbusier opens the wall in the garden, he offers a secure perch from which to view the dramatic spectacle.' Etlin[101] further defines the 'prospect–refuge' theory as 'the dialectic of small and large . . . the paired experiences of concentration and expansion' evident in almost all of Le Corbusier's work.

Philip Johnson,[102] writing 45 years earlier in the *Architectural Review*, makes a similar point in relation to Wright: 'the cumulative impact of moving through his organised spaces, the effect of passing through low space into high, from narrow to wide, from dark to light'. Interestingly he directly follows this comment with: 'Wright is also unique in his ability to adjust buildings to natural surroundings.' Again later in the same article he quotes Wright: 'We must learn to use the word nature in its proper romantic sense.' This raises the question as to whether romantic or picturesque design can be rational, or adequately so, since it is the rationality of how a building performs and relates to its natural surroundings that dominates in terms of green issues today.

We know, for example, that Le Corbusier linked his architectural promenade to a green rationale in buildings such as the Maison Curutchet. Wright's motives in leaving the willow tree in the linking corridor between his house and studio at Oak Park also seems to combine practical climate-sensitivity with a sense of romantic or picturesque, and he was prepared to take technical risks in so doing. In his autobiography[103] he states:

> An old willow tree still stood in the corridor connecting the house with the big work-room. I had succeeded in making the roofs around the tree trunks watertight in a manner that would permit the trees to grow, and the great sprawling old tree gave us grateful coolness in the studio in summer. I liked the golden leaves dropping above the amateurish buildings. If I could have covered the buildings all over with greenery, I would have done so. They were so badly overdone.

Similarly, there are very apparent differences in materiality comparing Wright with Le Corbusier (again more obvious with respect to the latter's 'male' line). The first part established Wright as an advocate of 'mono-material' and often 'mono-layer' as opposed to Le Corbusier's 'multi-material' (in Precisions: 'anything you like'[104]) and usually 'multi-layer'. Doremus[105] stressed a difference in approach in terms of Wright using sub-components from a factory, such as steel mesh to enable plastic continuity of reinforced concrete on site; whereas Le Corbusier liked the idea of whole components that were assembled on site. He states: 'Continuity as a Resource, then, is the kernel of disagreement with Le Corbusier about the nature of mass production.' However, Le Corbusier's roof at Ronchamp, by its nature bespoke, not mass produced, bears comparison with Wright's cantilevers at Fallingwater; and the former's statement of 1908 quoted by Etlin[106] – 'I saw what concrete is, what revolutionary form it requires' – could be applied appositely to Wright's dendriform columns for the Johnson Building. In terms of 'green' materiality, the importance lies in the shared belief in exploitation of local materials in imaginative and economic ways.

Thus it can be argued that Wright and Le Corbusier shared some philosophical ground, much of which might be interpreted as 'green'. Related *green roots and shoots* from other influential architects on both sides of the Atlantic have been identified. The question to pose is whether such sustainable strands emanating from the Modern Movement are being suppressed, forgotten or ignored with time, and whether this has a bearing on the environmental agenda of architecture today. In order to answer this, there are major gaps to be filled. The route by which some tenets survive or resurface at various stages up until the present has to be revisited. Correa[107] also makes the valuable point that the dialectics of small and large, discussed above in terms of spatiality, apply equally to process. He stresses that design is iterative going 'from the detail to the overall concept and back again' and 'that the kind of designs that emerge are dependent on the issues we feed in at the input end'. This aspect will figure quite strongly in the next part, especially within the concluding chapter 'spirit of the age'.

As a prelude to what is to come, and as a return to the starting point of this part, still acknowledging the 'light and air' aspect of a 'house is a machine for living in', it is opportune to return to the work of two other architects. Aalto has previously been discussed in terms of multi-layerism and transparency, and Kahn concerning his development of an inter-changeable opaque-transparent skin. Both also became renowned for their masterly and melismatic manipulation of natural light, particularly through roofs.

For example, Aalto's prismatic roof-lights in the Academic Bookshop in Helsinki (competition 1962, built 1966–9) do much more than a normal set of roof-lights of the same area. The inner facets of each prism refract and reflect in a purely physical way, but they also constitute a strong poetic or musical presence. They proclaim natural daylight and sunlight in *fortissimo* in the triple-height central atrium, even though the bookshop is reliant on artificial lighting. In other buildings, light spills in more discreetly, but no less dramatically. In the main auditorium of the Institute of Technology at Otaniemi (designed 1955, built 1961–4), and if black-out is not enforced, the audience is able to enjoy the benefits of southerly sunshine, but without any glare. A simple sectional device achieves this. Similar daylighting techniques are used in his later North Jutland Museum of Arts in Aalborg, Denmark, designed in conjunction with Jean-Jacques Baruel. Won by competition in 1958, this project was redesigned in 1963, but not completed until 1972. Shortly after comple-tion, the *Architectural Review*[108] describes Aalto's approach to lighting in some detail, emphasising the asymmetry of the section and the use of baffles or shields to cope with varying intensities of diffused daylight and direct sunlight both seasonally and diurnally. The commentary also draws attention to the manner in which Aalto places artificial lighting to simulate daylighting.

Likewise, Kahn's authoritative and sophisticated command over direct and indirect lighting in his projects has been recognised and docu-mented. In a book sub-titled 'Light and Space', Büttiker[109] examines this aspect of Kahn's opus in some depth; and usefully concludes with a chronological classification of the different typologies of light control – fairly basic up until the Weiss House in 1947, and becoming increasingly sophisticated during Kahn's last 15 years from 1959 (the analytical study extending to 1971).

Returning to Correa's point, light is the environmental input that satisfies function, uplifts emotions and displaces primary energy. The harnessing of light has a major impact on spatiality and form – all very topically relevant to the following theme of 'adventitious propagation' that takes us forward to the present.

References to Part Two

1   Vale B. and R. (1991), Case Study 6. In *Towards a Green Architecture*, RIBA Publications, London, 65–78.

2   Kugel C. (1998), *Exotic Prototype*, Architectural Review, Vol. CCIII, No. 1214, April, 80.

3   Tong D. and Wilson S. (1990), Ch. C5: Building Related Sickness – the Causes of Sick Building Syndrome. In *The Rosehaugh Guide to the Design, Construction, Use and Management of Buildings*, RIBA Publications, London, 266–71.

4   van Doesburg T. (1924), *Towards a Plastic Architecture*, Vol. VI, No. 6/7, Paris 78–83. Quoted in C. Jaffe, *De Stijl*. Thames & Hudson, London, 1970.

5   Smith C. (1997), In *Breakfast News* (verbal quote), 11/9/97.

6   Clean Air Act 1956 (1957), Ch. 52 In *The Public General Acts and Church Assembly Measures 1956*, HMSO, London, 379–415.

7   Clean Air Act 1968 (1969), Ch. 62 An Act to make further provisions for abating the pollution of the air [15th October 1968]. In *The Public General Acts and Church Assembly Measures 1968*, HMSO, London, 1523–38.

8   Le Corbusier (1923, trans. Etchells 1927), Eyes Which Do Not See: II Airplanes, The Manual of the Dwelling. In *Towards a New Architecture (Vers une Architecture)*, The Architectural Press, London and Frederick A. Praeger, New York, 114–15.

9   Etlin R. A. (1994), Ch. 1 The Architectural System. In *Frank Lloyd Wright and Le Corbusier, the Romantic Legacy*, Manchester University Press, Manchester and New York, 15–17.

10   Le Corbusier (1930, trans. Aujame 1991), Techniques are the Very Basis of Poetry, They Open a New Cycle in Architecture (Lecture 2, 5/10/29). In *Precisions on the Present State of Architecture and City Planning (Precisions sur un etat present de l'architecture et de l'urbanisme)*, The MIT Press, Cambridge, Massachusetts and London, 38.

11   Ibid. The Plan of the Modern House, 136.

12   Turrent D., Doggart J. and Ferraro R. (1980), Technical Appraisal. In *Passive Solar Housing in the UK*, A report to the Energy Technology Support Unit Harwell, 28.

13   Etlin R. A. (1994), Ch. 2 The Picturesque. In *Frank Lloyd Wright and Le Corbusier, the Romantic Legacy*, Manchester University Press, Manchester and New York, 112–29.

14   Le Corbusier (1930, trans. Aujame 1991), A Dwelling at Human Scale (Lecture 4, 10/10/29). In *Precisions on the Present State of Architecture and City Planning (Precisions sur un etat present de l'architecture et de l'urbanisme)*, The MIT Press, Cambridge, Massachusetts and London, 97.

15   Lapunzina A. (1997), Ch. IV Insertion into Le Corbusier's Oeuvre. In *Le Corbusier's Maison Curutchet*, Princeton Architectural Press, New York, 137–9.

16   Mackenzie C. (1993), *Le Corbusier in the Sun*, Architectural Review, Vol. CXCII, No. 1152, February, 71–4.

17   Evans J. M. and de Schiller S. (1998), *The Friendly City, the Sun and Le Corbusier: Form, Function and Bioclimatic Response*, proceedings PLEA '98, 'Environmentally Friendly Cities', Lisbon, Portugal, June 1998, James & James Ltd, London, 221–4.

18   Ali Z. F. (1998), *Le Corbusier's Chandigarh from an Environmental Point of View*, proceedings PLEA '98, 'Environmentally Friendly Cities', Lisbon, Portugal, June 1998, James & James Ltd., London, 183–6.

19   Aronin J. E. (1953), The Sun, Design and the Sun, In *Climate & Architecture*, Reinhold Publishing Corp., New York, 83.

20   (1938), *Ventilation and Air Conditioning of the Interior*, Architectural Review, Vol. LXXXIV, August, 80.

21   Yorke F. R. S. (1934), *The Modern House*, The Architectural Press, London, 73 & 78.

22   Le Corbusier (1930, trans. Aujame 1991), Techniques are the Very Basis of Poetry, They Open a New Cycle in Architecture (Lecture 2, 5/10/29). In *Precisions on the Present State of Architecture and City Planning (Precisions sur un etat present de l'architecture et de l'urbanisme)*, The MIT Press, Cambridge, Massachusetts and London, 64–6.

23   Banham R. (1969), Ch. 8 Machines a Habiter. In *The Architecture of the Well-tempered Environment*, The Architectural Press Ltd, London 1969, 1984, 158–62.

24   Kopp A. (1970, trans. Burton), Ch. 10 Dream and Reality. In *Town and Revolution*, George Braziller Inc., New York, 182.

25   Le Corbusier (1930, trans. Aujame 1991), Ibid. 54.

26   Yorke F. R. S. and Gibberd F. (1937), *The Modern Flat*, The Architectural Press, London, 191–3.

27   Etlin R. A. (1994), Ch. 1 The Architectural System. In *Frank Lloyd Wright and Le Corbusier, the Romantic Legacy*, Manchester University Press, Manchester and New York, 23.

28   Curtis W. J. R. (1986), Ch. 9 Regionalism and Reassessment in the 1930s. In *Le Corbusier: Ideas and Forms*, Phaidon Press Ltd, London, 115.

29   Sbriglio J. (trans. Parsons 1996), The Project's History, constructing a fragment of the 'Ville Radieuse'. In *Apartment Block 24 N.C. and Le Corbusier's Home*, Birkhauser, Basel, 76–8.

30   Taylor B. B. (1998), The House of Glass. In *Pierre Chareau*, Taschen, Cologne, 29.

31   Wright F. L. (1945), Book Four: Freedom. In *An Autobiography*, Faber & Faber, London, 277.

32   Ibid. 298–300.

33   Ibid. Book Three: Work. 140.

34   Ibid. Book Four: Freedom. 305.

35   Ibid. Book Five: Form. 426.

36   Ibid. Book Three: Work. 128.

37   Jacobs H. (1978), Part II: The Solar Hemicycle. In *Building with Frank Lloyd Wright, an Illustrated Memoir*, Chronicle Books, San Francisco, 69–142.

38   Drexler A. and Hines T. S. (1982), The Architecture of Richard Neutra. In *The Architecture of Richard Neutra: from International Style to California Modern*, The Museum of Modern Art, New York, 19.

39   Gebhard D. (1971), Ch. 4 Opportunity: California in the Twenties. In *Schindler*, Thames & Hudson, London, 47.

40   Ibid. 51.

41   Hines T. S. (1982), Modernity 1932–1940. In *Richard Neutra and the Search for Modern Architecture*, University of California Press, Berkeley and Los Angeles, 158.

42   Ibid. 121.

43   Friedman A. T. (1998), *Women and the Making of the Modern House*, Harry N. Abrams Inc., New York, 160–87.

44   Ibid. 143.

45   Schulze F. (1985), Revival: Modernism without Utopia 1938–49. In *Mies van der Rohe, A Critical Biography*, The University of Chicago, Chicago, 254–6.

46   Kudel Ková L. and Mácel O. (1998), The Villa Tugendhat in Brno. In *Mies van der Rohe*, Vitra Design Museum/Skira, 186–93.

47   Yorke F. R. S. (1934), *The Modern House*, The Architectural Press, London, 114–17.

48   Friedman A. T. (1998), *Women and the Making of the Modern House*, Harry N. Abrams Inc., New York, 141.

49   Yorke F. R. S. (1944), *The Modern House in England*, The Architectural Press, London, 82–4.

50   Joint Committee on the Orientation of Buildings (1932), *Orientation of Buildings: Being the Report of the Royal Institute of British Architects*, Journal of the Royal Institute of British Architects, 39 (10th September), 777–99.

51   Boyce R. (1993), Ch. 7 Development of a Passive Solar House. In *Keck and Keck*, Princeton Architectural Press, New York, 73.

52   Ibid. 79.

53   Butti K. and Perlin J. (1980), Ch. 15 An American Revival. In *A Golden Thread, 2500 Years of Solar Architecture and Technology*,

Cheshire Books, Palo Alto, California, and Marion Boyars Publishers Ltd, London (1981), 193–4.

54 Ford K. M. and Creighton T. H. (1951), *The American House Today, notable examples selected and evaluated*, Reinhold Publishing Corp., New York, 239.

55 Germany L. (1991), Ch. 3 Of Organisms, Machines, and the Illusion of Architecture, 1926–1931. In *Harwell Hamilton Harris*, University of Texas Press, Austin, 29.

56 van Doesburg T. (trans. Loeb and Loeb 1990), *Theo van Doesburg on European Architecture Complete Essays from Het Bouwbedrift 1924–1931*, Birkhauser Verlag, Basel, 94 (Het Bouwbedrift Vol. 6, July 1929, 305–8).

57 Ibid. 62–3 (Vol. 2, No. 5, May 1925, 197–200).

58 Ibid. 124 (Vol. 3, No. 15, November 1926, 477–9).

59 Ibid. 138–41 (Vol. 4, No. 6, March 1927, 144–5).

60 Ibid. 142–3 (Vol. 4, No. 6, March 1927, 144–5).

61 Germany L. (1991), Ch. 5 Jean Murray Bangs and a Career Takes Shape, In *Harwell Hamilton Harris*, University of Texas Press, Austin, 62.

62 Gropius W. (trans. Morton Shand 1935), Rationalisation. In *Walter Gropius and the New Architecture*, Faber & Faber, London, 30–2.

63 Hines T. S. (1982), Transition 1941–1949. In *Richard Neutra and the Search for Modern Architecture*, University of California Press, Berkeley and Los Angeles, 201.

64 Wright F. L. (1953), To the Young Man in Architecture (The Chicago Art Inst. Lectures, 1931) In *The Future of Architecture*, Horizon Press Inc., New York (and Mentor Books 1963), 213.

65 Wright F. L. (1955), Where Principle is Put to Work there will Always be Style (quote: talk to University Guild, Evanston, Illinois, 1894) In *An American Architecture*, Ed. E. Kaufman, Horizon Press Inc., New York, Horizon Press, London, 242.

66 Ibid., Architecture Presents Man and From Generals to Particulars (quote: Architectural Record, March 1908), 24, 48 and 53.

67 Wright F. L. (1945), Book Three: Work. In *An Autobiography*, Faber & Faber, London, 126.

68 (1984), In *Longman Dictionary of the English Language*, Longman, Harlow, Essex, 1034.

69 Wright F. L. (1945), Ibid. 130.

70 Ibid. 129–30.

71 Lipman J. (1986), Ch. 5 Innovations: Columns and Glass Tubing. In *Frank Lloyd Wright and the Johnson Wax Buildings*, Architectural Press, London, 68.

72 Ibid. Ch. 12 Using the Complex, 172.

73 Quinan J. (1987), App. G Frank Lloyd Wright, 'The New Larkin Administration Building' (from The Larkin Idea, 6, November 1906, 2–9) In *Frank Lloyd Wright's Larkin Building, Myth and Fact*, The MIT Press, Cambridge, Massachusetts and London, 140–4.

74   Ibid. App. L Frank Lloyd Wright, 'Reply to Mr. Sturgis's Criticism'(from 'In the Cause of Architecture, Buffalo, New York, April 1909), 168.

75   Ibid. App. K Russel Sturgis, 'The Larkin Building in Buffalo' (from Architectural Record, 23, April 1908, 310–21) 159–64.

76   Ibid. Ch. 4 Functional Aspects of the Design, 66–72.

77   Banham R. (1969), Ch. 5 Environments of Large Buildings. In *The Architecture of the Well-tempered Environment*, The Architectural Press Ltd, London 1969, 1984, 86–92.

78   Wright F. L. (1945), Book One: Family. In *An Autobiography* (Book 1 first published 1932), Faber & Faber, London, 20.

79   Vale B. and Vale R. (1991), Case Study 5. In *Towards a Green Architecture*, RIBA Publications, London, 53–64.

80   van Doesburg T. (trans. Loeb and Loeb 1990), *Theo van Doesburg on European Architecture Complete Essays from Het Bouwbedrift 1924–1931*, Birkhauser Verlag, Basel, 94 (Het Bouwbedrift Vol. 3, No. 5, May 1926, 191–4).

81   Ibid. 170–1 (Vol. 4, No. 24, November 1927, 556–9).

82   Brown T. M. (1958), *The work of G. Rietveld, architect*, A. W. Bruna & Zoon, Utrecht, 53.

83   Le Corbusier (1923 trans. Etchells 1927), Argument. In *Towards a New Architecture (Vers une Architecture)*, The Architectural Press, London and Frederick A. Praeger, New York, 10, 19, 32, 89, 257.

84   Ibid. The Engineer's Aesthetic and Architecture, 23.

85   Ibid. 19.

86   Ibid. Three Reminders to Architects I Mass, 33.

87   Ibid. Eyes Which Do Not See I Liners, 89.

88   Ibid. Architecture or Revolution, 357.

89   Ibid. Mass Production Houses, 232–3.

90   Le Corbusier (1954), *Une Petite Maison 1923*, Artemis Verlags-AG, Zurich, 5, 10–11, 39–59.

91   Sbriglio J. (trans. Parsons 1996), 'My Apartment' and The Project's History. In *Apartment Block 24 N.C. and Le Corbusier's Home*, Birkhauser, Basel, 62–6, 99–100.

92   Le Corbusier (1923, trans. Etchells 1927), Mass Production Houses. In *Towards a New Architecture*, The Architectural Press, London and Frederick A. Praeger, New York, 220–1.

93   Ibid. Mass Production Houses, 224–5.

94   Ibid. Mass Production Houses, 236–7.

95   Scholberg P. (1948), Plastics. In *New Ways of Building*, Ed. de Maré, The Architectural Press, London, 194–208.

96   Doremus T. (1985), Wright and Le Corbusier as Savants. In *Frank Lloyd Wright and Le Corbusier The Great Dialogue*, Van Nostrand Reinhold Co., New York, 67.

97   Ashbee C. R. (1911, trans. Goldstein 1995), Frank Lloyd Wright, a Study of his Work. In *Frank Lloyd Wright Early Visions*, Gramercy, New Jersey, 3–10.

98 Etlin R. A. (1994), Ch. 1 The Architectural System. In *Frank Lloyd Wright and Le Corbusier, the Romantic Legacy*, Manchester University Press, Manchester and New York, 55.

99 Doremus T. (1985), Wright and Le Corbusier as Kin, Ibid. 64.

100 Etlin R. A. (1994), Ibid. 35 and 73.

101 Ibid. 74.

102 Johnson P. (1949), *The Frontiersman*, Architectural Review, Vol. CVI, August, 105–6.

103 Wright F. L. (1945), Book Three: Work, Ibid. 125.

104 Le Corbusier (1930, trans. Aujame 1991), Techniques are the Very Basis of Poetry, They Open a New Cycle in Architecture (Lecture 2, 5/10/29), Ibid. 42.

105 Doremus T. (1985), Ibid. 64–5.

106 Etlin R. A. (1994), Ibid. 13.

107 Correa C. (2000), Foreword. In *Housing and Urbanisation*, Thames & Hudson, London, 6.

108 (1973), *Aalto at Aalborg*, Architectural Review, Vol. CLIII, No. 913, March, 155–61.

109 Büttiker U. (1994), *Louis I Kahn Light and Space*, Whitney Library of Design, New York.

Adventitious propagation?   PART THREE

Green trail to now – ecology vs economy   CHAPTER 8

Historical distortion or amnesia with respect to political matters is generally acknowledged as, or expected to be, deliberate. 'Spin' is a recent term for an old phenomenon. However, with architecture, it is more likely that such spin is less managed and more a result of natural selection. In any event, logic suggests that the volume and type of published material has some relationship with interest. Above all, with respect to the Modern Movement, or the New Architecture as Walter Gropius termed it, the interest appears to be primarily sustained by the revolution in redefining space supported by critical technological enablers in this process such as reinforced concrete and large panes of glass. The ends provided by these means – light, airy, buildings associated with a healthier more egalitarian way of life – tend to be remembered in terms of visual images, rather than detailed physical reality and social consequence. Other sub-movements arising from the main one are even more easily forgotten or mis-remembered.

Therefore, having noted that the first wave of passive solar design starting in the late 1930s was fairly short-lived due to increasingly cheap post-war fossil fuels, the perception of a student is quite likely to be that passive solar design starts with the Trombe[1] wall or perhaps the school at Wallesey[2] in the 1960s (if any date is remembered). The name of the co-designer of the Trombe wall, Jacques Michel, is forgotten, not because he was an architect, but because his name came after that of Felix Trombe. And the fact that the wall is a simplified version of the solar air collector of 1881 by a zoologist and Japanese enthusiast, Edward Sylvester Morse,[3] is probably not widely known (Fig. 8.1). Had the monitoring of the Duncan House in 1941–2 (see Chapter 6) been better remembered, perhaps designers in the 1980s and 1990s would not have spent so much time and effort wrestling with the same issues – thermal capacitance, response relative to auxiliary heating, and excessive infiltration of air. On the other hand, it may be simply inevitable that designers are drawn to reinvention, despite all the recent advances in information technology, or at least this may be another factor complicating the historical path of research.

Accepting then the apparently ephemeral nature of green modernist sources, this study is making a case for re-examination as part of the process of assessing today's variegated architectural foliage. The brief comparison above of two buildings completed over 80 years apart, the Larkin Building and the ING Bank (see Chapter 7), alone justifies

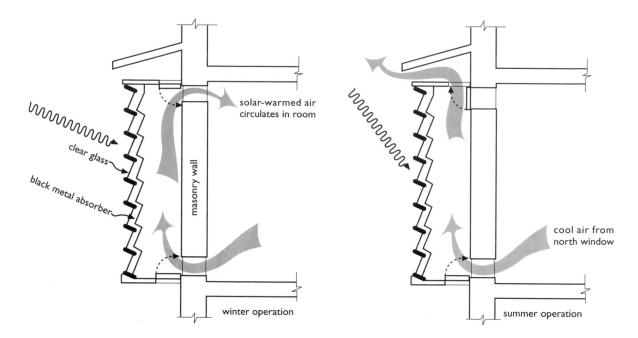

solar-warmed air
circulates in room

clear glass

black metal absorber

masonry wall

cool air from
north window

winter operation

summer operation

8.1 *Edward S. Morse's solar air collector, Salem, Massachusetts, 1882*

following through to the present time in more depth. This final part tracks a 'green trail' to the present mainly through individual architects who have explicitly engaged with ecology and energy-efficiency in their designs, variously responding to socio-political movements, socio-economic conditions, and pressure from geo-political phenomena. Longevity in the shape of figures such as Ralph Erskine and Albert Frey injects a degree of continuity into the casualness or collaterality implied by adopting the metaphor of *adventitious propagation* as its title.

The story picks up again in the 1960s and continues, with various peaks and troughs and with an increasingly broader green spectrum, until the present. The motivation for this is to try to pin down as far as possible aspects of modernism, regional modernism and any other *isms* that continue to be relevant to the green agenda of the 21st century, and to discuss how changing architectural theory and language may present opportunities or obstacles for such an agenda. For example, at the time of writing there is an increasing interest in expanding the architectural potential of glass. This is partly driven by technical advances and partly by a desire, perhaps romantic, symbolic or psychological, for maximum visual transparency in roofs, walls and floors. This then returns the debate to one of the primary ingredients of the Modern Movement. It is now possible to design a fully glazed 'crystal house' or *mur neutralisant* which can address thermal comfort without over-reliance on air-conditioning or other energy-intensive mechanical systems. However, it does not follow that such an emphasis on glass is in itself the most economically or ecologically desirable tactic. It may be that a strong practical case for a largely opaque external skin can only be countered by more subjective arguments based on emotional and illusional, as well as physical, aspects of light, air and spatiality – very much as embodied in the first of Wright's resources:[4] 'Well, like poetry, this sense of architecture is the sound of the "within".'

The German architect, Thomas Spiegelhalter, might be regarded as being on the horns of such a dilemma when he reconciles the theory of deconstruction with photovoltaic solar cells, flat plate solar collectors and sunspaces. In doing so he introduces a deceptive feeling of glassiness viewed externally, when the actuality is a building with a rather modest area of windows (Fig. 8.2). He also uses his fossil fuel-saving devices as prominent components in his visually deconstructed imagery when a more integrated approach might have been more efficient. For instance, flat-plate collectors could have doubled as roof coverings, and photovoltaic panels could have been integrated with roofs or walls so as to capture their by-product of thermal heat. However, there is a contra-technical argument with respect to photovoltaic panels in particular. Partial shading from obstructions will knock out complete 'strings', thereby reducing output. Arrays that are not physically integrated with the skin of a building may be more freely positioned to avoid such shading, while they remain an integrated part of the overall design and its 'alternative' signals. Such technical and aesthetic nuances evoke the addition of some appealing spice to what is sometimes perceived as an overly bland menu in terms of green imagery.

A reasonable hypothesis to be drawn from the review thus far is that the preoccupations of influential architects of the Modern Movement still have a 'green' relevance in the context of an inevitably dynamic 21st century theoretical *mise en scène*. This is increasingly engaging with an acknowledged need for more sustainable buildings. But thorny issues remain around wilful hedonism in architecture. This is becoming more prevalent today, and by its nature tends to compete with a necessary quota of rationalism. Such polemic should be stimulating rather than frustrating. The risk in taking too extreme an ecological position architecturally is that reaction halts any progress. It appears to be a truism that radicalism of any kind tends to be attractive only to the political periphery. In turn, this relates to a pressing frustration at the beginning of the new millennium. That is the apparent acceptance by the entire spectrum of society of an overwhelmingly conservative architectural recidivism, most acutely felt when it comes to dwellings.

Such populist reliance on the past for visual context and comfort, and lack of engagement with the present and future, is driven largely by commercial interest. The past is easier to sell than the future, and economic interests tend to be much more powerful than ecological ones. This is the case even though industries come and go with relative rapidity whereas ecology is here forever. Economic advantage is what drives technology forward. But the process also generates pollution and foments political and territorial disputes, which ironically can generate conditions whereby more altruistic, geo-conscious, green architectural surges may

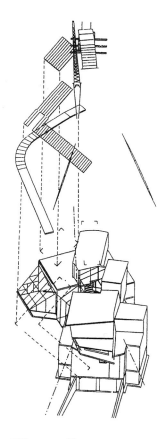

additive composition

8.2 *Solar House by T. Spiegelhalter, Breisach, Germany, 1996*

intermittently flourish. Hence the term 'adventitious propagation' is an appropriate metaphor in the sense that the abundant flowering of poppies in the shell-torn ground of the Great War has a correspondence in aspects of the Modern Movement. The underlying proposition is that design, which is explicitly green in some aspect or another, tends to be expressed in periodic peaks of activity. This can be attributed more to politico-economical traumas in the 1960–70s, and global scientific revelations in the 1980s, than to steadily progressing advances in technology or environmental conscience. There are nevertheless discernible threads connecting them all. Not only that, but the issues and outcomes impinge strongly on the polemic around architectural *isms* that cross climatic boundaries with and without respect, and those that cannot, or do not readily, cross such boundaries. The debate around the relative validity or value of international modernism, regional modernism and regionalism, with all their neo-versions and variables, is still ongoing.

One resource-based, socio-technological strand emanates from Buckminster Fuller – strength to weight ratios, recycling, reusing, self-building and so forth. It embraces some notable 'fringe' architectural figures, such as Bruce Goff with connections to Wright's 'organic simplicity', Lucien Kroll in relation to participatory design and, more recently, 'bio-functional eco-architecture', and Walter Segal with his 'small is beautiful' rational approach to self-building. These individuals strongly connect with anti-populist challengers of the norms of society. They may be hippies and new-age travellers, or disaffected groups of people housed in shanty towns proliferating around the downtown cities of Central and South America, Africa and Asia. On the other hand, individuals such as Lucien Kroll and Ralph Erskine have also connected forcibly with the first-world city of Graz in Austria, generating innovations in architectural thought and practice.

Ralph Erskine's climate-sensitive modernist strand has an adherence well beyond Europe, for example, emulated in Australia by figures such as Glen Murcutt. Now, with environmental issues such as global warming acknowledged in international agreements, together with the rising influence of green political policies and parties in individual countries, an environmentally conscious modernism is emerging and sharpening the interest of architectural stars. Rational, tectonic modernists such as Thomas Herzog in Germany and perhaps AARPLAN in Switzerland are rapidly gaining prominence, alongside the ilk of Rogers, Piano and Herzog & De Meuron. Bravely experimental engineers working closely with architects, such as Frei Otto and Ted Happold, have also impinged on green design; and today Patkau Architects in Canada and Spiegelhalter in Germany offer other green reinterpretations of architectural syntax. Subsumed in this more mainstream *mélange*, dating from the late 1960s with its multi-faceted and multi-disciplinary character, is a discernible second wave of passive solar and bioclimatic design.

Thus at the start of the third Christian millennium, although such shifts in attitude are still underpinned by economic realities, one may be cautiously optimistic about a more planet-conscious architectural outlook. However, market forces have fickle attitudes of their own, which justify the need for some regulation. The Thatcherite idea of a green built environment being compatible with zero-intervention in the market-place is not viable; and public aesthetic taste is as capable of being led or influenced just as much as any other opinion or view. For example, it is likely that German standards had something to do with the way Foster and his consultants addressed the new Reichstag's energy load. Will Rogers' proposed Welsh Assembly in Cardiff be renewably fuelled by rape seed oil or its equivalent, and its electrical load offset by solar photovoltaics?

Fuller life – hippies, junk and self-build CHAPTER 9

We can view Buckminster Fuller as an entrepreneur, inventor or global strategist. To at least some students of architecture in the early 1960s, he was as strong a force as Wright or Le Corbusier. If the Rio Earth Summit had taken place in 1963 rather than 1992, his Universal Requirements Check List[5] and Carbondale publication[6] would have been at the centre of it. 'Bibles' of the alternative movement stemming from the 1960s such as *Shelter*,[7] 1973, and *The Next Whole Earth Catalog*,[8] 1980, are more user-friendly descendants of Fuller's philosophy. The alternative movement in the 1960s and 1970s was largely drop-out and co-operative–community based in spirit. As information about passive solar design began to be disseminated in similarly digestible format, for example, Bainbridge's catalogues of 1978[9] and 1980[10] and the AIA's survey of 1978,[11] it became well absorbed within a sympathetic network in the USA.

In the context of 'adventitious propagation', Fuller's concerns were given a boost by the 1967 and 1973 Arab–Israeli wars, and their destabilising influence on the price of oil, followed by the Iranian Revolution of 1979. Deep unrest over the war in Vietnam, the Civil Rights Movement, and a growing awareness of the iniquities wrought by global capitalism in the Developing World, almost resulted in revolution in the USA and Europe in 1968. Although this was not energy-led, it fuelled the same alternative culture. Hornby Island,[12] off Vancouver Island, is a typical manifestation of these influences in the 1970s. The 'leaf retreat' by Lloyd House, 1970, exemplifies sensitive 'green' self-build (Fig. 9.1a);

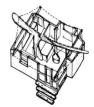

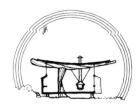

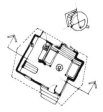

9.1a *Lloyd House's 'leaf retreat', Hornby Island, B.C., Canada, 1970*

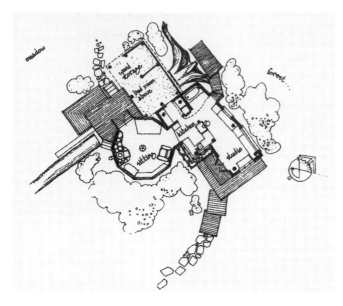

9.1b *Dean's 'metamorphic dome', Hornby Island, B.C., Canada, 1972–3*

and Dean's 'metamorphic' dome, 1972–3, is Fuller-derived (Fig. 9.1b), as were many others of this period. New Mexico was a popular location for specifically passive solar pioneering. In Albuquerque, Steve Baer's 1971 water-wall variant of the 1967 Trombe-Michel prototype (Fig. 9.2a), and in Santa Fe, Unit 1, First Village, 1975, with its attached sunspace, double-envelope and rock-store (Fig. 9.2b) received a significant amount of scientific attention.[13] Unit 1 soon became occupied by Susan and Doug

9.2a *Steve Baer's 'water-wall', Albuquerque, New Mexico, 1971*

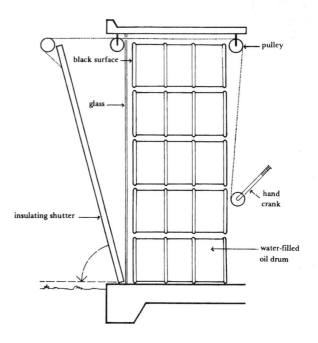

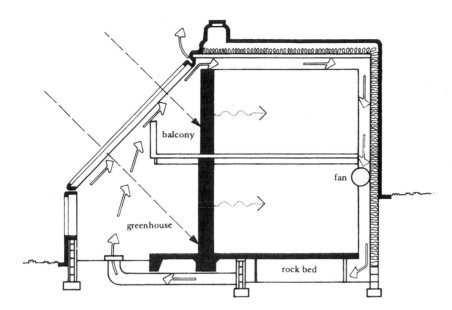

Balcomb, the latter playing a leading role on the international solar conference circuit from the late 1970s onwards. The Cape Cod Ark, publicised in 1977,[14] added autonomous living in terms of energy and food as a further dimension to solar architecture (Fig. 9.3), whereas the 'new alchemists' who designed the system were serious scientists. Two of the 'new alchemists, Nancy Jack Todd and John Todd, published another book in the mid-1990s,[15] *From Eco-Cities to Living Machines*, which relates strongly to more recent writings of Lucien Kroll.[16] In turn, at an earlier stage Kroll put 'participatory design' and 'community architecture' on to the architectural landscape with his student accommodation at Woluwé Saint-Lambert, 1970–82; leading again in the mid-1990s to *Housing without Houses* by Nabeel Hamdi,[17] which also draws from the much earlier ideas of Habraken,[18] and so on.

Thus there was a meeting of hippy culture on the one hand with

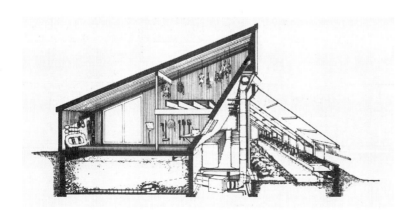

9.3 *The Cape Cod Ark, Massachusetts, 1970s*

academic research, not unexpected since students have often been activists for social change, and on the other with radical architectural practice. Sergeant[19] referred to Goff as an 'organic-expressionist', a label acknowledging a certain linkage with Wright. In fact his work has much in common with that of Hornby Island, both materially and in the way spatial organisation and the public/private realms were redefined. He used standard industrial products in new ways, for example the boiler tubing for the prefabricated frame of the Wilson House in Florida, 1953, and spun concrete columns in the Garvey House No. 2 in Illinois, 1954. The earlier Bavinger House in Oklahoma, 1950–5 (designed 1949), represented an entirely new way of life in the home. Rooms above ground level became suspended saucers within a rough sandstone logarithmic spiral. Finally, his even earlier Triaero House in Kentucky, 1941, was as advanced in terms of its environmental controls as any of the first wave of passive solar houses described in Chapter 6 (Fig. 9.4). There were elegant fixed louvres to shade the windows, plus counterbalanced venetian blinds internally rising from the floor, while pools in front of the main windows reflected light deep into the interior and cooled incoming fresh air.

If 'organic-expressionist' is an apt term to describe Goff, and in turn applicable to the self-building of drop-outs, the logical progression is to the mainstream of 'ecological-organic-expressionists' today. Of course the visual nature and texture of reused and recycled materials, together with amateur building skills and *ad hoc* extensions over a period of time, inevitably introduces a rough edge to the homes of the hippies. Even so, there are undeniable visual connections between 'hand-built Hornby' and Patkau Architects of Vancouver (Fig. 9.5); while the later work of Blue

9.4 *The Triaero House by Bruce Goff, Kentucky, 1941*

'Fishbones' house, Galiano Island, B.C., Blue Sky Architecture

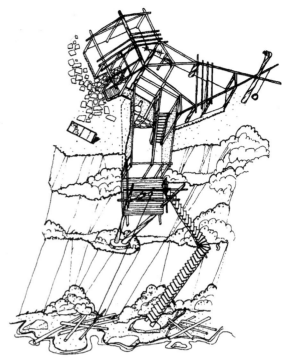

Cliff-top living on Hornby Island, B.C., Blue Sky Design

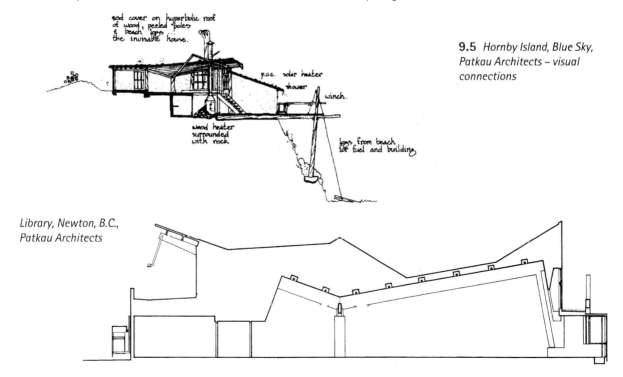

sod cover on hyperbolic roof of wood, peeled 'poles & beach' logs the invisable house.

p.v.c. solar heater

shower

winch.

wood heater surrounded with rock

logs from beach for fuel and building

9.5 *Hornby Island, Blue Sky, Patkau Architects – visual connections*

Library, Newton, B.C., Patkau Architects

Sky Design (which originated in Hornby in the 1970s and now operates from Vancouver) carries the tradition forward, albeit with rather more sophisticated outcomes. There is then a common regional aesthetic statement, from architectural practices of the 1990s back to the work of mainly lay-designers with a specific ecological attitude in the 1970s, which corresponds to a similar strand rooted in Europe – for example, Horst Schmitges's work in Stuttgart of the 1980s,[20] even if visually less flamboyant. It is a continuum. We start with Goff. Herb Greene is Goff's student in the late 1940s–50s. Greene's 1962 Prairie House shares materiality with the Shire Community on Hornby (Fig. 9.6), whereas formalistically the Prairie House has a strong vernacular reference to the tepee.

9.6 *Greene's Prairie House cf Shire Community, Hornby Island*

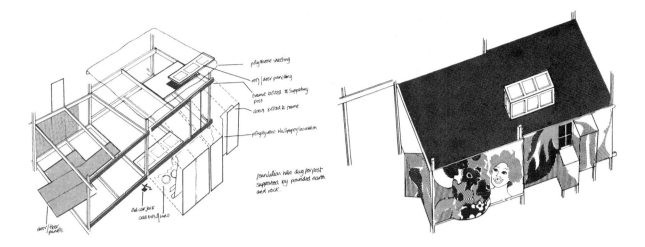

9.7 *Roland's £20 recycled nursery, 1969*

As stated, books such as *Shelter* have played a part. Techniques adopted by the alternative community, from Fuller's geodesic domes to sprayed ferro-cement and Baer's passive solar water-wall, are placed side by side with ancient indigenous techniques and forms. The self-build shanties of the urban poor also lock into this resource-frugal culture.

In 1971, Pawley[21] published an article in *Architectural Design* entitled 'Garbage Housing' which made connections between Fuller, Goff, post-war 'prefabs' and Watford 'semi-Ds' in the UK of the 1940s, Park Hill in Sheffield and Roland's £20 recycled Nursery (Fig. 9.7) in the UK of the 1960s, as well as Woodstock. Pawley[22] returned to the theme in 1973 with images of dwellings made from bottles, cans and even Sugar Puff packets, along with Hornby and vernacular log cabins. In the second part to his article, Pawley describes his role in a 'research programme into the possible value of garbage housing in the context of the explosive urbanisation of the Santiago region'. This had been carried out in the spring of 1973 before the military coup of Pinochet which deposed and killed President Allende. Pawley drew attention to 'the conflict between the organisational, economic and social requirements of a mass housing policy and the aspirations of the people the policy is intended to serve'. He illustrated a 35 m² dwelling for Santiago from standard Citroen 2CV parts (Fig. 9.8), as well as a stressed-skin roof vault system with a core of cans. The former represents a much more literal translation of production lines for vehicles or aeroplanes into prefabricated housing than that achieved by the UK's post-war 'prefabs'; while the latter endeavours to give structural and formal rationale to reusing everyday products. An experimental building made from blocks of sulphur by the Minimum Cost Housing Group (McGill University, Montreal), published in the same issue[23] as well as an earlier *Architectural Design*, is based on compatible industrial thinking that has its roots in figures such as Le Corbusier.

The important issue here, stemming from Fuller, is that a mix of

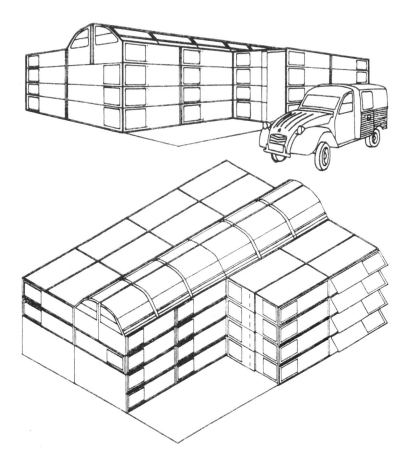

modern technology and reusing and/or recycling of waste products was seen as a way forward with respect to the world's urban poor. There was also the idea of connecting small, light components in such a way that they could cover very large areas, and thereby enable climatic change for whole sectors of urbanity, in tandem with the use of the same or similar elements for individual semi-permanent or temporary dwellings. Whereas the former scenario implies skilled contractors and relatively sophisticated plant, the latter is aimed at unskilled self-build. Politically the mega-concepts such as the geodesic dome for Manhattan, 1962, or gigantic structures shaped like cooling towers which Fuller proposed to replace Harlem in 1965, are hard to equate with a notion of self-reliance.

At any rate, apparently opposing socio-political agendas move forward in parallel. Apart from Buckminster Fuller speaking to the world from the USA, Frei Otto[24] in Europe was of the same visionary engineering mould. In 1971 he proposed an inflated, and otherwise unsupported, transparent membrane to cover an arctic town of three square kilometres. This apparently altruistically motivated intervention with nature ironically relied on an atomic power station for energy. Again like Fuller, Otto did not confine himself to large-scale projects, unrealised or

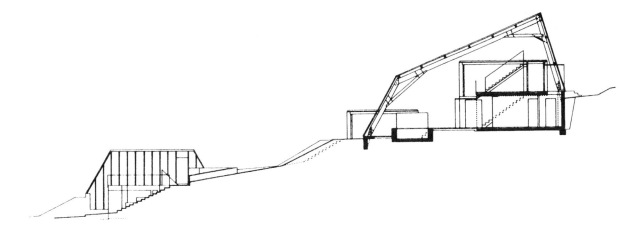

otherwise. While his light suspended net and fabric structures stretched engineering boundaries, his own home, completed by 1971 on a hill overlooking Stuttgart, comprised a compact core encased in a very simple and cheaply constructed greenhouse (Fig. 9.9). A large-scale variation of a standard up-and-over counterbalanced door enabled this to open to the garden in favourable weather. This extended the boundaries of passive solar design well beyond the simple attached sunspace of Brown[25] in 1945, and was in the spirit of the alternative experimenters in New Mexico and elsewhere.

Otto also became involved with timber gridshell structures such as that at the Mannheim Garden Festival, 1975.[26] Here small sections of timber are stitched together in such a way that a large free-form clear span was possible (Fig. 9.10a). Then by 1987 Otto and Ted Happold were both working on medium-span workshops at Hooke Park[27] in Dorset on buildings (with architects, Ahrends Burton and Koralek and later Ted Cullinan) which exploited young flexible sapwood. These were literally green structures, designed for unskilled rapid assembly, but also highly engineered (Fig. 9.10b). The techniques persist, as do the partnerships even after Happold's death. For example, Cullinan and Buro Happold in association with The Green Oak Carpentry Company recently designed a project for a gridshell museum in Sussex.[28]

Such buildings, from the humblest self-build shelter to large-scale public buildings reliant on computer-generated engineering, innately tend to express their structural logic more visibly than a right-angled, flat-planed 'de stijl' adherent. We may recall that van Doesburg found the 1919 design of a student with a catenary roof offensive and romantic. Neither, presumably, would he have been impressed by Gaudí's ingenious use of catenary chains to design his complex vaults. Engineers are not so discriminatory. They regard flat slabs and wavy gridshells as different structures fit for different purposes. On the other hand, they can influence to the point where we have 'architectural engineering' rather than 'engineered architecture'. Fitness for purpose also takes us beyond

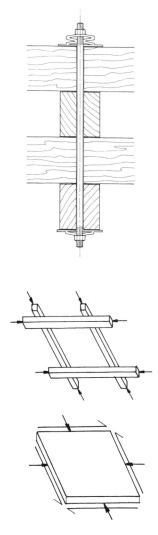

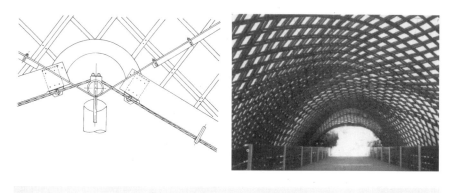

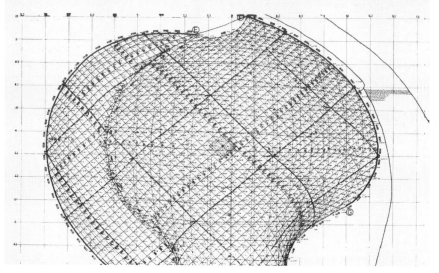

9.10a *Gridshell, Mannheim Garden Festival, 1975*

the client–architect relationship into the political arena where the Modern Movement was generally perceived as socially progressive and reformist. However, some strongly expressed attitudes within the movement ran counter to a left-wing ethos.

While van Doesburg, as a leading critic, espoused a form of aesthetic fascism, Gropius, as a leading practitioner and theorist, adopted different aesthetic outcomes according to fitness for purpose and team dynamics as he saw it. Now, at a time when the political scene is more open and

9.10b *Flexible sapwood, Hooke Park, Dorset, 1987*

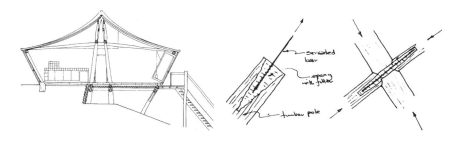

inclusive, at least in some influential parts of the world, so also the romantic rusticity of Hooke Park, or the exotically expressionistic green gestures of Blue Sky Design, sit comfortably with the formal environmental vision of the Californian winery of Herzog & De Meuron[29] (Fig. 9.11). Indeed there is a strong parallel between the use of young timber, grown and cut in the locality, to the caged local basalt; and the use of gabions, more commonly associated with the edges of rivers and roads, connects back to the spirit of Fuller and Goff.

Between these extremes in terms of image, we have Walter Segal, who left a self-build legacy that is still active in the UK 15 years after his death; and Glen Murcutt, who elevated modern indigenous materials such as corrugated tin to new architectural heights. The buildings of both architects belong to a school of tectonic rationality, and also have a literal lightness of touch that adheres very much to the principles of Fuller. Both architects have disturbed the ground as little as possible, and have exploited relatively cheap standard components. Segal's method in

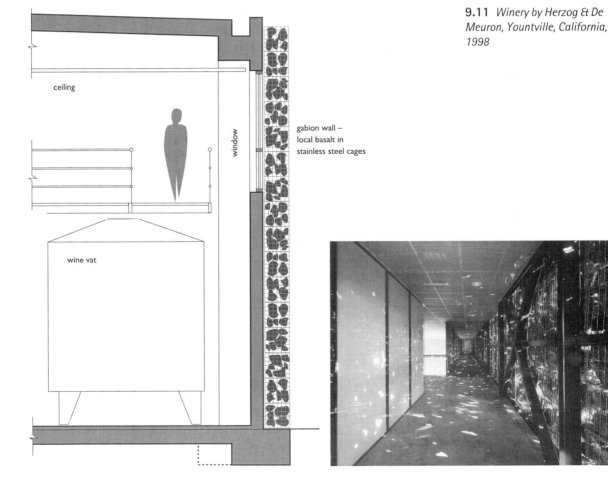

ceiling

window

wine vat

gabion wall – local basalt in stainless steel cages

9.11 *Winery by Herzog & De Meuron, Yountville, California, 1998*

particular advocates avoidance of waste by using modules of uncut boards as much as possible. Segal also approached archetypal practical problems, such as the reliability and longevity of waterproof membranes for flat roofs, with an innovative degree of lateral thinking.

There are other commonalities between Segal and Murcutt. Through his father, a builder and developer in Sydney, Murcutt[30] was exposed to the Farnsworth House at about the age of 10; whereas Segal, through his parents, was exposed from the age of 13 to a whole milieu of influential figures, including Mies van der Rohe and Gropius. Murcutt's father[31] believed in the 'economy of survival', and developed clever ventilation systems for roofs which left a lasting impact on his son. According to McKean,[32] Segal, exposed to much high-flown rhetoric from the avant-garde visitors to his parents' home in Berlin, 'developed an acute nose for pretention, for bluff and for jargon'. McKean[33] maintains that his 'guiding principles can also be characterised by a remarkable Zen-like ability to reject the inessential' which included 'cultural pre-conceptions to wasteful modes of architectural practice and building construction'.

However, although having had some similar influences, Segal's architecture seems confined by its pragmatic constructional methodology compared with that of Murcutt. Rather like the CLASP[34] system, which flourished in Nottinghamshire in the 1960s having been lauded at the Milan Triennial, it conveys a political expression, leaving the architectural juices understimulated. Murcutt, on the other hand, with the same attention to detail and structural asceticism as Segal, consistently achieves greater visual panache (Fig. 9.12). Also, although only some of Murcutt's work is designed specifically to be self-built, most of it is capable of it; and finally Murcutt's work is much more advanced than Segal's in terms of its climatic sensitivity.

Whatever their differences, as small-scale, small-practice achievers of practical, and eminently sustainable products, these two figures contrast sharply with the conceptual theorists who operated in the mega-Fuller mould, and who were engaged with tackling urban infrastructure in innovative ways – ways that would now be seen in terms of global sustainability. For example, Peter Cook's 'plug-in city' concept of 1964 accepted a high degree of short-life disposability for everything other than the primary lattice structure, but that did not preclude recycling. During the 1960s and 1970s, there were numerous other radical challenges to the urban norm. They were high on ideas and inspired by the 'space race', often concerned with some form of specific climatic modification, sometimes focussed on exploring new locations such as the sea, and, in terms of scale, owing much to the spirit of Le Corbusier's 'City of Towers' of 1920.

Such concepts had impact, for instance as in Centre Pompidou in Paris. But since none were fully realised, aspects of their relative sustainability remain abstract. Inevitably built projects more tangibly chart progress of the issues around climatically responsive and responsible

9.12 *Murcutt cf. Segal*

design. Nonetheless, unbuilt projects form a part of the scene-setting of linked influences from the 1960s and 1970s, which often have quite disparate formal architectural outcomes. The next chapter will move on to the solar oriented 1980s and 1990s, still including relatively primitive techniques side by side with those that seek out the latest technological developments.

Oil and water

Oil and water may not mix, but they do architecturally connect through global warming. All fossil fuels like oil are non-renewable. Although nuclear fuel is regarded by some as quasi-renewable, to most people the problems of waste-disposal and decommissioning pose an unacceptable environmental threat. Thus in spite of the nuclear dilemma and widely varying forecasts of untapped supplies, risks and costs of fossil fuels, it is now widely accepted that we should plan for gradual replacement with renewable sources. Architecture is deeply implicated because buildings at present consume so much non-renewable energy. If strident, although not uncontested, forecasts of increasing global warming[35] persist, usable land will shrink significantly due to encroachment from the sea, and may either become more prone to flooding or to drought.

Solar energy can and should help to both reduce CO_2 emissions by reducing the energy loads of buildings, and to supplement natural supplies of fresh water by means of techniques such as desalination and distillation. In terms of thermal demand that can be met by the sun, water has a conveniently high volumetric thermal capacitance. Because this property makes it easy to heat and store compactly, it is ideal for all hygienic and utilitarian purposes, and for space heating. Air is host to water vapour, the warmer it is the more it can hold. This can be exploited advantageously, for example to humidify in hot dry climates, but may also constitute a problem in terms of health and well-being. For example, where heating is unaffordable, relative humidity may rise to levels that support condensation, followed by mould spores, and also large numbers of dust mites, which may lead in turn to asthma and other respiratory disorders.

Although the volumetric thermal capacitance of air is some 3500 times less than that of water, we require a significant amount of air around us in order to function within buildings, and that air must also be replenished at regular intervals. Therefore, although air is not a good medium for storing heat, it does need to be heated and/or cooled and, in either case, solar energy can assist and so displace fossil fuels. Solar radiation in the form of light can also displace electricity, and since much of this power is generated inefficiently by nuclear and fossil fuels, this is a very efficient method of reducing their consumption. Thus light and air are not only relevant to a theme of 'oil and water', they are also critical environmental issues today, just as they were 70 or so years ago.

The fuel crises of the 1970s, followed by the growing alarm and knowledge with respect to greenhouse gases in the 1980s and 1990s, have instigated a discernible shift in the architectural scene. Comparisons with the 1920s and 1930s – a subtle mix of need, altruism and enthusiasm – are justified. In one important aspect, that of air quality, we are now beginning to circle back technologically to the beginning of the 1900s which signalled the loss of a science of ventilation that had prevailed for more than 60 years. Then there were many buildings that introduced air at low level and ran it past radiators or heating coils so that windows did not need to be opened, and fresh air was introduced without draughts. Finally it would be exhausted at high level by means of wind-assisted thermal buoyancy or stack effect.

One such example, where the method of heating and airing remains unaltered, is the former assembly hall of Glasgow High School. It is now used as a debating chamber by Glasgow City Council, occasionally by the Scottish Parliament, and is also hired out for conferences. The thermal comfort and quality of air in crowded situations is found to be of a higher standard than is the norm in mechanically ventilated buildings. However, such Victorian exemplars are all too often subject to much less satisfactory modern replacements. The recognised masterwork of Charles Rennie Mackintosh, Glasgow School of Art, is an example. When built, air was washed and filtered, warmed in winter, and delivered to every space. The power to do this came from a large belt-driven centrifugal fan in the basement, feeding from a main horizontal chamber into a series of vertical ducts embedded within walls. The vitiated air was then exhausted naturally through the roof by a further network of ducts. It was what is now termed a mixed mode system, part active and part passive. Today it might be regarded as inefficient since it involved continual throughput of fresh air, without any recycling or recovery of heat. But it was healthier than the present set-up, in reality a non-system, reliant mainly on fortuitous air-leakage, and under stress due to heat from computers, and off-gassing. The original ventilation of Glasgow's Kelvingrove Art Gallery is now threatened. Contemporaneous to the Art School and with a similar installation, it included some recirculated air and has worked very well for a century.

The history of such techniques is remarkably long. Ignoring the precedent of Roman hypocausts, one of the earliest, if not the earliest, modern warm-air central heating cum air-conditioning systems came about through the refurbishment of the temporary House of Commons in 1836, followed by the House of Peers some three years later.* This coincided with the change from lighting by candles to lighting by gas. However,

---

*It would appear that following the great fire of 1834, the select committee set up to oversee the procurement of the New Houses of Parliament wished to use the temporary accommodation as a test bed for the latest technology with respect to heating, ventilation, light and acoustics. The temporary House of Commons was located in the former House of Peers to the south of the Old Palace Yard, while the temporary House of Peers was located in the adjacent Painted Chamber above what was known as Guy Fawkes's vault.

exhausting the more vitiating combustion products of gas was only one of the problems faced by the consultants of the time. The River Thames was virtually an open sewer and smoke belched forth from much of its traffic, as well as the chimneys of housing and commerce. In other words, the pioneers of improved ventilation at that time had their work cut out. Interestingly such pioneers tended to be physicians, partly since they had a knowledge of physics, but more because they were in the forefront of tackling airborne infectious diseases. Dr David Boswell Reid gives a very thorough review of the general science in 1844,[36] as well as describing in detail the specific improved installation of the temporary Houses of Parliament installed eight years earlier. Measurements recorded in his book for May 1837 and 1843 indicated that it operated well, but these may not be altogether representative. At any rate we know that the relationship between Reid and Charles Barry was not easy, and that Reid was superseded in 1852.[37]

Apart from filtering the air to remove large particulates, washing it with lime-charged water to attract the smaller particulates, and heating it with batteries of steam-filled pipes, it was necessary to be able to control the flow of delivery through quite a large range. This was because the population of the chambers could vary from only a few MPs and spectators to 800 or more. The variable flow was achieved by balancing delivery through a series of chambers and adjustable valves. Delivery was at low level through the risers in the stepped floor of the chamber. The aim was to maximise diffusion of air through the natural fibres of the carpet and its backing, while minimising the introduction of dirt. It was effectively what would now be called a 'displacement' system whereby relatively cool air is introduced at low level, flowing around a room just above the floor until it encounters warmth, for example a person, when it will become less dense and move upwards in a plume. Once it encounters the ceiling, it will be further heated by light fittings before being exhausted. This was also the system of 1852 for the new House of Commons over which Reid retained control, but responsibility for heating and ventilating the House of Lords passed to Barry.[37] He introduced air at high level around the perimeter of the chamber and maintained that this avoided uncomfortable draughts. Variations of this technology appeared in many buildings throughout the remainder of the 19th century. This is what Frank Lloyd Wright inherited when he designed the Larkin Building in the early years of the 20th century, and it is what gave way quite rapidly to modern air conditioning and mechanical ventilation.

One might regard this simply as a natural progression in step with modern technology. Yet it was suggested above that it signalled a loss of science. It was undoubtedly an advance in terms of the sophistication of engineering. Where it represented a loss, however, was the transference of the knowledge from architects to specialists. This is not to deny a role for specialists, but rather to put forward the proposition that once architects are no longer in full control of an aspect of architectural design, it alters the way they design. Moreover, the ascendancy of air-conditioning coincided with the discovery of immense sources of natural gas and oil. Conservation of energy was not an issue. The additional cooling loads brought about by the 'heat sink' effect of cities, partly nourished by the waste heat from air-conditioning, could be solved by more and more air-conditioning. Buildings with sealed windows were compatible with skyscrapers. They were absolved from the excesses of 'stack effect' as well as the noise and pollution of traffic. Paradoxes, such as air-conditioning in the carriages of the Metro in cities like New York simultaneously super-heating the platforms in the stations, seem to go unnoticed. At any rate, until quite recently, air-conditioning has remained part of the techno-economic climate, with which the architect has had little control or input. If global warming had not started to develop political muscle, it is unlikely that this position would have changed at all. Even now, it is changing slowly, and reinvestigation of the 19th century ideas is only at an embryonic stage.

One example is the Woodgreen Community Health Centre by Mac-Cormac Jamieson Prichard, completed in 1994. The centre faces a busy road on one side and was designed so that office windows should not open directly on to it. Instead it breathes fresh air in at low level from the 'greened' back court and feeds it in and out of rooms by a series of ducts within a grid of cross-walls. The users are encouraged to interact with the system by adjusting movable flaps in their rooms. The system was well tested in the severe heat-wave of 1995, when apparently the only active assistance required to maintain comfort was that of desk-top fans. Another recent example, the 1998 Aden Theatre at Gresham's School in Norfolk designed by Arts Team, is very much in the mould of the century-old Glasgow High School (Fig. 10.1). Unlike the Woodgreen

10.1 *Auden Theatre, Gresham's School, Norfolk, 1998*

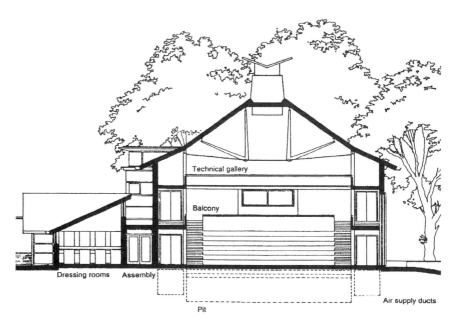

Technical gallery

Balcony

Dressing rooms   Assembly

Pit

Air supply ducts

project, where ventilation and heating are separated, here they are brought together. Lack of heat recovery or recirculation may be economically challenging. The client pays to heat the air in winter, only to use it once and dump it. Thermal mass can mitigate against such loss, but what this implies is a willingness to prioritise the well-being and comfort of the audience over typical prevailing attitudes on energy efficiency.

It may be inferred then that even if such projects do not signify a new era of altruism, they mark a return to a past methodology for ventilation which recognises environmental issues from a wider perspective. We have moved from a time when fresh air was treated as a priority relative to health, and mechanical systems were rather primitive; through one when mechanical systems became increasingly sophisticated and into one when energy-efficiency and economy in use are prioritised above all else. Now some architects and engineers are beginning to appreciate that we may have reduced air quality to unacceptably low rates in the quest for efficiency. The concurrent concerns over the environmental penalties of air-conditioning in terms of both global warming and the ozone layer, coupled with research into the causes and characteristics of sick building syndrome have underpinned a change of attitude. However, it is by no means universal, and in the UK the air-conditioning industry strongly and successfully lobbied against reforms to the building regulations[38] in the 1990s. If the proposed new standards had been introduced, it would have been much more difficult even to specify basic mechanical supply and return systems, let alone full air-conditioning, where more passive options were viable. However, even without this 'green' standard for ventilation in the UK, over the past two decades a new breed of passive solar and bioclimatic buildings has emerged, together with a more thoughtful steer towards mixed mode or hybrid heating and cooling by consultants.

The role of glass relative to the actuality and perception of ventilation is pivotal, the windows of early buildings of the Modern Movement fulfilling both. In other words spaces felt light and airy with the windows closed, but they could also be very fully opened, sometimes disappearing sideways or downwards. This is thermally and emotionally a very different experience to that of breathing clean but often undesirably dry air behind a sealed wall of glass. Even if the atmosphere is 'perfect', the loss of control may be resented.

The course of this change has reintroduced further debate concerning the compatibility of climatically sensitive design to any other 'aestheticism', which might well be relatively transient. It has also highlighted a new polemical dimension concerning the interface between architects and others such as mechanical engineers and physicists. Although there is much glib talk about successful multi-disciplinary teams and conferences, boundaries between interrelated skills still tend to be distinct, and cross-disciplinary understanding rather poor. In particular architects may feel that other non-design disciplines do not understand what they are attempting. Others, involved mainly in numeracy and science, sense reluctance on the part of architects to fully engage at that level. There is a tendency for such observations to be publicised more at solar conferences[39,40] than in the architectural press, and the issue is raised here so that it may be seen in parallel with the more general question of plurality within the architectural profession.

There are serious related questions. Is ecological design too prescriptive, or inhibiting, or not inspiring to students? Is design, which does inspire students and professes to be based on sound ecological premises, meeting its environmental expectations? The route to addressing such questions inevitably focusses first on the layers of the skin or outer clothing of buildings, whichever metaphor suits, since this is potentially a variable diode in terms of heat, humidity and light. For example, short-wave solar radiation is trapped due to the greenhouse effect, with movable insulation limiting nocturnal losses; rain and snow are excluded while water vapour breathes outwards; and diffuse daylight comes in while direct-beam sunlight is blocked. Consequently it is on the skin that most research, development and demonstration has been concentrated.

Skin-deep

Morgan's Wallasey school[2] is a 1960s symbol of direct passive solar gain, where a double-skin, south-facing glazing system is used to diffuse and moderate light into the classrooms, and is an effective acoustic shield. However, it is known that the electric lighting was an essential ingredient in terms of negating the need for further space heating. The aim was to meet the heating load by the combined input of solar gains, lighting and pupils. The first two tended to be self-regulating – i.e. on a dull day the lighting would compensate for the solar shortfall. The further opportunity to exploit the air between the two layers of glass, say to allow natural ventilation via the inner skin while the outer skin remains closed, was not taken up in a systematic manner, or at least not exploited to the full. This is a pity, especially since the drive for energy efficiency resulted in such low rates of air change that there were complaints of stuffiness and body odour.

In spite of such shortcomings, the uptake of double-skin façades during the 1980–90s, mainly to diminish reliance on air-conditioning without compromising sound reduction, has been considerable. Nelson[41] has described one such mid-1980s example, Briarcliff House, Farnborough, in some detail (Fig. 10.2). He acknowledges that the 'solar wall is a by-product of the response to the problem of noise and solar gain'. In other words insolation is regarded as a 'nuisance, rather than a benefit'. Despite this, in arriving at a twin-skin solution, the sun's energy is used to both preheat incoming fresh air in winter and to cool the façade in summer. An example, this time from the early 1990s with the common denominator of Arup Associates, is a school at Sossenheim. Carter and Warburton[42] recognise that it builds on the experience of Wallasey. The

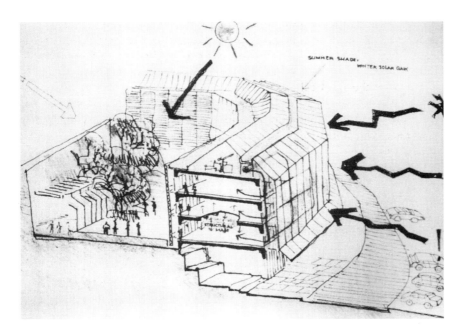

Outside air moving up the walling is either drawn into the air-handling units during the heating season, or vented at the top in summer.

twin-wall here assists natural daylighting and passive solar gain in winter, while again helping to cool the façade in summer (Fig. 10.3). This is a very different approach to that of *le mur neutralisant*.

The 1995-designed Photonics Centre in Adleshof, Berlin, by Sauerbruch Hutton,[43] raises some issues with respect to twin-skin performance. The southern and northern walls of the larger of two amoeba-shaped buildings are divided into alternate narrow sections for exhaust, and wider ones for intake. But, since inlets are at each of three floors and the exhaust at the eaves, natural thermo-circulation, assisted by the sun on one façade only, together with the influence of variable winds, may not ensure that air will move in and out as intended (Fig. 10.4). The ability of this buffer space to direct air in and out of the occupied zones is likely to be even more uncertain. Their recent east and west twin-skins of the 18-floor GSW tower in Berlin seems more convincing. Air-flow in the latter is wind-accelerated to address peak cooling loads in the afternoon, and a relatively narrow floor plate offers potential for controlled cross-ventilation, mainly from east to west.

However, although the use of double-skin glazing to allow natural ventilation in multi-floor buildings is intriguing, it is also potentially problematic. The fluid dynamics of a high continuous air space, functioning as a solar chimney in either preheat or cooling mode, with a large number of inlet variables, are complex. An alternative is to contain thermocirculation at each floor. Two commercial towers in Germany,[44] a bank headquarters in Frankfurt by Foster and the RWE headquarters in Essen by Overdiek Kahlen, employ this system. That of the former is very simple. The building is a hollow equilateral triangle, with façades facing

10.3 *School at Sossenheim, Germany, by Arup Associates, 1992*

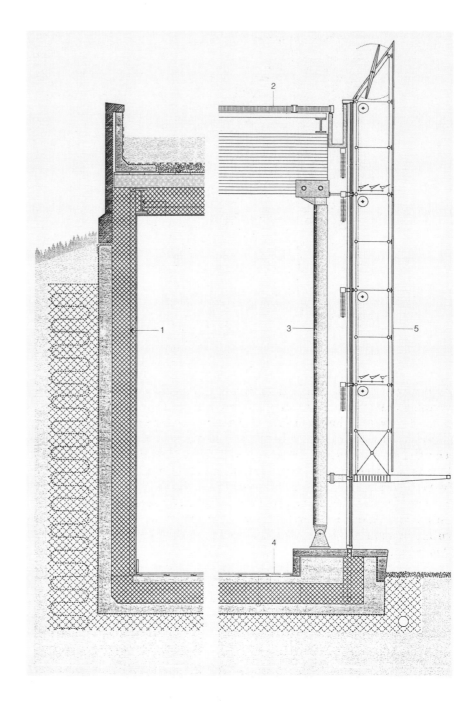

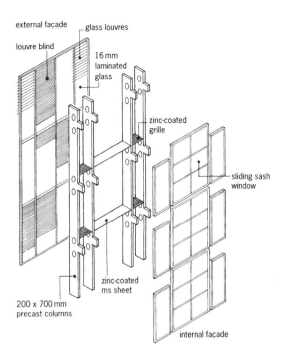

external façade

louvre blind

glass louvres

16 mm
laminated
glass

zinc-coated
grille

sliding sash
window

zinc-coated
ms sheet

200 x 700 mm
precast columns

internal façade

10.4 *Photonics Centre, Adleshof, Berlin, 1998*

30 degrees north of east and west, and due south. Air enters the space between inner and outer glazing through a slot at floor level and leaves through another slot at ceiling level. When the weather permits, inner windows can be opened to admit air, as can windows on the opposite side facing into a naturally ventilated atrium. In excessively windy conditions, windows can be closed and the air conditioning comes into play. In the Essen case, the tower is circular and the slots are reduced to one per floor by means of a staggered system whereby alternate slots function as intakes at floor level and exhausts at ceiling level (Fig. 10.5). In both cases the inner glazing is double, the outer single, and there are venetian blinds in the cavity.

These two buildings represent a major move away from the traditional sealed skyscraper, but one that still allows air-conditioning to play a minor role when the weather dictates. The twin-skin solution also deals effectively with external noise. Neither is a more passive approach confined to Europe. The bioclimatic tropical towers of Ken Yeang are well known. As in the German examples, although he cannot make air-conditioning redundant, he reduces reliance on it. He provides as many opportunities for natural ventilation as possible, and makes extensive use of planting to encourage biodiversity as well as enhance the quality of air. He also reduces cooling loads as far as possible by means of orientation and shading devices, and has convincingly persuaded commercial clients to come to terms economically with his dispersed building forms.

Richards[45] points out first that: 'Yeang's friendship with Kisho Kurokawa is important in providing both a critical and philosophical

10.5 *RWE HQ in Essen, Germany, by Overdiek Kahlen, 1997*

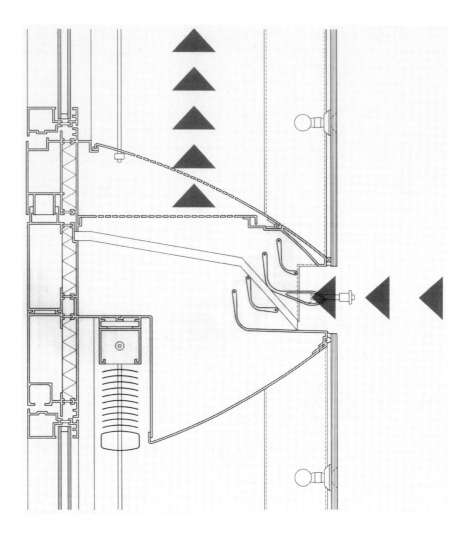

framework for the architect, rooted metabolist ideas of "change, biological analogy and organic architecture"'; and second, that Yeang's experience at the Martin Centre in Cambridge gave him the technical authority and confidence to pursue ecological architecture so vigorously. Partly because his buildings are often located in luxuriant parkland, he is also able to adopt a more flexible approach to the skin than implied by the German towers mentioned above. In their particular contexts it is difficult to see how else natural ventilation could have been accommodated.

That does not mean however that urban twin-skin solutions cannot be distinctively varied – formalistically, scientifically and texturally. Two other recent double-skin examples stretch composite environmental-visual boundaries in new and imaginative ways. One is the Art Museum in Bregenz, Austria, by Peter Zumthor.[46] Here, outer, overlapping glazing is a rainscreen, a light-diffuser and an acoustic baffle. In terms of daylight and sunlight the screen works in harness with a 2.2 m high space above a translucent ceiling. In winter, low-angle sunlight can penetrate deep inside this space, whereas in summer, it is nearly all excluded. In terms of air, it is simply a drained and back-ventilated rainscreen, while the gallery and the space above the ceiling work in tandem, but isolated from the peripheral buffer space. Displacement ventilation is delivered to the perimeter at low level from small air-ducts embedded in the slab; while warmed and partly vitiated air is exhausted at high level, by the same means (Fig. 10.6). Water also plays a part in tempering cooling and heating. In summer natural spring water circulating in coils within walls and floors cools the thermal mass. In winter the water is warmed to provide background radiant warmth.

Somewhat analogous to Zumthor's Art Museum, is a compact family house in Okayama, Japan, by Kazuyo Sejima and Ryue Nishizawa,[47] The outer skin here is itself double, two layers of corrugated polycarbonate sheeting set on either side of structural timber posts. Apart from occasional modestly sized windows and doors which pierce it for access and visual transparency, this is the main provider of light to the interior core. A narrow, double-height canyon of light accesses compartmentalised bedrooms and washrooms peripherally at ground level, while a stair leads up to the centre of a minimalist open-plan floor plate, this time bounded by a moat of light – at least when the dividing components are open. At first floor these are vertically pivoting, floor-to-ceiling timber louvres, while at ground level, there is the sliding-folding equivalent. If the system is fully closed, bedrooms receive no natural light or ventilation, the corridor receives less heat, and the living space is reliant for light and air on two 'sleeved' windows which bridge the gap, only one of which faces the sun. Practically, this means that bedrooms and wet rooms require to be mechanically ventilated. Furthermore, when their screens are open, moving round the corridor is rather difficult; and when closed, this narrow space may be uncomfortably cold in winter. Nonetheless, the concept is pure and interesting in the same way as the Farnsworth House, but promises much more in the way of environmental efficiency (Fig. 10.7).

As passive solar buildings (sunlight and/or daylight), the last two examples may still be considered as 'direct-gain', even though a gap separating two different menus of opaque and transparent surfaces is more usually associated with indirect systems. The museum simply provides diffused daylight or sunlight to the gallery through two vertical skins and one horizontal one. Within the house, when the louvres and folding screens are open, solar irradiation goes directly to the inhabited spaces, coming predominantly from the southern and western sides. When they are closed, thermal losses will be inhibited, with direct gain only available to the living room through the sleeved south-facing window. In a sense this serves to demonstrate that systems resist easy categorisation. In general 'direct' denotes useful solar gain immediately to an inhabited

10.6 *Art Museum in Bregenz, Austria, by Peter Zumthor, 1997*

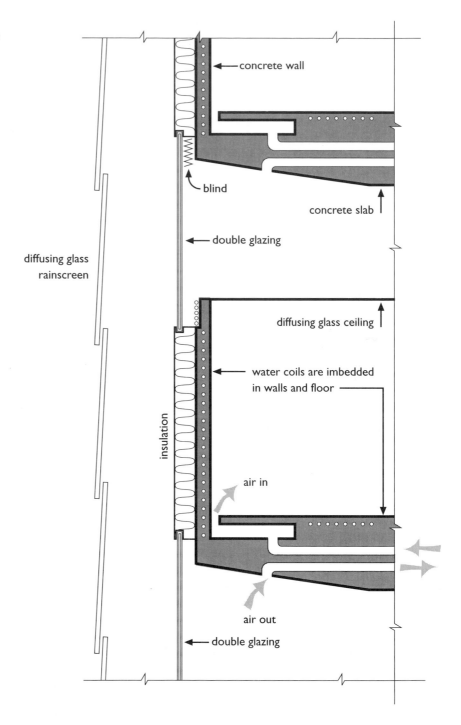

concrete wall

blind

concrete slab ↑

double glazing

diffusing glass rainscreen

diffusing glass ceiling ↑

water coils are imbedded in walls and floor

insulation

air in

air out

double glazing

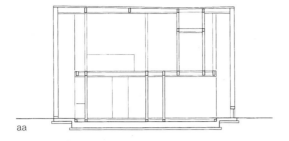

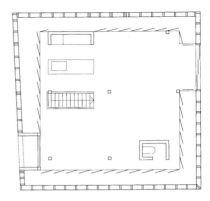

aa

space, while 'indirect' denotes an intervention by an absorber or thermal store prior to delivery.

Thus the Trombe-Michel prototype of 1967 constitutes an 'indirect gain' landmark corresponding to the 'direct' one of Wallasey in 1961. But since the former inherently denied most of the direct access to sun and view, the variant of the inhabited sunspace became a popular alternative, with a combination of direct and indirect gain. The distinction between this technique and that of the double-skin types described above usually lies more with use than thermal typology – i.e. the latter is not normally inhabited other than for maintenance. However, the house in Okayama breaks this 'rule', and any double-skin solution is capable of housing 'indirect' components such as solar air collectors. Indeed solar air collectors can readily be integrated[48,49] with a single-skin, 'direct gain' façade, or a façade that includes sunspaces. Gustav Hillman's 1988 housing project in Berlin (Fig. 10.8) is one of many examples. The combination of solar devices that operate on a closed loop without intervention, and open devices where thermal exchanges occur within the users' domain and may be controlled by them, has certain advantages that merit discussion.

The performance of unheated sunspaces may suffer significantly from misuse by the occupants. They are generally intended to function as solar-enhanced climatic buffers and reservoirs of preheated fresh air. The adventitious heating will come mainly from the sun in spring and autumn, and mainly from heat lost from 'host' spaces in winter. However, there is often a temptation to heat the space so that it can be used all the time. In this case it reverts to a 'direct gain' space, and its thermal viability will be dependent on the area, orientation and tilt of glass, as well as its specification. The passive ideal is high solar heat gain relative to low thermal losses, mainly by conduction. Also if the space is opened up too much or too frequently to the heated core, thermal merging between heated and unheated spaces will occur, with the same consequence. Additionally or alternatively, if opened too much to the outside, it will start to thermally merge with ambient climatic conditions,

10.7 *House in Okayama, Japan, by Sejima & Nishizawa, 1998*

10.8 *Solar housing in Berlin, by Gustav Hillman, 1988*

Either side of the conservatories are solar air collectors. Air passes through these on a closed thermal loop through cavities in floors and walls. This project represents an interesting combination of one closed system where users are not able to intervene, and an open system where they can.

and hence lose its effectiveness. For these reasons sunspaces of all types from small attached conservatories to large glazed arcades and atria have been controversial as savers of energy.

For example, a decision to heat the glazed arcades at the Technical University of Trondheim up to 21°C, rather than the intended 15°C, did result in a significant penalty.[50] In fact it was reported that buildings with heated glazed atria can be expected to have combined electrical and thermal loads as high as $500\,kWh/m^2$, when some $110\,kWh/m^2$ was predicted at the modelling stage.[51] On the other hand, the small sunporches of European projects such as that by Hillman (Fig. 10.7) as well as in Scotland[52] have been shown to provide significant savings. Since such savings are normally very reliant on successfully introducing preheated air to occupied spaces, control over air flow into and out of the sunspaces is important. The same rules apply as in the double-skin systems described above, and purely passive or natural systems can be over-optimistic.

AARPLAN's terraced housing at Zollikofen in Switzerland (Fig. 10.9) cleverly controls air flow by twinning cool northern and warm southern buffers to permit mechanically assisted passive preheating in winter and purely passive cooling in summer[53]: 'A ventilator in the rear basement section of the dwellings creates a state of low pressure which draws heated air from the conservatory zones into the living areas. . . . The action of the ventilator can also be reversed to circulate cooler air from the north side through the house.' The tilt of the south-facing façade maximises solar gain, while the system of ventilation, with generous opening lights at top and bottom as well as the air-flow from the north, will prevent overheating. The triangular section of the sunspace also suits function in terms of the space provided at each level. This small project also re-examines the retaining wall and ground floor slab in terms of

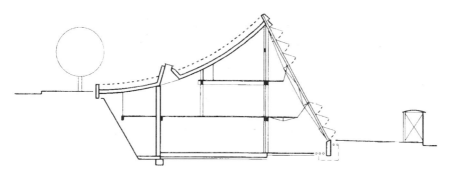

10.9 *Housing in Zollikofen, Switzerland, by AARPLAN, 1996–7*
Note combination of north and south buffer spaces with economic catenary roof
(250mm insulation on 50mm timber boarding on steel chords), lack of tanked retaining wall and low-concrete floor
(20mm asphalt slabs on 60mm stone chippings, 5mm separating layer, 250mm crushed foamed glass insulation, bituminous felt on 700mm lean concrete).

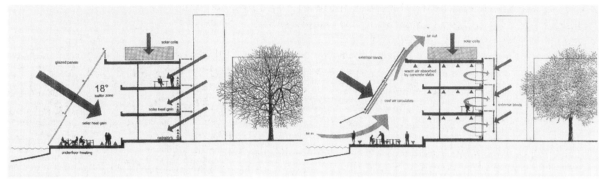

Energy management principles: winter day.   *Energy management principles: summer day.*

10.10 *R & D Building by Kiessler, Gelsenkirchen, Germany, c. 1996*

minimising use of concrete and reliance on membranes, while the ingeniously light timber and steel catenary roof structure is well able to support the load of moist turf, which in its turn minimises the effective footprint of the building.

A much larger building, which again employs a three-storey high glazed space with a tilted skin of glass, is the research and development building by Kiessler + Partner in the Rheinelbe Science Park at Gelsenkirchen to the north of Dusseldorf in Germany (Fig. 10.10). This is a building where it is tempting to comment that the architect has firstly created a problem and secondly solved it. To orientate a sloping façade of glass almost due west seems to be asking for solar overheating. This is then solved by lifting up large sections of the façade to permit evaporatively cooled air to enter at ground floor level, and then, after picking up heat, to exit through a clerestory window at roof level. If natural thermocirculation does not suffice, fans come into play to assist the process, and the entire glazed surface can also be shaded by external blinds. The power for these tasks comes from a large photovoltaic (PV) array mounted on the roof. Matching of supply to demand is therefore optimised. When electricity is required in warm weather to operate the motors that move the lower sections of the façade, and others to move the blinds, an adequate solar supply will be available. The location of the PV on the roof is logical, but it obviates the opportunity for a dual function – for example, as part of the envelope – and the thermal losses from the panels cannot be utilised. They are effectively a hidden asset, appearing only as a cornice from certain northern viewing angles.

There is of course an architectural justification for the orientation of this glazed concourse. The building is sited close to a road bounding the eastern edge of a north–south park. The concourse is used as break-out space and for relaxation, informal meetings and large social gatherings. Therefore it makes sense for it to enjoy maximum aspect to the park, and since the main usable space is at ground level, with access stairs, galleries and foyers overlooking it at first and second floor, the rake of the glass is also spatially logical. Since it is designed to be used throughout the year, it is a heated buffer zone, with the usual problems of responsively controlling the purchased heat so that it may be rapidly switched off to take advantage of the variable free heat from the sun.

However, the space has to be accepted on the basis that it will fluctuate considerably in terms of its resultant or radiant temperature, depending on the vertical and horizontal position occupied within it.[†] While it reportedly[54] consumes almost twice as much energy per unit area as the rest of the accommodation, it justifies its presence as a self-cooling amenity with a still satisfactorily low load for space heating of just under $50\,kWh/m^2$ for the building as a whole (some $17\,kWh/m^2$ less than the target). The value of 50 may be compared with that of $64\,kWh/m^2$ predicted[51] for the Technical University in Trondheim with the atria restricted to 15°C.

The closed rooms directly off the concourse face east into open courts bounded by short legs of office and laboratory accommodation. The south and east facades have movable awnings, also powered by the PV array. Windows normally remain closed but louvred panels with insulated internal shutters provide the means for users to control natural ventilation in the relatively shallow depth of offices. This then is a single-skin façade which aims to displace electricity: first by admitting as much natural light as possible, while using the awnings to automatically prevent overheating and glare; and second, they eliminate the need for mechanical ventilation or air-conditioning. However, it is possible that the frequency with which the awnings respond to variable conditions of sunlight and cloud could be irritating to the occupants. Automatic control and whether or not there are manual overrides is therefore an issue, particularly where personal workspace is concerned.

Another solar building that bears comparison with that in Gelsenkirchen is the new PV factory in Freiburg by Rolf and Hotz[55] (Fig. 10.11). It again has a glazed concourse which is triangular on section. This functions as the showcase for the factory, used frequently for parties of visitors as well as providing a breakout space for staff. However, it differs significantly in that it is oriented due south. The offices form a

---

[†]I experienced this building throughout a day in early September. It was a bright cool day with intermittent cloud, becoming gradually warmer and sunnier as the day progressed. The concourse had been used for a major function the previous evening, and on arrival at about 9.00 a.m., the lack of sunlight added to its 'morning after' bleakness. Naturally at this stage all the sliding glass sections of the façade were closed. As the day wore on the building management system selectively lifted some of these to a partially open, and some to a fully open position. By late afternoon, the temperature at second floor level within the concourse was becoming rather warm. It grew progressively more comfortable on descent. At ground level it was both comfortable and environmentally interesting. At the eastern 'movement' edge with stairs, lifts and landings, the feeling was of being inside a building, but very aware of the dissolving boundary between the concourse and the park. At the western edge, the feeling was of literally standing outside, although still within the floor plate. In the centre of the concourse, the fresh quality of the incoming air, cooled and moistened by the artificial lake, was very evident. Given the predominantly ambulatory nature of this space, particularly at the upper levels, the range of temperatures that I experienced within similar solar-radiant conditions, was acceptable, especially given the choices available with respect to location.

10.11 *Solar photovoltaics factory in Freiburg, by Rolf & Hotz, 1999*

linear east–west spine behind the concourse, enabling all of them to have an openable north-facing window, and obviating the need for sophistic-ated devices to control glare. In addition the concourse is shaded in summer by means of fixed PV louvres located outside the skin. These are spaced to provide maximum shading of the floor plate in summer and significant solar penetration on to the floor and wall in winter. The thermal mass of floors and walls together with efficient stack-driven natural ventilation do the rest of the work in maintaining a stable and acceptably low temperature on hot days.[‡] The lower stretch of opening windows again admit water-cooled air during the working day; while at night, in order to maintain ventilation and cooling of the fabric without

[‡]I visited this building not long after it opened in early July 1999. It was early afternoon on a very hot sunny day with the outside temperature in the order of 30°C. Inside floor shading was about 90% and the temperature was probably around 10°C lower – say 20–21°C. At any rate it was uncomfortably hot outside while comfortably cool inside, and a very good advertisement for passive cooling. It was also gratifying to learn that all of the energy needed for this building was supplied by the sun: 53 hectares of rape provide enough oil to fuel a combined heat and power (CHP) unit which meets about two-thirds of the 50 MWh thermal/electrical demand; 400 m² grid-connected PV provides the balance.

compromising security, the air is admitted via underground ducts. In winter, radiant panels mounted on the ceiling should provide an appropriate degree of comfort even though the air remains relatively cool. Although the precise tilt and spacing of the louvres to suit all seasons must involve some compromise, their triple purpose appears to be well justified. Not only do they generate electricity and provide a degree of passive environmental control, but they also advertise the product that is being made in the factory itself. The fact that they slightly reduce the level of daylighting to this space is not critical here due to the function of the space. However, had the same array been applied to the external skin

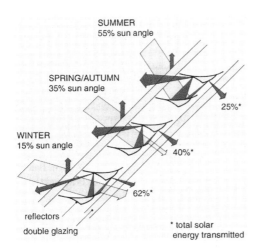

SUMMER
55% sun angle

SPRING/AUTUMN
35% sun angle

WINTER
15% sun angle

25%*

40%*

62%*

reflectors

double glazing

* total solar
energy transmitted

10.12 *Swanlea School, London, by Percy Thomas, 1993 Detail section through Okasolar double glazing.*
To prevent the mall overheating in summer, the south-facing, double-glazed roof has purpose-designed Okasolar louvres between the panes. These reflect direct sunlight in the summer months, but allow lower-angle sunlight into the mall at other times. During hot weather, the smoke-relief vents can be opened to increase ventilation.

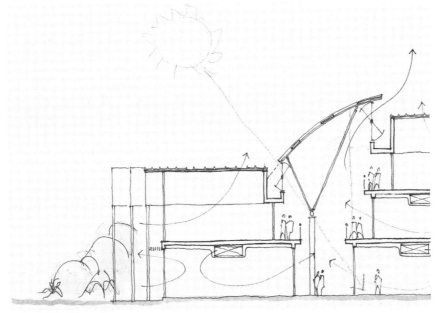

of offices, this could become a much more serious issue, possibly leading to increased use of electricity for lighting.

An alternative approach to such control is the development of advanced glazing which will admit light all the time, but limit the amount of heat gained according to solar geometry. The Okasolar glazing[56] used over the concourse of Swanlea School in London (Fig. 10.12) is such a product. The curved surfaces of the bespoke prismatic glass louvres between two panes of glass admit shortwave solar radiation in winter, but exclude it in summer. Although initially expensive, the life-cycle benefits, taking into account lack of maintenance of moving parts, make a case for such a system. Other developments in 'variable transmission' glazing[57] such as electrochromic glass and liquid crystal laminates, are likely to make some impact in the marketplace in due course. This is also the case for *aerogel*, a form of transparent insulation (TI). Although there are some built examples, such as Thomas Herzog's house and office,[58] development has apparently failed to provide adequate guarantees of long-term stabilisation of the aerogel filling. There are also less technically risky versions of TI including glazed sandwiches with polycarbonate honeycomb cores, and multiple-layer glazing, with gas fillings and/or low-emissivity coatings, which achieve remarkably low coefficients of thermal transmittance. Honeycomb TI sandwiches may be used either as normal glazing, or as the outer cover of a solar-mass wall. However, regardless of how technically sophisticated or 'smart' glazing becomes, there is likely to remain a demand for some form of control by the users, whether it be a manual override to an automatic venetian blind, or simply opening some device such as a window or shutter to admit fresh air.

The incorporation of PV cells into glazing has now become quite common. It can both actively generate electricity, perhaps with an immediate use, as described above, for opening large windows and controlling awnings. It will also generate some thermal heat which could be useful for a buffer space in winter to enhance its prewarming role, and possibly in summer to accelerate the flow of air for cooling, as in a solar chimney. If used in this way, there is no need for the glass to be double-glazed, which in turn assists the electrical efficiency. The glazing of the atrium of the Brundtland Centre[59] in Toftlund, in southern Denmark, was a relatively early example of this technique. A more recent one is a training centre, the Akademie Mont-Cenis in Herne,[60] by Jourda and Perraudin in association with Hegger, Hegger and Schleiff, and located a few miles to the east of the Rheinelbe Science Park. Here a pristine PV-glass box completely encapsulates a further education campus. It is the same principle as that established by Frei Otto with respect to his own house in Stuttgart in 1971. The climate of the interstitial space between the buildings and the glass is modified in several ways, all but one completely passive: first by the greenhouse effect through the glazed skin in conjunction with absorption and shading by buildings; second by heat lost from the buildings; third by the thermal characteristics of the ground cover which includes water and vegetation; and finally by the extent to which the glass skin is opened. Even though the last is not strictly passive, the energy is renewable and provided by a passive component.

Moreover, the balance of energy demand in this complex is met by 'fire-damp' gas from old coal workings below the site. This is used to power a small CHP plant similar to that of the solar factory in Freiburg. Even better, apparently in periods of low atmospheric pressure which coincide with low solar radiation, the pressure of the fire-damp is higher. In any event this is an inspiring example of regeneration and renewable energy at work. The green aspects of the design also go further than the fire-damp and solar skin. The supporting structure for this gigantic glass 'box' is almost entirely of timber. The combination of rows of columns, mature pine trees from the Black Forest, and their impressive trussed 'branches' diffuses the impact of the light inside in a manner reminiscent of a well-thinned forest glade. The project also sets up a paradigm in terms of control. The opening up of the outer glass skin can be triggered automatically by a number of climatic variables, whereas controlling the windows of the buildings within is much more in the domain of the users. There is also a choice of climatic experience walking from one building to another, and a choice of static experience – standing while chatting with a group, sitting alone reading, etc. Such choice is of course to some extent dependent on the weather, and one might argue that it is available in the vicinity of any set of buildings. Nevertheless the microclimate improves what has become known as the 'adaptive opportunity' for people. Exactly the same term might be applied to the buildings. Their adaptive opportunity is improved since they no longer have to withstand the rigours of precipitation in one form or another.

The Akademie Mont-Cenis is a particular solution for a particular complex on a particular site. In general, the balance between automatic electronic control and manual control by the user remains contentious. The appropriate mix naturally depends on the use and occupancy of a particular building, and the design of any manual control is also critical. It should be obvious and user-friendly. Research[61] has shown that, for housing at least, small controls such as trickle ventilators are seldom operated, unlike relatively large devices like louvres or normal windows which are frequently used to adjust both air and heat. More sophisticated devices to control the heat itself are frequently not well used, or not well enough understood, or both.

The management of buildings can also interfere with their thermal comfort. For example, the automatic actuators that operate high level windows in the glazed arcades of the Technical University at Trondheim tend to be switched off at the end of the caretaker's working day. For those remaining during periods of hot weather, the space can then rapidly become unacceptably warm. The temperament of users with respect to their living or working environment also varies widely. For example, some people seek out sunlit areas, almost regardless of other factors, and resent artificial light during daylit hours. Others actively seek to exclude sunlight and switch on electric lighting. In other words, the co-operation of all the users in any passive situation that allows their interaction is always going to disappoint to some extent. This then supports the idea of having at least some user-free 'closed loops' in any system of environmental control.

In general the aspect of control in solar architecture is locked into the capture, storage and transfer of the sun's energy. Capture in particular axiomatically implies an influence on form, orientation and materiality, the last strongly associated with transparency. Having suggested in the previous chapter that 'green architecture' can thrive within a very diverse aesthetic framework, surely this must be more limited in the case of 'green solar architecture'? However, the issue of constraints is more complex depending on the relative priority afforded to solar energy for heat, light and electricity.

Three variables, which can be addressed separately, with and without bias to one or the other, or in various groupings or sets, with or without a hierarchy, again gives great scope for aesthetic plurality. If the emphasis is on light, orientation is likely to be less dominant as in the Bregenz Gallery. If the emphasis is on thermal and electrical collection, geometry comes into play, but this does not prevent the contrasting approaches adopted for the Akademie Mont-Cenis and the PV factory in Freiburg. The former collects both thermal and electrical energy on the east and west walls and the roof. Almost perversely it seems the south wall is heavily shaded by the entrance canopy. But this canopy is there to mark the threshold, which faces the town and allows a gentle transition from outside (the park) through outside/inside (the 'forest glade') to completely inside (the room). In contrast the factory entrance is modestly announced by a much smaller canopy and located centrally in the south façade. Access could equally have been through one of the triangular gables or through the office wing, as was the case in Gelsenkirchen. None of these options would have affected solar collection. The entrance to the RWE tower in Essen is associated with its urban context, and irrelevant to the solar aspects of the offices above. Towers of course suit the corporate image as well as exploiting high land values to the full. But such clients are becoming increasingly conscious of the value of promoting the well-being of their workforce, and recognise that green solar architecture can play its part in this respect. Here, since the emphasis is on daylighting, the circular form is appropriate, and the detached lift tower not critical, while the twin-skin design deals with overheating and ventilation.

The plan form of the Brundtland Centre was also generated by a circle, more than probably for abstract ecological associations with closed cycles. These have a very long history, and one that is partly spiritual due to inevitable links with ecology. The parkland setting at the edge of Toftlund also has a generosity that suits the notion of concentric echoes of the building rippling out into the landscape. It also allows the core to loosen up. The circle is excavated on plan to provide straight-forward, vertical, south-facing surfaces, leaving a circular arc of wall to the north. The roof is then partly serrated to optimise solar collection and daylighting into the central exhibition space. In contrast to this, the tight almost square plan of the house in Okayama is dictated by a typically constrained Japanese site, while the issue of maximising daylight without compromising privacy led to the nature of the mainly translucent twin-skin envelope.

Thus it can be said that although this new generation of solar buildings is concerned with the same issues of light, air, health and comfort as were those of the Modern Movement, the approaches to tackling the issues have become more technically sophisticated as well as more subtly intriguing in terms of contextual form-making. Today one might reasonably expect all buildings to engage with sunlight and daylight, but not to the exclusion of other major eco-indicators of architectural process and product. It does not necessarily follow that a new 'spirit of the age' is discernible, but it is nevertheless tempting to explore this thought.

Spirit of the age CHAPTER 11

Chapter 8 began by being cautiously optimistic about the 'green' architectural outlook, at least in terms of 'adventitious propagation' by a
significant number of architects. However, it also recognised that
economy is more powerful than ecology. This reality is extremely perva-
sive with respect to the built environment as a whole, and hence to any
attempt to come to architectural grips with a term such as 'spirit of the
age', especially if the term is held to embrace green aspects of design.

The previous chapter, in a brief browse through the second wave of
'passive solar, climate-conscious' design that is still ongoing, attempts to
highlight trends and themes. It is paradoxical that Wallasey School relied
on a poor quality of air to meet its objective of no fossil-fuel space
heating, whereas many of its descendants are concerned with improving
the quality of air, *and* reducing dependency on mechanical ventilation,
and lowering, but not necessarily eliminating, heating loads. In some
countries such as Norway[62] thermal standards are changing in favour of
increased rates of ventilation, but further reduced U-values. Such a step
acknowledges that excessive recirculation and low rates of ventilation are
a contributory factor to sick building syndrome. However, there is an
opposing lobby that strongly criticises the return to more naturally ventilated buildings in terms of poor control and distribution, and hence, it is
argued, poor quality of air.

Thus the ventilation and breathability of buildings is hotly disputed
environmental territory, with energy-efficiency and well-being jostling
and sometimes competing for priority. Natural ventilation can reduce
energy needed to run fans, but increase fuel required for heating. Its
adherents also advocate it on the grounds that people can work more
productively, but this is refuted by its detractors. Passive solar techniques
in general have had a mixed history in terms of performance. However,
we are now at a stage when the amount of research, development and
demonstration is more than enough to make a solid case for particular
techniques. For example, based on experience in Scotland, 'solar ventilation preheat' by means of air collectors or sunspaces should be able to
save in the range of 20–40% when any savings from further insulation
have diminished to an uneconomic point. Also, advances continue in
glazing and its attached components, which serve to both conserve
energy for heating and displace energy for lighting.

More attention is now being paid to the 'embodied energy' of materials as well as their polluting characteristics during and after production.

Imaginative new construction is emerging which relates strongly to the early days of the Modern Movement, when architects improvised with natural materials in order to insulate their buildings. A small studio in Darmstadt (Fig. 11.1) is an example of this, with its construction including casein-lime render, recycled newspapers, and reed matting, but without resorting to overt regional artifice in terms of its appearance. Could this represent a typology for a new 'spirit of the age' at the dawn

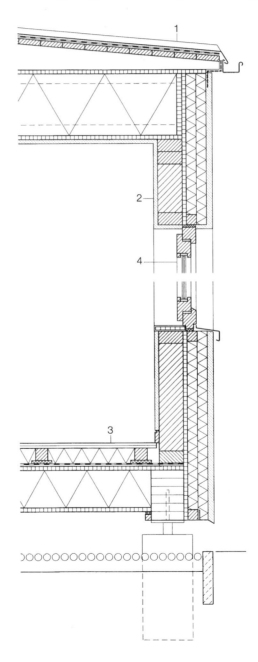

11.1 *Studio in Darmstadt, Germany, by Schauer & Volhard, c. 1997*

1 roof construction: zinc sheet, standing-seam roofing, bituminous sheeting on 24 mm timber boarding, 40/40–280 mm bearers, 18 mm plywood boarding, cellulose-fill insulation between 302 mm deep composite timber I-joists, 18 mm plywood boarding, fibre-clay plaster undercoat on reed matting (16 mm thick), 4 mm lime plaster setting coat with casein-lime finishing coat.

2 wall construction: casein-lime finishing coat, lime plaster setting coat on fibre-clay undercoat (20 mm thick), 120 mm vertically-stacked lightweight clay block wall between timber studs, 18 mm plywood boarding, 2 × 50 mm reed matting with sprayed lightweight plaster and 30 mm external rendering.

3 floor construction: 20/140 mm oak tongued and grooved boarding finished natural resin oil and beeswax, loose-fill insulation between 50/70 mm wood battens on 10 mm insulating strips, bituminous sheeting, 18 mm plywood boarding, cellulose-fill insulation between 100/180 mm timber beams, 18 mm plywood boarding.

of the new millennium? It is incidentally a role model in terms of working from home, and hence reducing the need to commute from its park-like site to a city or town.

In contrast, market-led forces, apparently responding to the demands of consumers, build most of our new housing stock in the UK as ticky-tacky icons of yesteryear. These voraciously continue to consume green-field land, while setting in place heavy reliance on cars for the mobility to meet most day-to-day needs. This situation has been made even worse in the 1980s and 1990s by the public reaction to bad copies of the work of leading modernists. Glasgow's version of Le Corbusier's Unité by Sir Basil Spence was blown up in 1993. Ironically, it had won an award and been opened by Queen Elizabeth in the 1960s. Then, only a few years before demolition, it suffered the ignominy of being 'improved' by a 'tin hat'. While it is true that many people do aspire to their own detached 'castle' with a front and back door, it is also true that many people respond favourably to good design, and alternative planning strategies, if and when presented to them.

An urban infill scheme, although at a completely different scale compared with the Unité in Marseilles or Spence's ill-fated copy, does however have a formalistic connection with Le Corbusier, not to mention a materialistic connection to Frank Lloyd Wright. It is designed by an architect called Rick Joy and located in Tucson, Arizona, and conforms to a 'home and castle' model (Fig. 11.2). Walls are homogeneous – 460 mm thick rammed earth placed in standard slip shuttering in 250 mm lifts, and reinforced with some steel bars and 3% Portland cement. This is a variant on the adobe that is traditional to the region and works well

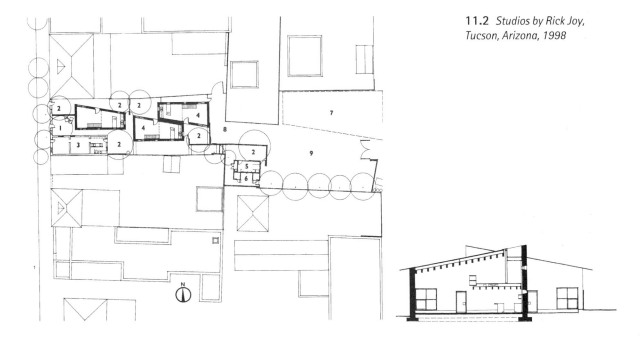

11.2 *Studios by Rick Joy, Tucson, Arizona, 1998*

in the climate in terms of thermal damping and resistance. The pallet of other materials is also carefully limited in the Usonian spirit, for example Corten steel for fences, Douglas fir for roof and floor joists. Although it may be argued that the materiality could be attributed to many architects, including Le Corbusier, the enclosed volumes are almost pure Esprit Nouveau or Unité. The difference lies in a slight shift of geometry on plan and section, and the sideways turn of the double-height space into private outdoor courts, which are in turn aided and abetted by the diagonal on plan. This is a 'green' project in the best spirit of modernism.

The overwhelming uptake of bad design, which is also usually environmentally irresponsible, could reasonably be held to be the consequence of a misdirected, but effective, marketing campaign, rather than the consequence of consumers actually wishing bad design. This explains the popularity of good design, which is also environmentally conscious, in other European countries such as Germany, Austria, Holland, Denmark and Sweden. Dense urban infill is a sustainable, and potentially popular model, especially when uses are mixed. The Sijzenbaan scheme by Theo Bosch[63] at Deventer in Holland is a good example (Fig. 11.3). An ingeniously compact layout includes some shops and small businesses with a vibrant range of dwellings. Despite tight planning, most of these cleverly combine mechanical heat recovery with passive solar preheat.

The 'green', low-energy, rented housing in the town of Gelsenkirchen (Fig. 11.4), whose Science Park was instanced above, is a comparable exemplar to that of Sijzenbaan. Apart from the more explicit passive solar features, Peter Blundell Jones[64] points out that water is a potent symbol of the ecological approach by Szyszkowitz-Kowalski:

> All the surrounding buildings disgorge rainwater into a series of high-level aqueducts, which deliver their contents in turn via open chutes into the watercourse. The water flows on into the oval space, whose sunken floor becomes a temporary lake. The elaboration of the rainwater apparatus celebrates the green theme by reminding people that water is a precious asset; it recovers the memory of lost pre-industrial rivers and, as a symbol of purity, it also opposes the memory of pollution. The aqueducts round the central space give it much stronger definition, looking almost like a series of giant order columns supporting a thin entablature.

This scheme also includes shops and other shared facilities, while the plan permits many variations to facilitate 'a rich social mix'. Although its form, which takes its cue from ground contours as well as solar orientation, looks expensive, Jones points out:

> The dynamic geometry of the plan cleverly conceals the fact that the housing is economically built largely with straight buildings between standard parallel walls. With rooms looking out to back and front, the middle band of each block carries kitchens and bathrooms, allow-

11.4 *Housing by Szyszkowitz-Kowalski, Gelsenkirchen, 1998*

ing economical service runs from a central duct crossing party walls. All this is good rational Modernist practice, but the architects do not switch over to auto-pilot. They humanise and individualise with a series of variations.

The reference to the rationalism of modernism is apt in terms of 'spirit of the age', as are Jones' musical and financial metaphors: 'The whole operates like a well-played fugue, maintaining the rhythm for economy's sake but turning every given difference to account.'

This level of praise by a critic, or endeavour on the part of the architects, might be construed by low-income residents as patronising. Their concerns tend to be rooted at a more pragmatic level. However, public concern and responsibility with regard to the environment is undoubtedly much higher in Germany than in other parts of Europe. For example, in the UK vulnerable sectors of the urban population have suffered disproportionately from low progressive taxation and under-investment in public-sector housing.

Notwithstanding its past, it would be reasonable to expect the UK's prominently located Millennium Village[65] next to the Millennium Dome to embody something of a new 'spirit of the age'. Indeed the involvement of Ralph Erskine boded well: 'The village was intended to: set new standards in construction efficiency, quality, innovation and sustainability; act as a blueprint for Environment secretary John Prescott's brownfield regeneration programme; and serve as a showcase village of the future, drawing thousands of visitors from the nearby Millennium Dome.' The specific comment of Bullivant[65] similarly favours the choice of Erskine as architect: 'The housing proposals for 1000 intelligent, green homes, are not revolutionary in design terms, but they do address the concept of flexibility to meet changing needs over time, offering a similar kit-of-parts (clip-on balconies and conservatories) style of adaptability that Erskine provided for the Ark office building in Hammersmith.' However, it is later reported[66] that 'the £250 million project's much-vaunted sustainability and innovation targets will be ignored until the final phases, with the first dwellings showing only modest improvements on current housing performance.' Also the first phase was planned as a commercial development of luxury flats and penthouses. Erskine[65] himself became very concerned about the delivery of this project: 'It's not all plain sailing; it hasn't been from the beginning. It's slipped quite a bit. Quite what's going on I don't know, and I don't want to know. I think it's a hell of a shame if it doesn't develop properly. I still hope that there will be a reasonable degree of innovation.' In the event, although the first part of the second phase by Proctor Matthews may not be especially innovative, it is laudably energy-efficient, transparently light-hearted and reassuringly modest in terms of layout and scale.

Further north in Glasgow, Baxter[67] was bullish about a project with similar intentions, 'Scotland's Home of Tomorrow' by Ian Ritchie for Thenew Housing Association. This is one of the main elements within the larger 'Homes of the Future' development, a flagship of Glasgow 99, City of Architecture and Design. Making a comparison with a green office building in Dublin, Baxter lauds:

> Glasgow will have a much larger literally and metaphorically green building [referring to its copper cladding once oxidisation has taken place]. The aspiration towards heating and servicing efficiency is high ... The fact that the various components of Scotland's Home of Tomorrow will be brought to the site and simply bolted together will allow for an extraordinary rapid construction programme ... This would be a coup not merely for Thenew and its designers, but also for Scottish Homes who originated the Scotland's Home of Tomorrow idea and for Glasgow's celebration of 1999.

The reference to rapid fabrication harks back to one of the main concerns of the Modern Movement, whereas its green, environmentally efficient aspects are more topical.

Bullivant[68] moves on from the 'Homes of the Future' development of Glasgow 99 to refer to an 'intelligent housing' project in London: 'Integer, a project organised with housing associations introducing 200 low-cost intelligent homes in London this year, offers new integrated systems, a reminder of the technological package cars are equipped with could be applied to the home.' This brings us back to the issue raised towards the end of the previous chapter. There is no doubt that electronic controls are already very important to environmental control of buildings, and computerised building management systems (BMSs) will increasingly become more sophisticated, and cheaper. This latter aspect will then make itself more strongly felt in the rented housing sector, and could have a large role to play in improving overall efficiency, as well as informing the user in the process. This is also appealing at a time when computers and information technology (IT) have become a way of life for many people; and have the potential to make a significant impact on the built environment – where and how we work, live, shop, bank and so forth.

But however certain we are about becoming increasingly reliant on electronic widgets, and knowing that this will introduce changes to future cities, towns and villages in a broad planning sense, it is more difficult to see how, if at all, it may manifest itself in terms of visual architectural syntax. For example, are electronically controlled louvres on the outside of a building an expression of that control, compared with the anonymity or neutrality of 'smart' glass? Also, if the solution does involve an explicit adjustable overlay such as louvres, would users prefer to override a BMS with a button-operated electric motor, or even by means of manual winding gear? The answer may lie in the extent to which users feel in control of, and advantaged by, the electronic system. With respect to the former, the technology allows a building or space within it to be controlled remotely, possibly by someone other than the user, or directly by the user. On the other hand, although remote automation might seem advantageous in theory, in practice a user may feel disadvantaged.

Returning to Scotland's Home of Tomorrow on this particular issue of energy and its control, Ritchie[69] himself states: 'Transfer of energy occurs continuously in our homes, but the obvious sources – our own bodies, cooking appliances, light fittings – have to be understood together with solid and transparent walls, ceilings and floors. This synergy can be understood, and it can be managed by IT, though it is potentially better if managed by natural and intuitive responses from the occupant.' He adds: 'Too little research has been done working with the natural psychology of users in energy-saving technology.' These comments are prefaced by a statement about basing the design upon the selection of our five human senses together with the 'material and immaterial ingredients: light, air, energy, water and time'. In fact the systems specified for heating and ventilating these dwellings have an active and automated bias, but should be able to both respond quite rapidly to passive influences and allow sensory interaction with the occupants.

Ritchie's work could be labelled as that of a rational, tectonic modernist, with minimalist overtones. He has worked with outstanding engineers, for example, Peter Rice on the glazed Serres at La Villette,[70] and IPP Köln with Ove Arup on the 'biggest glass palace in the world' at Leipzig,[71] where the structural concept and its detailed resolution is extremely bold and refined. In such examples, the capabilities of the materials and their supporting structures are stretched to new limits, passive environmental ideas are embraced, and the completed buildings invoke the same kind of spirit at the end of 20th century as that of Paxton's Crystal Palace in 1851. Indeed there appears to be a late 20th century surge or renaissance in the potential of glass for structural, thermal and visual *tour de forces*.

Glass and its relationship with the socio-political agenda of the Modern Movement has been discussed earlier in *the glass is greener....* Light and air were acknowledged as promoting physiological and psychological health; and the provision of clean, light and airy modern buildings for all purposes for all people had a self-evident political dimension. This was partly illusory since large areas of glass signalled problems of discomfort due to excessive heat gain as well as loss, with which we are still grappling. However, setting this aspect to one side, this spirit of the inter-war period, extending over most of Europe and parts of North and South America, bears comparison with a much more recent body of work, of a much narrower geographical focus. That it has occurred in Graz, the second largest city of Austria, a country steeped in conservatism, is perhaps surprising. It has been termed New Graz Architecture, and appeared as the result of an artistic-cum-political fermentation during the 1960s. Jones[72] writes: 'The New Graz Architecture – sometimes designated Grazer Schule against the wishes of its members who insist there is no coherent "school" – is recognisably a "movement" and it certainly centres on the city. This movement is not just architectural but related to other arts, and it is in no sense narrow-mindedly regional.' He expands on this point, suggesting it is 'a microcosm of the international architectural debate, a local well-fertilised bed in which international seeds grow and cross-fertilise'. He also makes the point that its built outcome is relatively recent: 'The New Graz Architecture has its theoretical roots in the 1960s, but the political conditions that allowed the commissioning of most of the work ... were not in place until around 1980.'

An important thrust in the 1980s was that of user-participation in the procurement and design of rented housing. Two connections to Graz occurred in 1972.[73] First, Lucien Kroll introduced such ideas at the 'Styrian Autumn' festival in Graz. Second, the work of Ralph Erskine made a sudden impact on Hubert Reiss, at that time a student in Graz. In 1980 Reiss began to work for Erskine, and persuaded him to enter a housing competition which he won. Reiss was the job architect. For Erskine, user-participation first came to public notice through his Byker Wall project in Newcastle in the mid-1970s.

Another Graz architect who took up the participatory banner through Kroll is Eilfried Huth. Huth at one time worked with Günter Domenig who is regarded as the father of the new movement in Graz, through both his practice and professorship of the architectural school in the Technical University. However, Jones[74] tells us that Huth was 'more interested [than Domenig] in architecture as the expression of a social process'. The plan and section of Huth's housing at Graz-Algersdorf (Fig. 11.5) not only embraced the sun, but also provided much scope for individualisation within a strong overall framework, especially at each end. In a later scheme at Ragnitz, Graz, completed in the early 1990s, Jones[75] reports that the participatory process is more muted:

> In the early days the difficulties of participation were not fully understood, says Huth. It seemed merely a case of sharing the creative act, but in reality it is less a matter of creativity than of political control, which is not so easily changed. Like others with plentiful experience in the field, he talks about all the difficulties of educating people into an awareness of what is possible, talking them out of naive and ill-founded decisions, putting up with their comings and goings and changes of mind, and trying to guide them towards making decisions as a community rather than as individuals.

An example of choice for the users in this scheme of parallel blocks lay between projecting balconies or sunspaces.

The degree of participation is inevitably an issue. Returning to Erskine's protégé in Graz, Jones[73] tells us: 'For Reiss, effective participation is much more a question of giving people choice within set limits, of allowing some flexibility of internal layout, for example, but also creating and turning over to them certain defined territories in outdoor space – for example, the planting of beds along the alleyways – which they then feel obliged to reinterpret.' Regardless of literal green participation, a critical commonality in the work of the Graz movement with respect to housing has been green, climate-sensitive, passive solar outcomes.

11.5 *Housing by Huth, Graz-Algersdorf, Austria, 1988*

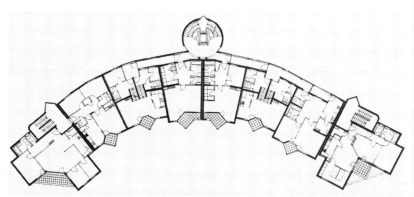

It has been mentioned that Huth and Domenig grew apart in terms of political attitude. Interestingly, while still together and before the respective influences of Kroll and Erskine, they designed a large infrastructural housing project for Graz (1966–9)[76] which owed much to the 'plug-in city' concept of Peter Cook (1964) and the 'living pod' of David Greene (1966). Although the latter may have offered a degree of choice for occupants, the concept of user-participation lay in the future for Huth at this time.

Coming up to date, the work of one of the most important Graz partnerships, Szyszkowitz-Kowalski, has already been cited above – their recent housing scheme in Gelsenkirchen in Germany. All along, their work has been typified by restrained geometry on plan, and rather more dynamic sections. As with Huth, this combination allows much individual tailoring without sacrificing the visual strength of the whole. Their early housing at Eisbach-Rein near Graz, won by competition with future inhabitants on the jury, and completed in 1986, exploits 45° shifts on plan, while the roof section is a combination of monopitches and curves (Fig. 11.6). In their later Sandgasse[77] housing, initiated by the couple

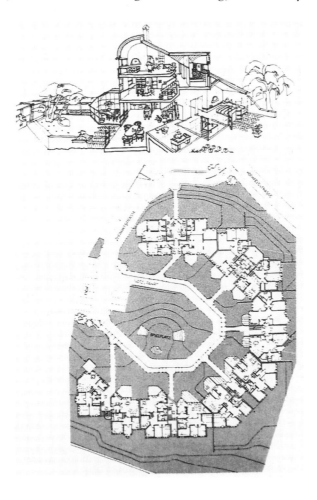

11.6 *Housing by Szyszkowitz-Kowalski, Eisbach-Rein, Graz, 1986*

through a building society, the level of participation is mainly confined to the placing of internal walls; while in describing their housing at Voitsberg in western Styria, Jones[78] does not mention participation. But he does again emphasise the attributes of the scheme, in terms of luminance and orientation – in this case with the main aspect slightly north of east; and he also draws attention to its multi-layerism: 'a rough load-bearing carcase that becomes invisible, clad both inside and out.' This again alludes back to many of the early examples of modernism in Europe, where the opaque surfaces inside and outside would conceal layers of structure, infill and insulation, as well as the use of translucent glass and glass blocks to vary the quality of luminance, visual outlook and privacy. At Voitsberg, selective use of Profilit sheeting to parts of the south-west façades of main rooms takes on the same role as glass blocks, providing a U-value around that of double-glazing, while allowing some solar heat gain with the diffused light.

With the repetition of Peter Blundell Jones in a series of references, it might be said that this is a very one-sided view of what he acknowledges as a wider movement, and hence relevant to a spirit of the age. However, it is not difficult to find examples of other building types by other architects that have been described and analysed by other authors who share the same perspective.

For example, the work of Behnisch has a vigorous political dimension. This is recognised by Reid and Hauser[79] in their analysis of the Herbert-Keller Haus in Stuttgart (Fig. 11.7) relative to some other buildings by the same practice. The democracy of these buildings is the common theme: 'They [Günter Behnisch and his colleagues] seek a democratic architecture which is found not in external appearance but in the generative processes involved.' Significantly, they also state: 'In Behnisch's design process, individual parts are given precedence over the whole.' This is not to deny the whole, rather to shift the emphasis so that individual parts may respond freely to user-driven needs, and change

11.7 *Herbert-Keller Haus by Behnisch, Stuttgart, 1985*

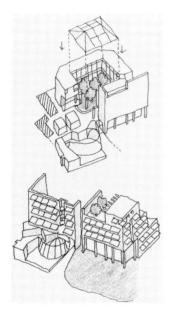

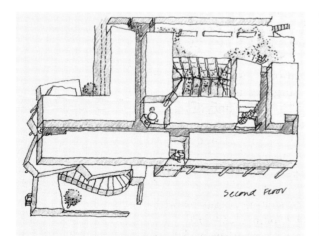

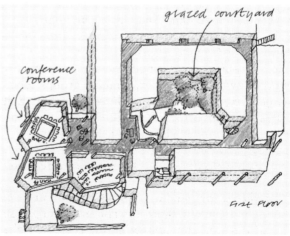

over the life of the building, without compromising either the aesthetic or democratic intent: 'For Behnisch architecture is the mirror of the diversity inherent in society.' Reid and Hauser also attribute quite widely divergent modernist sources of inspiration or influence to Behnisch's work – Häring, Scharoun and Aalto concerning the organic tradition, Schindler's constructivist tendencies, and Duiker with regard to a preoccupation with *skin and bones*. They also assert: 'Another essentially Modernist aspect of Behnisch's work is the importance he attaches to a direct and honest expression of materials.'

The Herbert-Keller Haus was designed for a charity that deals with the 'old and handicapped, children and teenagers from deprived backgrounds, the sick and the addicts'. Reid and Hauser discuss the aspects that become the province of people such as planners and building control offices, relative to those that remain within the sphere of the client and the users: 'Another contradiction arose between the need to make the most intensive use of the compact site, yet also to respond with generosity to the charity's requirements.... Those elements and aspects of the building however, that were not predetermined, and over which the charity still has control, can be ranged alongside the predetermined, inaccessible elements.' The glazed courtyard, and its relationship to bounding and diagonally interconnected spaces, exemplifies the approach to this dichotomy:

> The interior courtyard was not merely the result of an arbitrary formal decision – rather it was an attempt to counteract the restrictions of the intensively developed site by providing well-lit and pleasant offices here too. This is the most generous and atmospheric part of the building, because of the busy interrelation of spaces with offices visible around the interior courtyard; and the juxtaposition of hard and soft contours, of light and shadow, of quiet and animation. The 'open house' feeling sought by the charity to express its inner purpose and architecture are one: form is identified with content.

Dawson[80] describes a similar type of urban building in terms of both its somewhat anarchic 'individual parts having precedence over the whole' (Fig. 11.8) and the overtly political nature of its client. In this case the latter is the Communist Association of West Germany, and their building, the Öko-haus, accommodates some thirty organisations including a worker-owned newspaper, feminist groups, doctors' surgeries and green associations. The project architect, Joachim Eble (of Eble & Sambeth), has a reputation for architecture that is both user-friendly and environmentally sensitive. This latter aspect is described quite fully by Dawson, and the resultant building shows that the literal 'green' spirit of buildings such as the Herbert-Keller Haus can be ratcheted up significantly:

> I visited the building on one of the hottest days of summer. Surprisingly the micro-climate in and around the building remained comfortably warm; the circulating air smelt of foliage; trickling water and

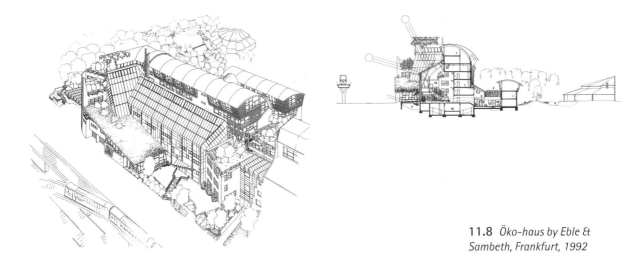

11.8 *Öko-haus by Eble &*
Sambeth, Frankfurt, 1992

rustling leaves formed an aural background. It seemed remarkably peaceful for a working background. . . . Both greenhouses also contribute towards the circulated air quality. Thick planting boosts the oxygen content of the air and filters out carbon dioxide. A stream in the southern greenhouse and a water cascade humidify air recycled from the printing works. . . . What distinguishes eco-architecture is its complex interaction and multi-functionalism. Landscaping, for example, is an integral part of the building services, a recreational and aesthetic ingredient in the environment. The sub-strata of the roof planting beds hold enough moisture to avoid the need for extra watering, filter the rainwater and insulate the building.

The echoes of Le Corbusier are self-evident in this description.

However, although the Öko-haus is exuberantly inspiring, probably constitutes Utopia in terms of its working environment and may on the surface appear to express romantic green idyll, it has in fact holistically and pragmatically tackled all critical aspects of green design. There were four main strands – materials, micro-climate, rainwater and energy – and these are completely interactive. For example, the dividing wall of lime plastered calcium silicate brick between the main southerly facing wintergarden and the offices has an adequate thickness of 50–60 cm to deal with thermal resistance, thermal damping and time lag to the benefit of both spaces over a daily cycle, and the materials are environmentally benign. All rainwater is collected into a 25 000 litre tank in the basement and used for both flushing WCs and irrigating the 1500 m² of planting on roofs and inside the building. Reducing the amount of impermeable surface generated by buildings is a major aspect of sustainability in Germany today. In this case, the roof gardens have as much as 50 cm of soil in order to allow quite substantial growth. Offices are heated at skirting level with one finned tube at 60°C and a return pipe at 40°C behind a metal panel. The resultant mix of radiant and convective heat apparently works well. It is this sensitive attention to detail in order to provide what is required and what will enhance working conditions that is impressive. Robust end-grain wood blocks are used for flooring in the printworks and there is a special clay acoustic lining to the walls. Waste heat from this part of the building is recovered, although it did not quite come up to expectations. Overall however, the total annual energy load of $70\,\mathrm{kWh/m^2}$ is rather impressive.

Organisationally, the Öko-haus might be viewed as a more relaxed and embellished version of the solar factory in Freiburg. The layers of the factory from south to north were: road, watery green outdoor strip, solar concourse, office spine, link and production block. The corresponding sequence for the Öko-haus from south-west to north-east is: raised railway with station, road, watery green outdoor strip, glazed garden, office spine, greenhouse, ancillary block. Unlike the solar factory, the Öko-haus has strong end-conditions, the main spine terminating in a 'hammer-head' at the northerly end. The west end of this wraps round to gather up special accommodation such as a lecture theatre, and finally cascades down gently over a cafe, while the lower east extension accommodates the printing works and buries itself into the landscape. The presence of the station means that the building is very accessible even though it is by no means central, and the cafe seems to be a commercial success with a clientele extending well outwith the immediate locality. The negative aspect of the railway – noise – makes the main southerly glazed space an important acoustic as well as thermal and ecological buffer for most of the main working zones. Overheating in the buffer is prevented partly by being convectively linked to the smaller north-east facing greenhouse, as well as by running water, opening glass panels and some fixed Okasolar glazing. In addition the north-east facing greenhouse makes a wonderfully cool breakout space for the printing staff.

A final ironic aspect of this building in terms of *realpolitik* rather than 'spirit of the age' is that its procurement was due to the Commerzbank wanting to acquire the original premises of the Communist Association. These were in an old industrial building, but in a valuable commercial location in the centre of Frankfurt. Thus a deal was struck whereby a contaminated brownfield site nearer the edge of Frankfurt was acquired for the new Öko-haus, but with good access and with a budget that was not particularly constrained. Neither of course was that of Foster's new tower for Commerzbank. The differences and commonalities between that building and the Öko-haus offer food for thought. Both attempt to improve the quality of the working environment, but only one offers more than a totem to the wider community.

Twelve years prior to the 1992 opening of Öko-haus, another remarkable urban building was inaugurated, the refuge for the Hubertus Association in Amsterdam by Aldo van Eyck. Like both the Herbert-Keller Haus and the Öko-haus, the client had a very specific social brief, on this occasion for single women and their children who were often traumatised or at least having difficulty in coping independently. The particular duality of its ethos was fundamental:[81] 'it would also have to be a building which reflected our personality. This meant that it would have to be an "open" building, totally devoid of any centralist or hierarchical structure, and at the same time a "closed" building, providing the residents with a shelter and a place they could call their own.' We know that van Eyck welcomed this challenge:[82] 'The Hubertus "style" above all breathes equality. Open – yes, but in no way vague or fluctuating. In fact *open and protective at the same time*.' This is not simply a matter of this particular building's agenda. His passion for *reciprocity* was widely recognised and influential. Herman Hertzberger[83] refers to the unusual relationship between the old and the new: 'One might say that the division into two building elements, each leaning against the one next to it on either side, creates a sense of ambiguity as in syncopation.' With respect to the architectural significance of this syncopation in the context of the 'open–closed', unhierarchical ethos of the client, Hertzberger goes on: 'the main implication lies in the way this shifting of focus and this sense of relativity in spatial organisation stresses the use and the experience of that use in such a way that the pattern of relationships between people become less hierarchical'.

In environmental terms, although it is not that energy efficient by the standards of today, it is a building on a very tight site that still manages to exploit light and sunlight to the full, where there are secluded terraces and courts outside, and where the single-access section enables cross ventilation. In terms of procurement, the process of designing was very participatory, and the occasional disagreements are frankly exposed.[81] It is also significant, given the brief, that Aldo's wife Hannie is credited with doing 'much for the interior'.

All these examples suggest a metaphorical spirit in terms of 'adventitious propagation' which involves the displacement of non-renewable contaminants such as oil by an approach imbued with the life-giving and renewable resonance of water. Such a spirit is not encapsulated by time other than by influential events, usually geo-political in nature. Hence there is a slant at the end of the 20th century that is not identical with that between the two World Wars, but which shares a common concern over resources. A client with a socio-political commitment, and an architect who is sympathetic to this, are complementary ingredients of a participatory process, whereby the outcome is now more likely to be green or environmentally sustainable than otherwise. In support of this position, there are conversely still countless examples of buildings today that have no altruistic purpose and which are often underpinned by commercial avarice. In these situations the architect is likely to be constrained by the requirements of the client over and above the negative effect that business pressures have on motivation or inspiration. The outcome is thus often harmful to its context and the wider environment. The euphemistically named Buchanan Galleries in Glasgow is a recent example. The shopping complex destroys the urban grid, is aesthetically lumpish, worsens the congestion and pollution of traffic, makes no effort towards energy efficiency and provides a hostile, low-grade environment for its users. It also flouts Glasgow's stated Agenda 21 commitments – in particular the gigantic car park relative to its location at a public transport interchange. Unfortunately other equally horrendous examples are not hard to find. Accountancy generates briefs that are devoid of other insights and social concerns; and collusion between local politicians, officials and the architectural team is a sad but all too frequent reality.

Such buildings are the architectural hooligans of an unfettered market-led economy, whereas the eco-spirit exemplars instanced above respect and embrace responsible controls and ambitions. This spirit of living in tune with ecology has been shown to have a respectable history, and having given some space to the work of architects such as Szyszkowitz-Kowalski in the 1990s, it is worth returning to some words contained in the Team 10 Primer of 1962.

First, the reprimand and warning of Aldo van Eyck[84] has special resonance given what followed as the European game of housing numbers stepped up in the 1960s and 1970s:

> Instead of the inconvenience of filth and confusion, we have now got the boredom of hygiene. The material slum has gone – in Holland for example it has – but what has replaced it? Just mile upon mile of organised nowhere, and nobody feeling 'he is somebody living somewhere'. No microbes left – yet each citizen a disinfected pawn on a chessboard, but no chessmen – hence no challenge, no duel and no dialogue. *The slum has gone. Behold the slum edging into the spirit.*

As it turned out van Eyck was over-optimistic about hygiene. The prevalence of fuel poverty with ensuing condensation and mould, and other infestations, was unhealthy . . . and also dispiriting.

Second, the living analogy of John Voelker,[85] first published in 1957, is as fitting today as it was then:

> The formal significance of housing is matched by its ecological significance. The house is the centre from which living extends and to which it returns; it contains in embryo all the organs of the village, town and city; the kitchen, for example, becomes the workshop, factory, warehouse and multiple store of the great city, the living room becomes the cinema, library and dance hall. If village, town and city are to be comprehensible extensions of living and not unknowable forces within which the house is nothing but a refuge, the connections between the embryo and its development need to be apparent. The design of the house must imply what lies outside.

There were other relevant propositions, hypotheses or manifestos towards the end of the 1960s. For example there were the 'Eight Alternative Futures' of Peter Cook in 1969,[86] all of which retain topicality; the 'arcology' of Paolo Soleri,[87] also in 1969 and a manifesto for ecological architecture; and the 'biotecture' of Rudolph Doernach in 1970,[88] with the self-defining organic agenda of blending biology and architecture.

Now it is time for a fresh Team Primer to take sustainably green architecture forward through a renewed perception of the past.

There are several arguments to support this position. One concerns information. While ecological issues are more strongly represented in the media, including the specifically architectural outlets, there is a counter tendency for less analysis and polemical debate than formerly. With one or two exceptions, the architectural periodicals are now less likely to demonstrate how buildings are put together, as well as less likely to strongly criticise. In combination, together with a proliferation of laudatory monographs which promote particular buildings or architects, this represents a trend towards *house styles* which praise more than probe.

There are also numerous technical conferences of relevance to ecological design in general, and to architects in particular, but which are poorly attended by them. Dissemination from these to the profession is then limited, and the consequence is that many architects never receive the knowledge and confidence to exploit green technology to its fullest potential. Ironically, during a time of expanding litigation arising from aspects of the building process that go awry, architects continue to take much higher risks with constructional detailing than with passive energy-conserving design, which carries a low risk of failure. This is partly due to over-reliance on specialist consultants who are notoriously conservative, but it is also driven by lack of information. This seems extraordinary in an era of IT, but the reality is that mainstream sources of information about new buildings provide very little about their performance, either in terms of measured data or in terms of the subjective experience of their users. The tendency to publish at, or soon after, completion must take part of the responsibility for this state of affairs; and since there is an inevitability about such immediacy in a competitive journalistic market, this suggests a need for more revisiting of buildings once they have been occupied for a year or so – perhaps a dedicated journal.

It also suggests a need on the part of the owners or users of buildings to monitor the readily measurable aspects of performance, such as fuel consumption and temperature. Electronic technology, with devices such as the 'heat mirror' developed by Ecofys[89] in Utrecht, provides the capability for such monitoring on a routine basis. This would both allow users to adjust their performance where it is perceived to be weak or profligate, as well as allowing complete records for external agencies. Nowadays, when the activities of most workers are regularly audited for quality, it makes sense that such audits should include a much more thorough and user-sensitive assessment of the environmental performance of their workplaces than is usual at present. And if we are to be serious about reducing global warming and increasing reliance on renewable sources of energy, the same kind of scrutiny of performance would be required for dwellings. For example, in the rented sector managed by housing associations, this would become part of their 'quality assessment'.

At a time when leading architects are increasingly and opportunistically opting into green design, continued momentum is reliant on adequate information, debate, accountability and, most importantly, political support. The last could well fade out, mainly because of the USA's prevailing reluctance to endorse international commitments on sustainability. On the other hand, with evidence of green performance 'in the face' of architects, the pace of its uptake should in itself become more politically influential.

Green priming could also ride on the back of the power of imagery with cultural clout. People in general, respond to icons or totems. Jørn Utzon's opera house in Sydney is an integral part of the economy of Australia as well as universally known. The temporary Dome of Discovery and Skylon of 1951 sang a duet of the time. The Millennium Dome promised much, but financially and popularly failed to deliver. The Pompidou Centre in Paris is as much part of Paris as the Eiffel Tower. More contextually, the new extension to the museum in Edinburgh by Benson and Forsyth is a breath of fresh air in an overly staid city. However one would have to search hard to find evidence of green strategies in any of these buildings. For example, although the plan and section of the last exploits daylight, as does the original museum by Francis Fowke, a much more subtle game of 'hide and seek' is generally played. Routes and inter-spatial relationships are a complex labyrinth, and similarly, neither structure nor servicing is readily legible as in the engineered rationality of Fowke's building. This raises the debate of whether *being seen to work* has any relevance to a building's green credentials, or indeed its presence in any other respect. Thomas Spiegelhalter's house at Breisach am Rhein, referred to earlier, which celebrates working technology in an even more unrestrained way than the Pompidou Centre did in the 1970s, is a case in point. It engenders overt but deconstructed science. Wet, electric and passive solar pieces tug at emotions in a trichotomy of attention-seeking, functional brutalism and subtle deception.

Renzo Piano's new Kanak cultural centre at Nouméa in New Caledonia (Fig. 11.9), is again potently iconic, and it adds emotional value to pure rationale. It is likely that already it is widely circulated on postcards and contributing to the local economy. The fact that the totems are perfectly structured and beautifully assembled wind shields is an architectural bonus, especially when this assists the natural ventilation of the buildings that snuggle up to them. As Piano puts it, the wind gives the buildings a 'voice' as it surges through the slats. Ecologically spirited and inspiring buildings such as this deserve more than a few words and photographs. How they perform over time merits the widest possible architectural audience.

If we accept then that the time is ripe for priming green attitude, partly by means of improved information and visual assertiveness, it seems important not to appear to be too prescriptive. On the other hand,

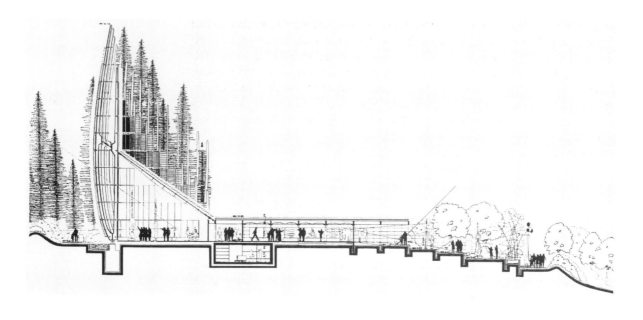

11.9 *Jean-Marie-Tjibaou Cultural Center, Nouméa, New Caledonia, 1991–8*

Client: Agence pour le Développement de la Culture Kanak
Consultants: Competition stage, 1991: A. Bensa; Desvigny & Dalnoky; Ove Arup & Partners; GEC Ingénierie; Peutz & Associés; Scène. Design Development and Construction phase, 1992–8: A. Bensa; GEC Ingénierie; Ove Arup & Partners; CSTB; Agibat MTI; Scène; Peutz & Associés; Qualiconsult; Végétude; Integral R. Baur.

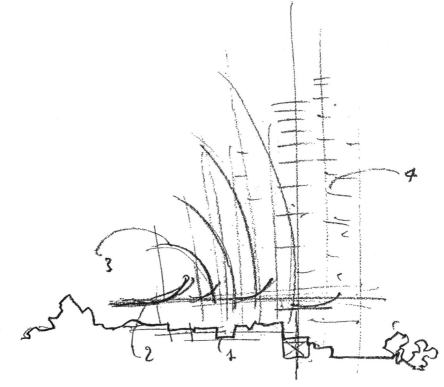

green attitude implies a need for some rational constraint to overly wilful design, which may deservedly be lionised in terms of organisation and spatiality, but which fails ecologically. The issue then is whether the underlying thrust of such an aesthetic is capable of adaptation to a green programme. Above all, we need to enthuse our students and practitioners. In part this will be by reference to historical precedents, bearing in mind that we should not be looking back through green-tinted spectacles, but rather moving forward with memory.

Specific architectural careers have their place in this. One, whose working life spans the decades from the 1920s to the 1990s, is that of Albert Frey. According to Golub:[90] 'For over 75 years Frey has sought to think about architecture and nature together, to learn to understand for architecture the economy, the discipline, the functionality, the creativity and the richness of nature.' It is interesting to speculate as to the part played by his early influences – Le Corbusier's Five Points, then Mies van der Rohe, Schindler and Neutra – with respect to such an ecological stance. His own house of 1941 in Palm Springs bears the imprint of Neutra in particular, although the more expressionist addition to this house in 1953 brings Goff to mind. Then the early passive solar rationality of California prevails in his second house in Palm Springs of 1964.

Talking to Golub in March 1995, Frey[90] states: 'I studied the position of the sun for a whole year.... The plan was designed so that, for instance, the glass walls are not exposed to the sun in the heat of the summer.... That's what determined these overhangs. In winter, when the sun is much lower, it comes in and helps to heat the house. I never need any heat after the sun comes up because the sun warms it.' He also talks about the visual value of reflected sunlight: 'And at this time of year, when the sun is low, the water from the pool is reflected on the ceiling and makes interesting patterns.... Everything is pretty rigid in the design of the house itself, so you have the movement from the water.' Over 30 years after its building, Frey appears contented with its design, and he is disparaging about certain intervening directions taken in architecture: 'There's some good work. But of course there was this terrible post-modern period – just picking up things from the past and putting them together like a decorator's stew. Then there was the deconstruction period too. We don't need that in California. Nature takes care of that.'

Accepting the facetiousness of the last sentence, his comments reinforce the need for more critical discussion about architectural theory in the context of the current green thrust. Nature takes care of much, but architects still require to intervene. Frey's own words in response to a question about an ecological ethic were: 'You are responsible for your actions.' Of course sometimes such actions may be compromised or even flawed. For example, the cold bridging through the steel of the insulated roof of his 1964 house is mentioned in Part 1.

So 'deconstruction' may also be incompatible with green design if it entails extreme cold bridges or excessive heat gain through tilted glazing, but the theory in itself does not deem such shortcomings inevitable. The same might be said of highly individualistic architects such as Frank Gehry and Zaha Hadid. They might be regarded as sharing the spirit of expressionism or deconstruction, but heavily translated through their own rules and boundaries, and their geometrical attitudes should not be lightly dismissed as innately un-green. Conversely, it is not difficult to find prominent recent examples of buildings that conform to very orthodox geometry, but which are overtly perverse environmentally. Perrault's library in Paris is such an example. One would have expected the books to have been protected from as much thermal impact as possible, for example, located in a deep-plan building or in a basement. But Perrault chooses to flaunt them in tall, slim, glass-clad, symbolic 'open-book' towers. He then has to deal with the problem of solar impact for various orientations, and does this by means of vertically pivoting timber shutters located behind the glass. This strategy will not eliminate a heavy reliance on mechanical cooling and heating, depending on the weather.

Then there are buildings such as the new library by Mecanoo for the Technical University of Delft. The twist in the geometry is expressionistic, but it also happens to be functional (Fig. 11.10). The backward slope of the northern-facing glass wall of the computer suite maximises the view of the sky and hence scope for natural lighting, but without excessive glare problems from the sun. Given the heat gain from computers, reducing the thermal gain from lighting is very advantageous, let alone the saving in primary electrical energy. Even so, some cooling is sometimes required in this space. The same twist tilts the glazed walls of offices to the east and south outwards. This then allows more passive reflection of sunlight as the incident angle exceeds 50°. In turn this means that the working spaces are not subject to excessive thermal stress, and a twin-skin system of ventilation is viable. Vollaard[91] refers to this as a 'climate façade'. It is separated vertically floor by floor, in the same way as the towers in Essen and Frankfurt (Chapter 10). In the closed condition, air from the offices is drawn into a 140 mm cavity through a slot between the floor and the inner window. It is drawn out into voids in the precast concrete flooring at intermediate levels and into the roof void at the top. This is a mechanical system of ventilation that uses spaces within and between building components passively. When desired by occupants, inner sliding windows and outer top-hung hoppers can be opened, although this would compromise the mechanical system to some extent in cold weather.*

The air supply is tempered in all seasons by means of air-to-water heat exchangers/pumps, the water coming from two underground tubes

---

*When visiting the building on a cold, but bright, day in March, several of the inner and outer windows were open. This may well have been triggered by a 'feel-good' factor associated with the look of the weather, rather than a response to the temperature outside or lack of thermal comfort inside. It is quite likely that in dull, mild weather, the windows are more likely to remain closed. Again it raises the issue of enhancing well-being by giving users some control, even if it runs counter to optimum energy efficiency.

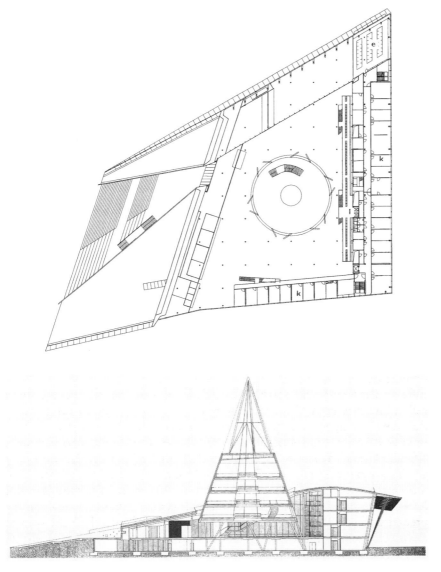

buried in sand at a depth of 45 to 70 m. In winter water from one tube at 17°C or so is pumped up to yield its heat to the supply of fresh air, and is returned to the second tube at around 6°C. The water from this cooler tube is then used in summer to cool the incoming air. The glass façades, facing north-west, east and south, play their part as described. Finally by allowing what would have been the western façade to become a gently tilted part of the green landscape, the usual problem of overheating in hot sunny afternoons has been avoided, as well as any aesthetic confrontation with the lecture theatre of van den Broek and Bakema. The green sward is dramatically punctured by an iconic cone. This allows natural light deep into the heart of what is a large floor-plate, at the same time allowing the successive layers of reading galleries their own spatial identity. The literal green element is fundamental to the concept. The library is in essence natural permeable landscape with a sculpture, the cone, and glass edges. Rainwater absorbed in the turf of the roof has a passive climatically moderating role which complements the semi-active role of the underground aquifers. Vollaard[91] states:

> One of the key departure-points of the design for the library was to realise a building that would be 'green' not only in architectural terms but technically too, though without sinking into eco-clichés. From the very first sketches this dual green characteristic has determined the basic make-up of the design. When it was decided during the fleshing-out stage to give the library the status of pilot scheme for sustainable building, it transpired that the initial design was in fact quite green enough already.'

In terms of 'spirit of the age', the resonant phrase in this statement is 'without sinking into eco-clichés'. The architectural idea and the eco-strategy are as one.

Other spirited architects such as Will Alsop do not ignore climate, but indulge in thermally rational geometry alongside thermally irrational, the latter requiring additive fixes in the same way as Perrault's library. For example, the south-facing upper half of the ferry terminal in Hamburg designed with Me di um Architekten slopes inwards from the eaves, thus passively reducing solar gain, while the lower half slopes the other way, necessitating a series of external louvres. Similarly, Alsop's Hôtel du Département in Marseilles, fondly nicknamed Le Grand Bleu, passively protects the atrium from southern sunlight, but not the south edge of the offices in the Administratif; while the shape of the Délibératif and its external awnings has been criticised in terms of climatic appropriateness. While acknowledging that the original proposal for passive heating and cooling had been lost in the transition from competition-winning design to built reality, Davies[92] nonetheless challenges:

> The typical citizen of Marseilles is acutely aware of the direction of the wind – the cold Mistral from the north or the hot, humid Sirocco from the south – and its likely effect on his or her physical well-being. Alsop therefore makes some attempt to justify the design in aerodynamic terms. The justification is not very convincing, however. If the basic forms were generated by wind tunnel tests, why was it necessary to bolt on a variety of baffles and deflectors? In any case the analysis seems to contradict Alsop's basic principle of irrationality. Isn't this precisely the kind of post-rationalisation that he seeks to undermine?

The Minaert Building at the Technical University of Utrecht by Neutlings Riedijk might be regarded as somewhere between Mecanoo's library in Delft and Le Grand Bleu. The 'worms' that crawl over the external skin are quirky to say the least, as are some internal features such as the shape of the openings to the seating booths in the main foyer. But, although the pool in the same space also might be regarded as quirky and is certainly atmospheric in the abstract sense, it does have a thermal and environmental function.[93] In wet weather, the pool will fill up to a maximum level, fed intermittently by dripping rainwater from the roof and, especially in dry, warm weather, the water will act as a climatic moderator, evaporatively cooling and restricting excessive rises in temperature. Then the light pipes cum ventilating 'columns' in its refectory evoke an allusion to ancient Egypt, while serving two interrelated purposes. The natural light will help to reduce incidental thermal gains, and will thus lessen the requirement for ventilation.

Similarly, although perhaps not immediately evident in the Educatorium almost opposite the Minaert Building, the designs of OMA/Rem Koolhaas tend to be underpinned by an intellectual rationale that embraces structure and servicing.[94] The issue for Koolhaas is for the architect to be in command of these aspects to the extent that they do not compromise the desired spatial order. He is forthright about the gap between architects and their consultants alluded to in Chapter 10: '(the architect) ... confronts the sabotage of engineers, his supposed *team-mates* with their tantalisingly vague (if not outright poetic) indications from what is supposedly the domain of pure science'. A good example of how he wrests the control back to the architect is his developmental designs in 1989 for both the TGB (Très Grande Bibliothèque) in Paris and ZKM (Zentrum fur Kunst und Medientechnologie) in Karlsruhe.

The latter in particular included 6 m high vierendeel beams on alternate storeys to deal with 30 m spans within a 43 m square plan and a total height of 58 m. Some of the peripheral space left over between the 43 m and 30 m dimensions could then accommodate what he termed a series of 'atomised plant rooms'. Koolhaas objects to the normal commercial sandwich, where the 'free zone for human occupancy alternates with inaccessible bands of concrete, wiring and ducts ... expropriating ever larger parts of the section'. He accuses the 3 m deep trusses of Beaubourg (Centre Pompidou) by Piano and Rogers of consuming 43% of the cross-section (although this may be considered spurious since it implies the necessity of a continuous ceiling below the trusses). His dispersed plant rooms serve spaces horizontally by the most direct route possible, the need for continuous vertical shafts or ducts is avoided, and alternate floors are completely free of columns. His approach to the simple cuboid of ZKM is reminiscent of the 'bold buccaneer' logic of Wright with respect to the Larkin Building (Chapter 7), which also innovatively moved service stacks to the periphery. The Educatorium in Utrecht is a much more horizontal edifice, again contained within an ordered rectilinear plan. However it has a section that sings the *promenade architecurale* of Le Corbusier in the way it engages with route. The structure is allowed an occasional descant. Examples are the diagonal struts and ties outside the main lecture theatre and, inside it, the expressed steel tensioning below the concrete roof slab. However, unlike Mecanoo's library in Delft, the shifts in geometry in the Educatorium do not in this case correspond with any environmental strategy. Indeed the sloping west-facing wall of the refectory is thoroughly irrational in terms of inevitable solar overheating.

Rem Koolhaas may be deservedly credited with having sparked a fresh surge of experimentation in Dutch architecture, to a great extent usurping the former strong influence of Aldo van Eyck. However, there are also analogous aspects to their respective work, just as there are between Le Corbusier and Frank Lloyd Wright. Reciprocity, manifested by van Eyck in terms of form, occurs with Koolhaas's materiality. He uses cheap modern materials side by side with expensive traditional ones, for example. Both exploit routes in comparable ways. We could take the orphanage and Hubertus refuge in Amsterdam on the one hand, and the Kunsthal in Rotterdam and Educatorium in Utrecht on the other. Returning to reciprocity, both also employ contrasts – narrow to wide, small to large, open to closed, light to dark and so on. However, it might also be said that although both start with a set of rules or constraints, Aldo plays a clever hand of 'bridge' while Rem plays a more anarchistic hand of 'cheat'. It is perhaps this aspect that made the former so critical.

Here then is another case of a dialectic that may have more general application – the other side of van Doesburg's coin which was expressed at the outset of the first part. Van Doesburg rigidly held that 'international modernism' could readily cope with climatic variations and that more expressive forms of regionalism were an aberration. But matters become much more difficult when there is a complex weave of rationality with irrationality, the Educatorium of Koolhaas being one of many examples. Also, architects are not necessarily consistent with respect to a green approach. The aspects described with respect to Mecanoo's library cannot be said to be representative of the entire body of work of this practice. Neutlings Riedijk's Minaert Building explicitly mixes rationality with irrationality. Again Alsop liberally espouses irrationality and form as an end in itself, but simultaneously flirts with climate-sensitivity while puristically banning planting in the atrium of Le Grand Bleu.

In terms of spirit of the age in the 21st century, it is Alsop's dichotomy of liberal purism that may be more likely to receive popular acclaim than stiff neo-modernists with historical overtones of fascism. Hussell[95] provides a glimpse of this which is a fitting *fin* from a city that is also home to Le Corbusier's still-thriving Unité (albeit with more middle-class occupants than when first built). Referring to the comments of a dozen councillors leaving a tense meeting he reports: 'They are almost unanimous in praising their working conditions as comfortable and convenient.' This could of course be due to efficient air-conditioning. Nevertheless, respective quoted comments of a left-wing and a right-wing councillor suggest that the ambience is such that the building has a feel-good factor, which must surely be essential in terms of green sustainability: 'I was on the jury that chose Alsop and the building is as marvellous as I hoped it would be' and 'I used to think it was a monstrosity from the outside, but now I find it both convivial and an excellent place to work. However, I can't say so publicly because we're in opposition and we vote against everything.'

Having obliquely brought up Le Corbusier again at this stage, and having stirred around the issues of today that seem to make green connections with a new 'spirit of the age', it is tempting to give him the last word. After all the title is attempting to trace the ecological architecture of today from the crucible of 'The New Architecture' and Le Corbusier provided much of that crucible's heat. His enthusiastic comments made with regard to Prouvé's pure form of prefabricated rationalism have already been mentioned (Chapter 4). Paradoxically it might seem, he is equally generous in his attitude with respect to one of the world's most famous expressionists, Antoni Gaudí:[96]

> What I had seen in Barcelona was the work of a man of extraordinary force, faith and technical capacity.... Gaudí is 'the' constructor of 1900.... Architecture whose meaning shines forth at the moment when lofty intentions dominate, triumphant over all the problems assembled on the finishing line (structure, economy, technique, utility) triumphant because of an unlimited preparation – 'that' architecture is the fruit of character – properly speaking, a manifestation of character.

The issue of fitness for purpose was raised earlier, and the point made that since this was the focus of concern for engineers, they tended to be formalistically neutral or non-discriminatory compared with architects. Le Corbusier appears to adopt just this stance in his even-handed praise of two very different designers – at least very different in terms of the overt aesthetic of respective built outcomes. His inclusive recognition of fundamental strengths, regardless of such differences, sits well with the ecological spirit of the 21st century as it starts to gather a critical physical and political momentum for the procurers and enablers of the built environment, and enters the psyche of the population at large. It also seems to have a distinct correspondence with the cryptic comment of Koolhaas and Mau: 'Most aesthetic absolutes prove relative under pressure.'[97] Of course, one might argue that an aesthetic absolute is a contradiction in terms, and one might also argue that van Doesburg misguidedly believed in aesthetic absolutes. Above all, 'absolutes' and 'alternatives' are by definition conflicting propositions, whichever meaning is attributed to the latter word, and which is in more than one sense embedded in a NEW eco-ARCHITECTURE.

However, relativity and pluralism are generic abstractions that require some degree of control or limitation in order to achieve *reasonably* sustainable architecture as suggested at the outset. The valuing of an integrity of approach as a prerequisite of an eco-spirit for our age is tempting, but does still beg this question of whether irrationality can have green integrity alongside rationality. Apparent lack of order, randomness or even chaos can be visually invigorating at a populist level, and may have a serious artistic or emotionally uplifting value. But sustainable or green architecture seems to axiomatically demand a rationale. The common ground might well be the stimulation of the senses. Zumthor's gallery at Bregenz has been cited as environmentally innovative. It clearly belongs to the technically rational mould, but equally clearly like other buildings by the same architect, it has a strongly poetic dimension. Words of Le Corbusier, such as those quoted with respect to Prouvé and Gaudí, strike a common chord alongside thoughts expressed by Zumthor:[98] 'Architecture needs to be executed. Then its body can come into being. . . . All design work starts from the premise of this physical, objective sensuousness of architecture, of its materials. To experience architecture in a concrete way means to touch, see, hear and smell it.' His feelings towards the joining of materials, which must stem partly from his early training as a cabinet maker, again describe a sensory rationale which stresses that apparently mundane physical connections can be architecturally uplifting:

> Buildings are artificial constructions. They consist of single parts which must be joined together. To a large degree, the quality of the finished object is determined by the quality of the joins. . . . Details express what the basic idea of the design requires at the relevant point in the object: belonging or separation, tension or lightness, friction, solidity, fragility. . . . Our attention is caught, perhaps for the first time, by a detail such as two nails in the floor that hold the steel plates by the worn-out doorstep. Emotions well up. Something moves us.

For the architect, details must be expressed at some critical stage in the process of design through the medium of working drawings. Again quoting Zumthor, this is the stage when spatial ideas come to life and prove themselves:

> Among all the drawings produced by architects, my favourites are the working drawings. . . . Working drawings are like anatomical drawings. They reveal something of the secret inner tension that the finished architectural body is reluctant to divulge: the art of joining, hidden geometry, the friction of materials, the inner forces of bearing and holding, the human work which is inherent in man-made things.

Delving further into the emotional side of creating architecture Zumthor suggests that what architects say about their buildings tends to only express the rational processes, which often seem to be at odds with how their buildings appear to others because they suppress the emotional aspects. His position is made clear: 'The design process is based on a constant interplay of feeling and reason. The feelings, preferences, longings, and desires that emerge and demand to be given a form must be controlled by critical powers of reasoning, but it is our feelings that tell us whether abstract considerations really ring true.'

Perhaps the clue to how such expressions of personal attitude to architecture link up with the topic of environmentally sensitive design lies most in his feelings expressed with respect to place: 'When I come across a building that has developed a special presence in connection with the place it stands in, I sometimes feel that it is imbued with an inner tension that refers to something over and above the place itself.' Slightly further on he talks about a converse response: 'If a work of architecture speaks only of contemporary trends and sophisticated visions without triggering vibrations in its place, this work is not anchored in its site, and I miss the specific gravity of the ground it stands on.'

Standing on firm ground, but with vibrations, provides for this discourse a timely sense of finality with undercurrents. The avoidance of eco-clichés while remaining focussed on green issues, as espoused by Mecanoo, also seems to represent a fundamental strength, and one that invites the maximum amount of participation from both architectural students and practitioners. Overall the review supports a tendency to anchored determinism in the sense of a continuity of green precedents, although mega-politics and economic crises do to some extent validate the metaphor of adventitious propagation. There is compelling evidence of architectural responses to oil-price hikes after the 6-Day and Yom Kippur wars in the Middle East, and the Iranian Revolution. Then at a time of lowered and relatively stable oil prices, the growing intensity of concern over ozone depletion and global warming in the mid-1980s, together with the Chernobyl nuclear disaster in 1986, melded the issue of energy-efficiency with wider ecological concerns. There is equally compelling evidence that an awareness of global warming, associated with the rapid expansion of industrialisation in the second half of the 19th century, dates back to the beginning of the 20th century.[99] However, this was regarded at the time as a potentially benign phenomenon. The literal environmental fall-out of soot from burned coal and its ill-effects on public health, together with new technical possibilities afforded by industry, was the tangible motivation for a new, healthier architecture. While the complexion of industry has changed, the issue of its positive and negative attributes has not. This aspect continues to nourish architectural thought and action, some of it experimentally innovative. For all the generic acuteness of socio-economic problems globally, it is the specific will of individuals to experiment and take risk that can project us positively into the 21st Century. For example, Bill Dunster's Beddington Zero Energy Development promises much in terms of reasonable sustainability. If it helps to promote replication, it may assist in aligning the UK more closely with its European neighbours in terms of 'green' commitment.

If not exactly a conclusion, this position is at least an optimistically open verdict from which to develop a new generation of sustainably green, solar-conscious buildings, which also constitute excellent and challenging architecture, and embody fresh ideas in keeping with the spirit of this book's title.

References to Part Three

1   Trombe F. *et al.* (1979), *Some Performance Characteristics of the CNRS Solar House Collectors*, proceedings The Passive Collection of Solar Energy in Buildings, Conference (C19) at the Royal Institution, April, International Solar Energy Society, UK Section, London, 402–9.

2   Davies M. G. (1986), *The Passive Solar Heated School in Wallasey. I*, Energy Research, Vol. 10, 101–20.

3   Butti K. and Perlin J. (1980), Ch. 16 Solar Collectors for House Heating. In *A Golden Thread, 2500 Years of Solar Architecture and Technology*, Cheshire Books, Palo Alto, California, and Marion Boyars Publishers Ltd, London (1981), 197–200.

4   Wright F. L. (1945), Book Four: Freedom. In *An Autobiography*, Faber & Faber, London, 298.

5   Fuller B. (1960), *Universal Requirements Check List,* Architectural Design, March, 101–10.

6   (1963), *UIA Cuba-Mexico – Buckminster Fuller* (News), Architectural Design, December, 557.

7   (1973), *Shelter*, Shelter Publications Inc., Bolinas, California.

8   (1980), *The Next Whole Earth Catalog*, Ed. S. Brand, POINT, Random House Inc., New York.

9   Bainbridge D. A. (1978), *The First Passive Solar Catalog*, The Passive Solar Inst., California.

10   Bainbridge D. A. (1980), *The Second Passive Solar Catalog*, Ibid.

11   (1978), *A Survey of Passive Solar Buildings*, AIA Research Corp., Washington DC.

12   Helliwell B. and McNamara M. (1978), *Hand-built Houses of Hornby Island*, Architectural Design, Vol. 48, No. 7, 451–79.

13   Lebens R. M. (1980), Ch. 2: Classification and Comparison of Passive Systems. In *Passive Solar Heating Design*, Applied Science Publishers Ltd, London, 5–26.

14   (1977), *The Book of the New Alchemists*, Ed. N. J. Todd, E. P. Dutton, New York.

15   Todd N. J. and Todd J. (1994), *From Eco-cities to Living Machines, Principles of Ecological Design*, North Atlantic Books, Berkeley, California.

16   Kroll L. (1998), *BIO PSYCHO SOCIO ECO 1*, The Sensitive Future, No. 34–5 January–February, 7–12.

17   Hamdi N. (1991), *Housing without Houses, Participation,*

flexibility, enablement, Van Nostrand Reinhold. (pb Intermediate Technology Pub., London, 1995)

18 Habraken N. J. (1961, trans. Valkenburg 1972), *Supports, An Alternative to Mass Housing*, Scheltema and Holkema N. V. (pb Architectural Press, 1972)

19 Sergeant J. (1978), *An Introduction to Bruce Goff*, Architectural Design, Vol. 48, No. 10, 3–6.

20 (1988), The Architectural Review, Vol. CLXXXIII, No. 1092, February, 27–33 and 42–5.

21 Pawley M. (1971), *Garbage Housing*, Architectural Design, Vol. XLI, February, 86–94.

22 Pawley M. (1973), *Garbage Housing*, Architectural Design, Vol. XLIII, December, 764–84.

23 Rybezynski W. (1973), *From Pollution to Housing*, Ibid. 785–9.

24 Crosby T. (1971), *Frei Otto at Home*, Architectural Design, Vol. XLI, March, 138–9.

25 Butti K. and Perlin J. (1980), Ch. 15 An American Revival, Ibid. 193–4.

26 Addis B. (1997), Design Methodology. In *Happold, the Confidence to Build*, Happold Trust Publishers Ltd, London, 86–95.

27 Addis B. (1997), Design Research and Development, Ibid. 130–6.

28 Evans B. (1998), *Shell Suits Museum*, The Architects' Journal, Vol. 208, No. 10, September, 60–2.

29 Lecuyer A. (1998), *Steel, Stone and Sky*, The Architectural Review, Vol. CCV, No. 1220, October, 44–8.

30 Fromonot F. (1995, trans. Campbell 1995), Pt. 1: Background and Influences. In *Glenn Murcutt, Works and Projects*, Thames and Hudson, London, 12.

31 Ibid.

32 McKean J. (1989), Guiding Principles. In *Learning from Segal, Walter Segal's Life Work and Influence*, Birkhäuser Verlag, Basel, 22–4.

33 Ibid. 14.

34 (1960), *News from Milan, United Kingdom Proven Prefab*, Ed. P. Rawstorne, Architectural Design, August, 302.

35 Bell M., Lowe R. and Roberts P. (1996), Ch. 2: Energy, Climate Change and Housing. In *Energy Efficiency in Housing*, Avebury, Aldershot, 8–20.

36 Reid D. B. (1844), Ch. VIII: Causes Modifying the Supply of Air Required for Ventilation, Ch. IX On Vitiated Air, Pt IV: Ventilation of the Present Houses of Parliament. In *Illustrations of the Theory and Practice of Ventilation with Remarks on Warming, Exclusive Lighting and the Communication of Sound*, Longman, Brown, Green & Longmans, London, 184–208, 270–99.

37 Port M. H. (1976), Ch. XI: The Building Services. In *The Houses of Parliament*, Yale University Press Ltd, London, 218–31.

38 (1993), Proposed Amendments to Regulations 22, 23 and the

Interpretative Regulations and Parts J, K and A of the Supporting Technical Standards, Appendix 3: The Use of Air Conditioning and Mechanical Ventilation in Non-domestic Buildings. In *Building Standards (Scotland) Regulations 1990, a Consultation Paper*, The Scottish Office, Edinburgh.

39   Porteous C. D. A. (1997), *Solar Designing that Counts*, proceedings North Sun '97, 7th International Conference on Solar Energy at High Latitudes, Espoo-Otaniemi, Finland, June 9–11, Ed. P. Kontinnen and P. D. Lund, Helsinki University of Technology, 402–9.

40   Porteous C. D. A. (1999), *Integration of Active and Passive Solar Components Reviewed*, proceedings North Sun '99, 8th International Conference on Solar Energy at High Latitudes, Edmonton, Canada, August 11–14, Ed. K. G. T. Hollands and J. Wright, Solar Energy Society of Canada Inc., Ottawa, Ontario, 122–7.

41   Nelson G. (1995), Ch. 13: Case Study: Briarcliff House. In *The Architecture of Building Service*, B. T. Batsford Ltd, London, 117–24.

42   Carter B. and Warburton P. (1993), *The Development of a Solar Architecture*, Detail, Serie 33, No. 6, 671–5.

43   Allen I. (1998), *Optical Spectrum*, The Architects' Journal, Vol. 208, No. 8, 3rd September, 39–47.

44   (1997), *Bank Tower in Frankfurt-on-Main* and *Company Headquarters in Essen*, Detail, Serie 37, No. 3, 349–62.

45   Richards I. (1993), *Tropic Tower*, The Architectural Review, Vol. CXCII, No. 1152, February, 26–31.

46   (1997), *Mystical Presence*, The Architectural Review, Vol. CCII, No. 1120, December, 46–53.

47   (1998), *House in Okayama, Japan*, Detail, Serie 38, No. 7, 1180–3.

48   Sharpe T. R., Porteous C. D. A. and MacGregor A. W. K. (1998), *Integrated Solar Thermal Upgrading of Multi-storey Housing Blocks in Glasgow*, proceedings PLEA 98, Environmentally Friendly Cities, Lisbon, Portugal, James & James (Science Publishers) Ltd, London, 287–90.

49   Jørgensen O. B. (1997), '*The Yellow House*', *an Innovative Solar Renovation of Multi Storey Housing*, proceedings North Sun '97, Ibid. 364–71.

50   Thyholt M., Aschehoug Ø., Bryn I. and Monsen P. (1998), *Glazed Atria Revisited – Energy Savers or Wasters*, proceedings EuroSun 98, The Second ISES-Europe Solar Congress, Portoroz, Slovenia, September, 14–17, ISES – Slovenian Section, Ljubljana, II.2.2-1-7.

51   (undated – c. 1987) N Technical University. In *Passive and Hybrid Solar Commercial Buildings*, *IEA Task XI*, Pub. The Renewable Energy Promotion Group, ETSU, Harwell, Oxfordshire, 181.

52   Porteous C. (1996), *Airing Energy Efficiency: Home Truths*, alt'ing, the Scottish Journal of Architectural Research, Vol. 1, No. 1, March, 17–28.

53   (1997), *Housing Development in Zollikofen, Switzerland*, Detail, Serie 37, No. 3, 327–30.

54   (1996), *Arcadian Assembly* The Architectural Review, Vol. CC, No. 1195, September, 30–5.

55   (1999), *Solar Factory in Freiburg*, Detail, Serie 39, No. 3, 407–11.

56   Hampton D. (1993), *Swanlea Secondary School – Energy Comment*, The Architects' Journal, Vol. 198, No. 15, 20th October, 43.

57   Brookes A. and Stacey M. (1991), *Product Review, Theme: Glazing and Curtain Walling*, AJ Focus, Vol. 5, No. 4, April, 29–34.

58   Dawson L. (1995), *Light Spirited*, The Architectural Review, Vol. CXCVII, No. 1175, January, 20–21.

59   Esbensen T. and Höi T. (1998), *Brundtland Renewable Energy Network*, proceedings North Sun '97, Ibid. 511–15.

60   (1999), *Academie of Further Education in Herne*, Detail, Serie 39, No. 3, 386–9.

61   Porteous C. D. A. and Ho H. M. (1997), *Do Sunspaces Work in Scotland? Lessons Learnt from a CEC Solar Demonstration Project in Glasgow*, The International Journal of Ambient Energy, Vol. 18, No. 1, 23–35.

62   Aschehoug Ø., Andresen I. and Arnesen H. (1997), *Energy Performance of Advanced Windows in Office Buildings at High Latitudes*, proceedings North Sun '97, Ibid. 754–60.

63   (1990), *Sijzenbaan, Deventer*, The Architects' Journal, Vol. 191, No. 24, 13th June, 48–53.

64   Jones P. B. (1998), *Experimental Community*, The Architectural Review, Vol. CCIII, No. 1214, April, 46–50.

65   Fairs M. (1998), *Is that it?*, Building Design, Issue 1375, November, 27, 1–2.

66   Bullivant L. (1998), *Spatializing New Labour*, Archis, Issue 5, 20.

67   Baxter N. (1998), *International expertise can help us shape our cities. . .*, The Herald, July 13.

68   Bullivant L. (1998), *Spatializing New Labour*, Archis, Issue 5, 22.

69   Ritchie I. (1998), *New Life in the City*, 1999, Glasgow 1999, G1 3DN, Spring, 12–16.

70   Rice P. and Dutton H. (1995), *Structural Glass*, E. and F. N. Spon, London.

71   Ritchie I. (1997), *The Biggest Glass Palace in the World*, Ellipsis, London.

72   Jones P. B. (1995), *New Graz Architecture*, The Architectural Review, Vol. CXCVIII, No. 1184, October, 4–7.

73   Jones P. B. (1995), *A Place for People*, Ibid. 70.

74   Jones P. B. (1988), *Participative Huth*, The Architectural Review, Vol. CLXXXIV, No. 1102, December, 81–3.

75   Jones P. B. (1993), *Urbane Participation*, The Architectural Review, Vol. CXCIII, No. 1161, November, 45–9.

76 Dahinden J. (1971, trans. Onn 1972), Projects. In *Urban Structures for the Future*, Pall Mall Press, London, 104–7.

77 Jones P. B. (1993), *Restrained Szyszkowitz-Kowalski*, Ibid. 40–4.

78 Jones P. B. (1995), *A Concatenation of Places*, The Architectural Review, Vol. CXCVIII, No. 1184, October, 59–62.

79 Reid R. and Hauser D. (1985), *Towards a Democratic Architecture*, The Architectural Review, Vol. CLXXVII, No. 1060, June, 51–5.

80 Dawson L. (1993), *Working Environment*, The Architectural Review, Vol. CXCII, No. 1152, February, 20–5.

81 van Roijen-Wortmann A. (1982, 2nd edn 1987), Building with van Eyck. In *Aldo van Eyck*, Stichting Wonen, Amsterdam, 28–37.

82 van Eyck A. (1982, 2nd edn 1987), Building a House, Ibid. 38–95.

83 Hertzberger H. (1982, 2nd edn 1987), The Mechanism of the 20th Century and the Architecture of Aldo van Eyck, Ibid. 7–27.

84 van Eyck A. (1962), *Team 10 Primer*, Ed. A. Smithson, Architectural Design, December, 572.

85 Voelker J, (1957/62), Architectural Association Journal, June 11; and Ibid. 595.

86 Dahinden J. (1971, trans. Onn 1972), Theories and Working Hypotheses. In *Urban Structures for the Future*, Pall Mall Press, London, 189–91.

87 Ibid. 210–14.

88 Ibid. 194–6.

89 (undated, c. 1995), *Energie Spiegel*. Pub. Ecofys, Kanaalweg 95, 3503 RK Utrecht, Holland.

90 Golub J. (1998), *Albert Frey/Houses 1 + 2*, Princeton Architectural Press, New York, 73–81.

91 Vollaard P. (trans. Kirkpatrick 1998), Integral Architecture. In *Mecanoo Architecten Bibliotheek Technische Univeriteit Delft*, 010 Publishers, Rotterdam 43–4.

92 Davies C. (1994), *Big Blue*, The Architectural Review, Vol. CXCVI, No. 1172, October, 26–35.

93 van Cleef C. (1999), *Earth Science*, The Architectural Review, Vol. CCV, No. 1225, March, 58–60.

94 Koolhaas R. and Mau B. (1995), Last Apples. In *S, M, L, XL O.M.A.* Monacelli Press Inc., New York, 662–85.

95 Hussell L. (1995), *Making Waves in Marseille*, The Architects' Journal, No. 3, Vol. 202, 29–35.

96 Le Corbusier (1957), On Discovering Gaudí's Architecture, In *New Free Style*, Ed. I. Latham, Architectural Design Profile, Academy Editions, 1980, 88.

97 Koolhaas R. and Mau B. (1995), Introduction. In *S, M, L, XL O.M.A.* Monacelli Press Inc., New York, xx.

98 Zumthor P. (1998), *Thinking Architecture*, Lars Müller Publishers, Baden, 9–59.

99 Christianson G. E. (1999), Ch. 9: Native Son. In *Greenhouse, The 200-year story of global warming*, Constable London, 105–15.

Personal post-script

This book started with a narrow focus on constructional layers from a straightforward physical viewpoint. Really it was about starting with details and placing them in a wider context – the kind of reciprocity of an iterative process from small to large that Charles Correa talks about. Reciprocity inevitably brings up Aldo van Eyck, who was a huge presence and influence during my student years. He simply could not be ignored, and his sensitive brand of architectural politics struck home. Indeed I used his 'slum edging into the spirit' quotation to preface my final thesis on urban regeneration. Then a series of primary schools I designed in the 1970s were my versions of his Amsterdam orphanage, perhaps with overtones of the Louisiana Museum by Jørgen Bo and Vilhelm Wohlert. The briefs derived from new methods of team-teaching and open-closed planning was as gripping to me as the realised interconnections between volumes and components.

Architecture inevitably engages with and reflects socio-political thinking, nowhere more positively than with primary education, where the loosening up of old structures in the 1970s was intended to enhance the environment for pupils. But just as the new way of teaching and learning still involved some constraints, so also did the architecture. I devised an architectural game-plan, with its own set of rules, to complement the educational one as closely as possible – thus partly open and partly closed planning, inside-outside transparency, legibility of structure, techniques to deal with acoustic demands, etc. Specifically green and energy-efficient architecture came later for me as a driving concern, but there is no reason why it should not have been part of a strategy where the design of the building supports and empowers what goes on inside it.

I also strongly relate now to Peter Zumthor's approach touched on at the close of the last chapter in terms of putting oneself in touch with ones feelings in the design of buildings. For example, his reference to 'details such as two nails in the floor' is tremendously evocative for me. I am more 'deep detail' within 'decisive concept' than 'deep ecology'. In fact I am noted as obsessive about 'nice wee details', using *nice* formally to imply precision, and the Scottish *wee* more to emphasise this aspect than small specific dimensions. I have demanded fine tolerances of contractors which have caused on-site consternation; and, as a self-builder with a bent for joinerwork in the tradition of Walter Segal, I have used particular devices to achieve visual accuracy, while recognising the necessity for realistic physical tolerances. In my first self-built house in the late 1960s,

where the aesthetic spirit owes quite a bit to the Oslo houses of AD
March 1956, I used aluminium trims and cover pieces to accommodate
the shortcomings and needs of the nailed timber framing and weather-
boarded cladding. In the second one, ten years later, I shifted from nails
to bolts. Prefabricated frames and trusses were drilled to the same dia-
meter as the bolts, and the completed assembly fitted together, plumb
and level, with satisfyingly clamped tightness. More recently I have
applied the same rigour to built-in furniture and other refinements within
my present 19th century home.

I have found the experience of self-building demanding. The risks
sometimes manifested themselves in nightmares. But it was one of
significant architectural discovery from nailed, screwed or bolted connections to the spatial whole. The physical and emotional investment yields
experiences that are quite transitory, but which can live on as perfect
memories. The rootedness of buildings are played against the un-
rootedness of people, sometimes the occupants and sometimes visitors,
together with the dynamics of the light, the sunlight, the shadows and the
air that moves within them. This is the game that Le Corbusier used to
talk about, and it has come out in some of the descriptions quoted above
as a defining issue when experiencing a truly green building. When constructing my second home in the Outer Hebrides, designed to be climate-
sensitive, energy-efficient and reasonably green, I was very conscious of
both the rootedness of the location and the transience of the supreme
qualitative experience. The new building was attached to an older one,
which had been built adjacent to an even older one, which in turn was
built on top of one older still. The location was at the head of a river
valley. Slightly further down was a small stone circle, and below that was
a Norse water mill . . . layers of history in a relatively timeless landscape.
Most of the building work took place during the long daylit hours of the
Hebridean summer, starting not long after dawn. The new and the old
were separated by a short flight of steps, at the top of which was a
narrow strip of glass. Around 6.00 a.m. I regularly sat at the top of the
steps in the direct line of a shaft of sunlight through this separating
window, and looking down the stairs through another small window on
the south edge of the old cottage directly to the river. These are special
moments that endure, the kind of moments which represent 'eco-spirit of
the age' for me . . . and hopefully for many others.

Picture credits

6.6   Source: Le Corbusier, La Plata: villa Curutchet 1949, ©
        FLC/ADAGP, Paris and DACS, London 2001.

6.7   Source: Architectural Review, August 1938, Part 2 ref. 20; repro-
        duced courtesy of The Architectural Review.

6.8   Detail redrawn by The Graphics Co. from The Modern Flat,
        F. R. S. Yorke and F. Gibberd, 1937, © FLC/ADAGP, Paris and
        DACS, London 2001; photograph by author.

6.9   Sources: Le Corbusier, Paris: immeuble 24 rue Nungesser et Coli
        1931 © FLC/ADAGP, Paris and DACS, London 2001.

6.10a   Source: Pierre Chareau, Part 2 ref. 29, © B. Bauchet, Architecte.

6.10b   Source: Le Corbusier, Paris: immeuble 24 rue Nungesser et Coli
        1931 Archive FLC H2(2)488 © FLC/ADAGP, Paris and DACS,
        London 2001.

6.11   Source: Le Corbusier, La Celle Saint Cloud: maison de Week-End
        1935 Plan FLC 9249 © FLC/ADAGP, Paris and DACS, London
        2001.

6.12   Source: The Natural House, Frank Lloyd Wright, 1954, © ARS,
        NY and DACS, London 2001.

6.13   Source: Photograph by Ezra Stoller in Building with Frank Lloyd
        Wright, an illustrated memoir, H. Jacobs, 1978, Ezra Stoller © Esto.

6.14a   Source: Frank Lloyd Wright and the Meaning of Materials, T. L.
        Patterson, 1994, © ARS, NY and DACS, London 2001.

6.14b   Source: Frank Lloyd Wright and the Meaning of Materials, T. L.
        Patterson, 1994, © ARS, NY and DACS, London 2001.

6.15a   Drawn by The Graphics Co.

6.15b   Drawn by The Graphics Co.

6.16   Source: Schindler, ref. 39, © University Art Museum, University
        of California.

6.17   Source: The Modern House in America, J. Ford and K. M. Ford,
        1940, per Dover Publications Inc, New York, © Dion Neutra,
        architect.

6.18a   Source: Walter Gropius: Works and Projects, P. Berdini, 1994,
        © Zanichelli Editore, Bologna.

6.18b   Source: Walter Gropius: Works and Projects, P. Berdini, 1994,
        © Zanichelli Editore, Bologna.

6.19   Sources: section – The Modern House, F. R. S. Yorke, 1934,
        © DACS 2001; and MIES van der ROHE, Ludvig. Tugendhat
        House. Brno, Czechslovakia. 1928-30. Lower-floor plan. Drawn
        for Philip Johnson's book. Ink on illustration board, $30 \times 40\frac{1}{4}''$
        (76.5×102 cm). The Mies van der Rohe Archive, The Museum
        of Modern Art, New York. Photograph © 2001 The Museum of
        Modern Art, New York, © DACS 2001.

6.20   Source: The Modern House in England, Part 2 ref. 49, © Ivan
        Chermayeff.

6.21   Redrawn by The Graphics Co. from Keck and Keck, Part 2 ref. 51.

6.22a   Redrawn by The Graphics Co. from Keck and Keck, Part 2 ref. 51.

6.22b   Drawn by The Graphics Co.

6.23   Source: A Golden Thread, Part 2 ref. 53, © photograph Marion Boyars Publishers; section redrawn by The Graphics Co.

6.24   Redrawn by The Graphics Co. from Harwell Hamilton Harris, L. Germany, 1991.

6.25   Source: The American House Today, Part 2 ref. 54.

7.1   Source: Louis I. Kahn, Light and Space, © U. Buttiker, 1994.

7.2   Sources: Richard Neutra and the Search for Modern Architecture, Part 2 ref. 63; and The Modern House in America, J. Ford and K. M. Ford, 1940, per Dover Publications Inc, New York, © Dion Neutra, architect.

7.3   Source: Frank Lloyd Wright and the Meaning of Materials, T. L. Patterson, 1994, drawn from Frank Lloyd Wright Archives, drawing 3601.012, © ARS, NY and DACS, London 2001.

7.4   Source: Frank Lloyd Wright and the Johnson Wax Buildings, Part 2 ref. 71, © S. C. Johnson – Racine, Wisconsin.

7.5   Source: Frank Lloyd Wright's Larkin Building, Myth and Fact, Part 2 ref. 73, J. Cahill drawings courtesy J. Quinan, © ARS, NY and DACS, London 2001.

7.6a   Source: Le Corbusier, Corseaux: villa 'Le Lac' 1923 © FLC/ADAGP, Paris and DACS, London 2001.

7.6b   Source: Le Corbusier, Corseaux: villa 'Le Lac' 1923 © FLC/ADAGP, Paris and DACS, London 2001.

7.7a   Source: Le Corbusier, Paris: immeuble 24 rue Nungesser et Coli 1931 Plan FLC 13373 © FLC/ADAGP, Paris and DACS, London 2001.

7.7b   Source: The work of G. Rietveld architect, T. M. Brown, 1958, © DACS 2001.

8.1   Redrawn by The Graphics Co. from A Golden Thread, Part 2 ref. 53.

8.2   Source: Architectural Review, October 1996, © Thomas Spiegelhalter.

9.1a   Source: Architectural Design, July 1978, Part 3 ref. 12, © Bo Helliwell.

9.1b   Source: Architectural Design, July 1978, Part 3 ref. 12, © Bo Helliwell.

9.2a   Source: Passive Solar Heating Design, Part 3 ref. 13.

9.2b   Source: Passive Solar Heating Design, Part 3 ref. 13.

9.3   Source: From BOOK OF THE NEW ALCHEMISTS, edited by Nancy Jack Todd, copyright © 1977 by New Alchemy Institute Inc. Used by permission of Dutton, a division of Penguin Putnam Inc.

9.4   Source: The Architecture of Bruce Goff, J. Cook, 1978, © photograph by J. Wallace.

9.5   Source: Architectural Design, Part 3 ref. 12, The Architectural Review, January 1967, © Bo Helliwell; and The Architectural Review, May 1993, © Patkau Architects.

9.6   Source: Mind and Image, H. Greene, 1976, © photograph by Bob Bowlby; and Architectural Design, Part 3 ref.12, © Bo Helliwell.

9.7   Source: Architectural Design, Part 3 ref. 21, © Jon Rowland.

9.8   Source: Architectural Design, Part 3 ref. 22, © Martin Pawley.
9.9   Source: Architectural Design, Part 3 ref. 24, © Frei Otto.
9.10a   Source: Happold, the Confidence to Build, Part 3 ref. 26, © The Happold Trust.
9.10b   Source: Happold, the Confidence to Build, Part 3 ref. 27, © The Happold Trust.
9.11   Redrawn by The Graphics Co. from The Architectural Review, Part 3 ref. 29, © photograph by Margherita Spiluttini.
9.12   Source: Glenn Murcutt, works and projects, Part 3 ref. 30/31, © Max Dupain & Associates; and Learning from Segal, Part 3 ref. 32/33, © the architects' journal.
10.1   Source: Building Design, November 6th, 1998, © The Arts Team.
10.2   Source: The Architecture of Building Services, Part 3 ref. 41, © Arup Associates.
10.3   Source: Detail No. 6, 1993, Part 3 ref. 42, © Arup Associates.
10.4   Source: AJ September 3rd 1998, Part 3 ref. 43, © the architects' journal.
10.5   Source: cover graphic, Detail No. 3, 1997, Part 3 ref. 44, © Detail.
10.6   Drawn by The Graphics Co. from Architectural Review, December 1997, Part 3 ref. 46.
10.7   Source: Detail No. 7, 1998, Part 3 ref. 47, © Detail.
10.8   Photograph by author.
10.9   Source: Detail No. 3, 1997, Part 3 ref. 53, © Detail.
10.10   Source: The Architectural Review, September 1996, Part 3 ref. 54, © Kiessler + Partner.
10.11   Source: photograph by author, and Detail No. 3, 1999, Part 3 ref. 55, © Detail.
10.12   Source: AJ October 20th, 1993, Part 3 ref. 56, © the architects' journal.
11.1   Source: Detail No. 2, 1997, © Detail.
11.2   Source: The Architectural Review, November 1998, © Rick Joy Architect.
11.3   Source: AJ June 13th, 1990, Part 3 ref. 63, © the architects' journal; photographs by author.
11.4   Photographs by author.
11.5   Source: The Architectural Review, December 1998, Part 3 ref. 74, © Eilfried Huth.
11.6   Source: The Architectural Review, December 1988, as Fig. 75, © Szyszkowitz-Kowalski.
11.7   Source: The Architectural Review, June 1985, Part 3 ref. 79, © R. Reid.
11.8   Source: The Architectural Review, February 1993; © Joachim Eble Architektur, Dipl.-Ing. Freier Architekt dwb BAU BDA, Berliner Ring 47a, D-72076 Tübingen.
11.9   Source: The Architectural Review, December 1998, © Renzo Piano Building Workshop architects.
11.10   Source: The Architectural Review, March 1999, © Mecanoo architecten.

Index of projects and propositions

Index of people